The Virgin Queen

Africa Explored
Agincourt
Benito Mussolini
Corunna
The Court at Windsor
The Destruction of Lord Raglan
The Dragon Wakes: China and the West 1793-1911
Edward VII: A Portrait
The English: A Social History, 1066-1945
The French Revolution
Garibaldi and his Enemies
George IV
The Grand Tour
The Great Mutiny: India 1857
London: The Biography of a City
The Making of Charles Dickens
The Personal History of Samuel Johnson
Queen Victoria in her Letters and Journals
Redcoats and Rebels: The War for America
The Rise and Fall of the House of Medici
Rome: The Biography of a City
The Roots of Evil: A Social History of Crime and Punishment
Venice: The Biography of a City

The Virgin Queen

Elizabeth I, Genius of the Golden Age

Christopher Hibbert

DA CAPO PRESS

A Member of the Perseus Books Group

Library of Congress Cataloging-in-Publication Data

Hibbert, Christoper 1924–
    The virgin queen : Elizabeth I, genius of the Golden Age /
Christopher Hibbert.
       p. cm.
    Includes bibliographical references and index.

    ISBN-10: 0-201-60817-0   ISBN-13: 978-0-201-60817-5

    1. Elizabeth I, Queen of England, 1533–1603. 2. Great Britain—
History—Elzabeth, 1558–1603. 3. Great Britain—Kings and rulers—
Biography. I. Title.
DA355.H53 1991
941.085'092—DC20
[B]   90-23275
                                                          CIP

Perseus Books is a member of the Perseus Books Group

Cover design by Thomas Strong
Text design by Wilson Graphics & Design (Kenneth J. Wilson)
Set in 10-point Sabon by Shephard Poorman Communications, Indianapolis, IN

Find us on the World Wide Web at
http://www.perseuspublishing.com

Contents

List of Illustrations

ILLUSTRATION CREDITS

COLOR

His Grace the Duke of Atholl's collection at Blair Castle, Perthshire, 20; Bodleian Library, 8; Bridgeman Art Library, 5, 12, 13, 23, 26, 29, 30; British Museum, 22; Bulloz, 5; National Maritime Museum, 24, 25; National Portrait Gallery, 3, 9, 16, 28; The National Trust, 18, 19, 21; Private Collection, 11; By gracious permission of Her Majesty The Queen, 1, 2; By courtesy of the Marquess of Salisbury, 4, 7, 10; Scala, 17; Mrs P. A. Tritton, 27; Victoria and Albert Museum, 14; Jeremy Whitaker, 6.

BLACK AND WHITE

Ashmolean Museum, 13, 18; British Library, 10, 22, 29; British Museum, 5, 6, 19; Burghley House Preservation Trust Ltd, 21; Malcolm Crowthers, 31; Fitzwilliam Museum, 7; By permission of His Grace the Archbishop of Canterbury and the Trustees of Lambeth Palace Library (photograph Courtauld Institute), 8; Mansell Collection, 1, 4, 12, 14; Museum of London, 11; National Army Museum, 27; National Maritime Museum, 28, 30; National Portrait Gallery, 2, 9, 17, 23, 24, 25, 26; Norfolk County Library, 20; By gracious permission of Her Majesty The Queen, 16; By kind permission of the Marquess of Tavistock and the Trustees of the Bedford Estates, 3.

For John and Tessa
with love

Author's Note

For their help in a variety of ways I should like to express my gratitude to Margaret Lewendon and Alison Riley; to the staffs of the London Library, the British Library and the Bodleian Library, Oxford; to my agents Bruce Hunter and Claire Smith; to Peter Carson and Eleo Gordon of Viking; to Jane Isay of Addison-Wesley; to John Guest, my skillful editor for over thirty years; and to Judith Flanders, Penguin Books's meticulous editor. I am also most grateful to Hamish Francis for reading the proofs and to my wife for compiling the index. Donald Pennington, sometime Fellow of Balliol College, Oxford, has been kind enough to read the manuscript and has given me much useful advice for the book's improvement.

FAMILY TREE

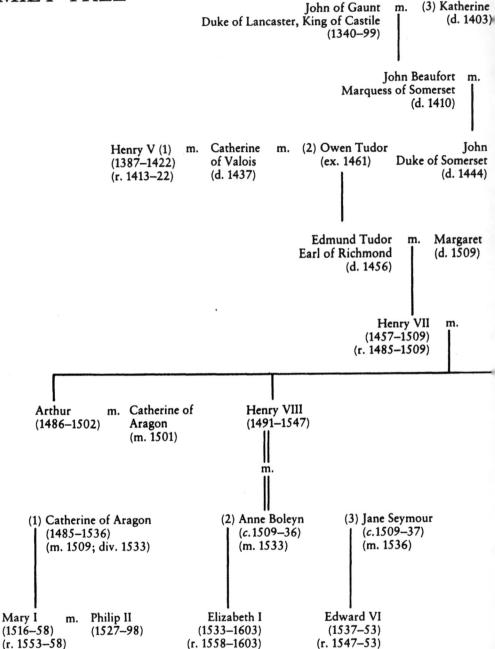

John of Gaunt   m.   (3) Katherine
Duke of Lancaster, King of Castile   (d. 1403)
(1340–99)

John Beaufort   m.
Marquess of Somerset
(d. 1410)

Henry V (1)   m.   Catherine   m.   (2) Owen Tudor   John
(1387–1422)   of Valois   (ex. 1461)   Duke of Somerset
(r. 1413–22)   (d. 1437)   (d. 1444)

Edmund Tudor   m.   Margaret
Earl of Richmond   (d. 1509)
(d. 1456)

Henry VII   m.
(1457–1509)
(r. 1485–1509)

Arthur   m.   Catherine of   Henry VIII
(1486–1502)   Aragon   (1491–1547)
(m. 1501)

m.

(1) Catherine of Aragon   (2) Anne Boleyn   (3) Jane Seymour
(1485–1536)   (c.1509–36)   (c.1509–37)
(m. 1509; div. 1533)   (m. 1533)   (m. 1536)

Mary I   m.   Philip II   Elizabeth I   Edward VI
(1516–58)   (1527–98)   (1533–1603)   (1537–53)
(r. 1553–58)   (r. 1558–1603)   (r. 1547–53)

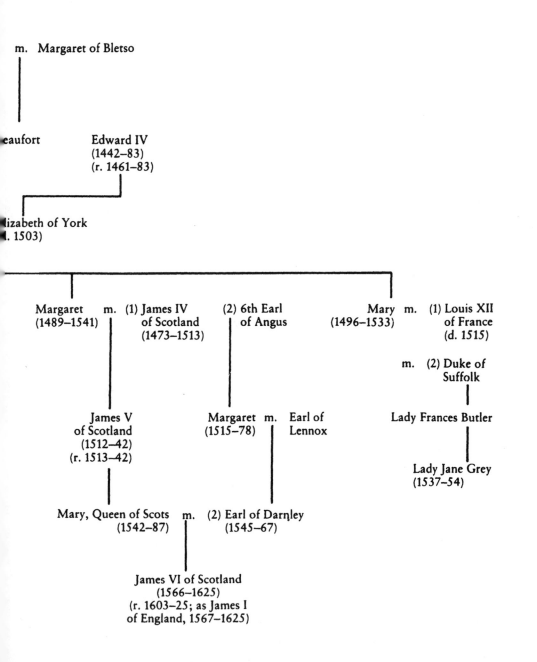

wynford

Margaret Holland

m. Margaret of Bletso

eaufort   Edward IV
(1442–83)
(r. 1461–83)

lizabeth of York
d. 1503)

Margaret   m.   (1) James IV   (2) 6th Earl   Mary   m.   (1) Louis XII
(1489–1541)   of Scotland   of Angus   (1496–1533)   of France
                   (1473–1513)   (d. 1515)

                                                                     m.   (2) Duke of
                                                                       Suffolk

James V   Margaret   m.   Earl of   Lady Frances Butler
of Scotland   (1515–78)   Lennox
(1512–42)
(r. 1513–42)

                                                                        Lady Jane Grey
                                                                      (1537–54)

Mary, Queen of Scots   m.   (2) Earl of Darnley
(1542–87)   (1545–67)

James VI of Scotland
(1566–1625)
(r. 1603–25; as James I
of England, 1567–1625)

Part One

I
Prologue

London was being prepared for "a great and glorious event." The fronts of houses had been washed and their windows cleaned; coats of arms, heraldic beasts and shop signs had been repainted, flags and banners unfurled, state barges and other river craft polished and gilded, railings garlanded. Conduits had been filled with wine, stands erected for spectators. Bell-ringers had practiced their carillons and trumpeters their fanfares. The bridge at Westminster had been repaired; fresh rushes had been strewn over the floor beneath the Norman hammer-beam roof of Westminster Hall, and in St. Paul's Cathedral the great stone pillars had been hung about with tapestries and a special gallery constructed so that the King, Henry VII, the first of the Tudor monarchs, and his Queen, Elizabeth, daughter of King Edward IV, could watch in private the wedding of their elder son, Prince Arthur, to Catherine of Aragon.

It was considered a splendid match for England: Catherine was the daughter of King Ferdinand of Aragon and Sicily and Queen Isabella of Castile, whose own marriage had helped to bring about the creation of the Spanish nation. She was an accomplished, well-educated young woman, pretty and lively, a skillful horsewoman and a graceful dancer. On the day appointed for her marriage, 14 November 1501, as she emerged from the west door of the cathedral on the arm of her new brother-in-law, Prince Henry, she seemed indeed the ideal princess. She and her husband were escorted separately to Baynard's Castle, the somber Norman fortress on the river front, whose approaches and courtyards had been graveled and sanded so that the horses' hooves did not slip on the smooth cobbles; and here in the great bedchamber, with the jocularity common to such occasions, the young couple were teased and encouraged as they climbed between the covers for their first night together.

Prince Arthur was fourteen years old, his bride a year older. From Baynard's Castle they left to keep court at the castle at Ludlow, close to the Welsh border, as was appropriate for a Prince of Wales; and, at Ludlow, Prince Arthur died a few months later of the sweating sickness.

He had once claimed with coarse boastfulness that he had been "six miles into Spain," but his bride maintained that she was still a virgin at his death.

As such, her parents requested that she either be sent back to Spain with the repayment of her dowry or be married to her brother-in-law, Prince Henry. And after a dispensation had been received from the Pope, permitting the marriage of a couple so closely connected, the new Prince of Wales and Catherine of Aragon were formally betrothed in the Bishop of Salisbury's house in Fleet Street five days before the Prince's twelfth birthday. Six years later they were married; and by then his father had died and Henry was King of England.

He was a young man of high intelligence, overriding self-confidence and of numerous accomplishments and interests that he pursued with a seemingly tireless energy. Despite a large and ugly high-bridged nose, he was considered extremely good-looking, with the fair skin, faint eyebrows and auburn hair that his contemporaries so much admired. His "round face" was so "very beautiful," one foreign envoy considered, "that it would have become a pretty woman." Every day he was up early, hunting, shooting, riding, jousting or wrestling. He was a most agile dancer, leaping about like a stag in the energetic English style. He loved singing; he could play the recorder, flute and virginals with equal facility and grace; he composed music; he wrote anthems. Dashing, strong, clever and charming, he was, on all occasions of state, gorgeously attired in jeweled glittering clothes that seemed at once to symbolize his power and emphasize his forceful masculinity. Standing with his strongly muscled legs splayed far apart, a dagger dangling beside a prominent codpiece, his arms encased in slashed sleeves puffed out to exaggerate the breadth of his powerful chest, he presented himself as the very image of a royal autocrat.

His marriage to Queen Catherine seemed happy enough at first. She shared his taste for open-air diversions and for music; she talked intelligently; she was obviously though not cloyingly devoted to him, and longed to give him a healthy heir. But this she failed to do. First she gave premature birth to a stillborn daughter, then to a son who died within a few weeks. Another son was born the next year. He too died, as did a fourth and a premature child in 1514. In 1515 a sixth baby was conceived. This surely, she was told, would be a boy. The birth took place on 18 February 1516. The baby was a girl, Princess Mary. After this the Queen gave birth to yet another premature child who did not long survive.

Her husband, while treating her with the public courtesy her position required, did not trouble to conceal from her his disappointment and displeasure. Nor did he hide from her his playful flirtations and occasional philanderings with the young ladies of his court. By one of these, Elizabeth Blount, the pretty daughter of a Shropshire landowner, he was to have a son. With none of them, however, did he appear to be much in love, until in 1522 there came to court from France a young woman for whom the King conceived a passion so intense that it was said she had bewitched him.

The charm of Anne Boleyn lay not in her looks. She had lovely eyes, so dark as to seem almost black, and thick hair so long that she could sit on it. But her complexion was swarthy; her nose too long, her bosom, in the words of an Italian envoy, "not much raised." Indeed, he added, she had little to recommend her other than the "King's great appetite." Rather small and thin, she seems to have had a prominent mole on her long neck or on her chin, what appeared to be a tiny, nascent sixth finger growing out of the side of her hand and, on another finger, a slightly deformed nail that she endeavored to hide with the tip of the finger next to it. But she was undoubtedly exciting as well as excitable, vivacious and sensual, quick-witted and sophisticated, supple in her movements and graceful in her manner. She wore her smart French dresses with confident style; and, while regarded by some as a coquette, she was too acute, ambitious and calculating to be dismissed, as the King of France dismissed her elder sister, Mary, as a whore, "the English mare."

Anne had learned her fluent French first as a *fille d'honneur* at the decorous court of Margaret of Austria, Duchess of Savoy and Regent of the Netherlands, then at the court of King Francis I where her father, a self-seeking though cultured and courtly man, was ambassador and where her sister, Mary, had spent several nights in the French King's bed, as she was later to do in that of the English King who had already, so it was rumored, been to bed with her mother. This, however, was a liaison Henry denied: when asked in later life whether or not he had slept with them both he firmly replied, "Never with the mother."

Anne appeared so far to have escaped such entanglements, earning for this the approval of a Victorian biographer who praised her discretion in a world so "exceedingly corrupt." The French court was indeed not the kind of finishing school that would have been chosen for the girls by their great-grandfather, Sir Geoffrey Boleyn, hatter, mercer and Lord Mayor of London, who had bought Blickling Hall in Norfolk and created himself a country gentleman, marrying as his second wife one of the daughters and co-heiresses of Lord Hoo. In Sir Geoffrey's day France was ruled by Charles VII, whose court was lax enough; but the court of Francis I was believed, on no very sound authority, to be the setting for repeated sexual frolics, the lecherous King himself being "clothed in women," surrounded by unofficial mistresses, as well as a *maîtresse en titre* and those numerous young and middle-aged women about the court who played their parts in his erotic revelry. "It was generally recognized in those days that it was indeed a rare lady or girl, either a resident at court or a fresh arrival, who was not seduced," wrote Pierre de Brantôme, whose mother was a member of the household of Marguerite of Valois, Francis I's granddaughter. "Rarely or never did any maid or wife leave the court still chaste." But Brantôme was not remarkable for the accuracy of his reporting; and while his allegations may have been true of Francis's later years after the death of Queen Claude, the French court of Anne Boleyn's time, though certainly more easygoing sexually than England's, was scarcely the *bouge* of iniquity that Brantôme so pruriently described.

Anne Boleyn left France when she was about twenty, an accomplished dancer and lute-player; and she had soon, despite her rather unpromising appearance, made her mark at the English court, where she was appointed one of Queen Catherine's maids of honor. Her liveliness, her self-confident, strong personality, her tart, provocative manner, at once playfully flirtatious and mysteriously guarded, her ready wit and compelling if elusive sexuality caught the fancy of Lord Henry Percy who longed to marry her, although both his family and hers opposed the match, each having in mind marriages more profitable to their respective houses. Percy, in tears, was brought to heel by the King's minister, Cardinal Wolsey, in whose household he was then serving, and married off to the young lady of his father's choice; while, according to Wolsey's Gentleman Usher, George Cavendish, "Mistress Anne Boleyn" declared in her anger that, if it lay ever in her power, she would "work the cardinal much displeasure." For the time being she appears to have been banished from the court and told that she must stay in the country under her father's watchful eye.

It was not long before she was permitted to return; and soon another man had fallen in love with her, the dashing, handsome poet, Thomas Wyatt, who was separated from a wife he had married when he was seventeen. It was widely supposed that they became lovers and that his mistress had other bedfellows besides. But Anne was more discreet than her sister; and, while her character and attainments were not such as to endear her to the other maids of honor, it was clear that she already envisaged a future brighter and more distinguished than theirs and that, as her father's and brother's fortunes rose, so would hers. Her brother, George, a cupbearer to the King, was one of his Majesty's close companions; her father, now

Treasurer of the Household, holder of several other profitable offices, and husband of a daughter of Thomas Howard, Earl of Surrey, was soon to be created Viscount Rochford on the same day and in the same place, the royal palace of Bridewell, where the six-year-old Henry Fitzroy, the King's natural son by Elizabeth Blount, was created Duke of Richmond and otherwise so honored that it seemed he would soon be recognized as heir to the throne.

By now the King had come to accept that his Queen would never bear him a son. She was five years older than he was and already looking worn and fat. She was also becoming excessively pious. He no longer shared his bed with her, and was beginning to think of divorcing her and marrying another woman who would give him a son. After all, as he argued, there was biblical authority for maintaining that he should never have married Catherine, whose first husband had been his dead brother, Prince Arthur. The third Book of Moses called Leviticus was quite clear on the point: "And if a man shall take his brother's wife, it is an unclean thing: he hath uncovered his brother's nakedness; they shall be childless." The King set great store by this text. It seemed to him to point to the reason why God had denied him a son. His conscience deeply troubled him; and he must make amends. "All such issue males as I have received of the Queen died immediately after they were born," he said, "so that I fear the punishment of God in that behalf." Even if it were to be decided that the King's marriage to Catherine was a valid one, divorce was far from unknown. His own sister, Margaret, widow of James IV of Scotland, had been divorced from her second husband, the unsuitable Earl of Angus; his brother-in-law, the Duke of Suffolk, had also had an awkward marriage annulled; and Louis XII, King of France, had had his first marriage set aside after his accession so that he could marry his father's widow. Cardinal Wolsey was accordingly instructed to make use of his influence with the Papacy and to secure the required dispensation for the King of England.

Wolsey devised a clever scheme to bring this about. As papal legate, he summoned the King to answer the charge that he was living in sin with Catherine, his late brother's widow, thus enabling his Majesty to escape the undesirable process of bringing suit against the Queen. But, after long arguments as to the proper interpretation of divine and ecclesiastical law, this ingenious ploy came to grief; and it was then decided that a direct approach must be made to the devious, saturnine Giulio de' Medici, who had become Pope Clement VII in 1523.

The time seemed highly appropriate for such an approach, since the Pope, having quarreled with Charles V, had been driven from Rome by imperial forces and was living in exile in the episcopal palace of Orvieto, "a ruinous and decayed old place" as the English envoys discovered it to be, a palace whose remote fastness could be reached only by a mule track from the valley of the Paglia. In his parlous and penniless conditions, the Pope, it was hoped, would welcome the opportunity of obtaining the friendship of the English King, even though the Emperor Charles V, upon whom Pope Clement's future so much depended, was Catherine of Aragon's nephew.

At first King Henry's requests, put to the Pope by two members of Cardinal Wolsey's secretariat, were met with characteristic procrastination; but when a French army drove the Emperor's troops out of Rome, Clement cautiously agreed to authorize a hearing of the case in London. Two cardinals, one of them Wolsey, the other Lorenzo Campeggio, an acknowledged authority on canon law, were to listen to the conflicting arguments and to pronounce their verdict, which would be binding.

The King was deeply satisfied by this response and more impatient than ever to have the matter settled in his favor at the earliest possible opportunity, for he had now decided upon Anne Boleyn as Queen Catherine's successor. Indeed, he was now obviously deeply in love; and men who had noticed of late an unfamiliar lassitude and despondency in the King, a dimming of the commanding light of his presence, were aware of a renewed energy burning within him. But Anne was not to be seduced as easily as her sister Mary, who had borne the French King a son, a child now kept well away from court at the monastery of Syon. High-spirited and confident as she was, Anne had good cause to be in awe of the King, and good cause to fear that his passion for her might be extinguished as quickly as his passion for her predecessors. And while his absolute power was thrilling in itself, he was no longer the glowing, extremely good-looking youth of the recent past. He was still captivatingly attractive when he chose to be, still marvelously energetic and alert, splendidly masterful and gorgeously arrayed; but already at thirty-six there was a coarsening of those fair features, a tightening of the skin around the grey eyes, whose look could terrify as well as charm. Besides, Anne's father, ambitious and astute, was not a man to stand aside and allow his valuable daughter to succumb to advances which had resulted in the elder girl being married off as a discarded mistress to an impoverished and insignificant courtier. Anne clearly had the King in thrall; he was "struck," as he said himself in one of his letters to her, "by the dart of love"; and she was as unlikely as her father to let such an opportunity for advancement slip from her determined grasp.

King Henry's consuming love was by now common gossip, and Anne
Boleyn was closely watched for her reactions. It was noted that she
dressed more expensively and more elegantly than ever, that her jewels
seemed to glitter more brightly, that she appeared fully conscious of her
special status. Wolsey's Gentleman Usher, George Cavendish, who much
disliked her, said that once she knew "the King's pleasure and the great
love that he bare her in the bottom of his stomach, then she began to look
very hault and stout [haughty and proud], having all manner of jewels or
rich apparel that might be gotten with money." The King wrote her letters
of almost humble supplication, begging her to recommend him to her
good graces and not to let absence lessen her affection, assuring her that it
was more painful than he could ever have thought possible to be parted
from her and that her absence was tolerable only because of his hope that
her affection for him might be unchangeable. "If you remember my love in
your prayers as strongly as I adore you," he wrote in an illuminated book
of hours that was passed to her during morning Mass in the royal chapel,
"I shall hardly be forgotten for I am yours." He sent her a bracelet, wishing
that he himself could be in its place; he signed himself "your loyal servant
and friend." Her ambiguous replies, on occasions seeming to promise
much, at others withdrawn and cautious, elicited further protestations of
love and of "great agony of mind, not knowing how to understand them,
whether to my disadvantage as shown in some places, or my advantage as
in others."

At length some sort of understanding was reached. It was evidently
accepted that were the King and Anne to spend more time alone together
the path to marriage must be made clear; and guided, no doubt, by her
father and her uncle, the Duke of Norfolk and their friends, she played
the part of a favorite whose future was secure, not merely overshadowing
the Queen, who, despite the insult to her dignity, treated her rival with the
utmost courtesy "for the King's sake," but going so far as to speak on his
Majesty's behalf, as she did when a messenger from Wolsey came to court
with the news that the Cardinal had returned to England from a diplomatic mission to France. The messenger asked when the Cardinal should
come for the private audience with the King that was customarily granted
him on such occasions, and where should his master present himself. "The
King had with him in his chamber," so that Imperial ambassador reported,
"a certain lady called Anna de Bolaine who appears to have little goodwill
towards the Cardinal, and before the King could respond to the message
himself," the woman spoke on his behalf.

"Where else is the Cardinal to come?" she said in her most sharp-tongued and audacious manner. "Tell him he may come here, where the King is." The King made no comment and the messenger departed.

In Cardinal Wolsey's absence his rivals and enemies had been conspiring to poison the King's mind against him, and to worm their way more securely into his Majesty's favor. They had succeeded well in doing so: Thomas Boleyn, for one, had been created Earl of Wiltshire and Ormonde. It was clear that Wolsey's future rested upon his success in securing the King's divorce.

The King remained confident that this would soon be arranged. Absorbed in the doctrinal niceties of his case, which made a strong appeal to the pedantry of his intellect, he spent hours in the compilation of a thesis setting out the merits of his claims. He spent hours, too – he who hated the occupation – in writing letters to his beloved, his "own sweet heart" whom he now fondled openly before the court and gazed upon with manifest desire. He wrote of his longing for her when she was away from him, of his "fervencies of love," of his ardent need to kiss her "pretty dugs." He sent her present after present of rings and bracelets, diamonds and rubies and silver bindings for books. When he heard that she was suffering from the sweating sickness that raged in England that summer of 1528 he seemed distraught; it was the most grievous news he could receive; at the foot of a letter he wrote to her, between his own initials, he inscribed Anne's inside a heart. "The King," the French ambassador reported, "is so infatuated that none but God can cure him"; while the Spanish ambassador told his master, "Both the King and his lady, I am assured, look upon their future marriage as certain. It is as though that to the Queen had been actually dissolved."

The marriage, however, was not to be celebrated yet. The changing fortunes of Charles V's armies on the Continent had helped to persuade the Pope to bring the hearings in London to an end and to revoke King Henry's prolonged case to Rome, much to the satisfaction of the populace, who made no secret of their sympathy for Queen Catherine and their dislike of her usurper, the "goggle-eyed whore." "No Nan Boleyn for us!" they shouted in the streets. "No Nan Boleyn!"

Wolsey's downfall was now inevitable. For a time Anne had endeavored to make it up with the Cardinal, to turn him into an ally. She told Thomas Heneage, a Gentleman of the Privy Chamber who had recently been a member of Wolsey's household, that she would be most pleased to receive some carp or shrimps from the Cardinal's fishponds; and when the King sent to her table some special delicacy, she asked Heneage, as a protégé of

Wolsey's, if he would join her in her meal. By 1529, however, such overtures had ceased and Anne had become determined that there must be no
reconciliation between the King and the man who had failed him, the man
upon whom she was said to have vowed "to work displeasure" when he
had come between her and Lord Henry Percy. The Cardinal was summoned from York to London to face trial for high treason. On 29 November 1530 he died at Leicester on the way; and Anne's hold on the King
seemed more secure than ever. Indeed, she now behaved as if she were
Queen already. She sat beside the King at court festivities; she rode beside
him when the court moved from one of his palaces to the next; and in
these palaces her chambers were hung with tapestries and furnishings befit-
ting the state of his Majesty's consort. "The King's affection for La Bolaing
increases daily," reported Eustace Chapuys, a shrewd lawyer from Savoy
who had arrived in England as Imperial ambassador in 1529. "It is so great
just now that it can hardly be greater, such is the intimacy and familiarity
in which they live at present." He loaded her with more and more presents; he paid the bills for her clothes and her gambling debts; he sent her
bows and arrows and shooting gloves, saddles for her horses and harnesses
for the mules that carried her litter. One day, ignoring the disapproving
eyes of passers-by, he lifted her up onto his horse to ride behind him.

Mistress Catherine, as the Queen was now known, was banished for a
time to Bishop's Hatfield, a palace belonging to the Bishop of Ely, while
the King pursued his plans to divorce her, determined that if the Pope
could not be persuaded to help him he would turn to the English Church,
setting aside papal authority. He would "denounce the Pope as a heretic
and marry whom he pleased." The months went by; the King's health
began to fail him as he labored under the burden of business to which
Wolsey had so efficiently attended for him; Anne grew ever more impatient
and tetchy, quarreling with Catherine and her ladies when she could not
avoid their company, upbraiding the King for his continuing respect for
Catherine – whose household was still, in Anne's opinion, unnecessarily
large – and for his obvious affection for their daughter, the Princess Mary,
whom Anne said she would have as her maid or marry off "to some
varlet." She once annoyed the King so much that he had sharply to remind
her that "she was under great obligation to him since he was offending
everyone and making enemies everywhere for her sake." From time to time
she burst into tears and, on one occasion at least, she upset him so much
that he cried too. She was becoming increasingly neurotic, more frequently
prone to those outbursts of sudden and disturbing laughter that threatened to erupt into hysteria. "Will you send me some apples," she asked

Thomas Wyatt one day. "I have such a longing for apples! Do you know what the King says? He says it means I am with child! But I tell him, 'No, no, it couldn't be. No!' " And she ran out of the room in peals of laughter.

Exasperated by the painful slowness of the progress towards divorce, Anne eventually decided that she must take steps to force the pace; while the King, satisfied at last that a canonical marriage to her could shortly be arranged, took her to his bed. By the end of 1532 she was carrying his child; and in January the next year they were married, secretly and in haste. Soon afterwards Thomas Cranmer, a married man of reformist views, sympathetic towards the idea of the King's marriage to Anne, was confirmed as Archbishop of Canterbury in succcession to Queen Catherine's friend, Archbishop William Warham; and, in early May, an ecclesiastical court convened by Cranmer decreed that the King's marriage to Catherine of Aragon, now to be known as Dowager Princess of Wales, was null and void.

At the Easter celebrations that year Anne appeared in royal state, covered in jewels, wearing a cloth-of-gold cape and attended by sixty maids of honor as she proceeded to Mass, the Duke of Norfolk's daughter holding her train, courtiers bowing as she passed, trumpeters sounding their shrill salute. The respect accorded her was, however, granted unwillingly; and when at Whitsun she was carried in a litter of white damask through lavishly decorated streets to Westminster for her coronation, the cries of greeting were muted and the bared heads few. "I think you all have scurvy and dare not uncover your heads," Anne's fool called out to a group of men who declined to remove their hats. Around them women shouted, "Good Queen Catherine!" or "Witch!" and "Harlot!" and, pointing at the initials H and A painted upon the banners fluttering above their heads, cried out, "Ha! Ha!"

Comforted by "physicians, astrologers, wizards and witches," who alike assured him that the child Queen Anne was bearing was a boy, the King, so foreign envoys thought, was doing his best to ignore the disapproval of his people, persuading himself that his wife was all he had at first considered her to be, that he was still as much in love with her as ever, that she was worth his quarrel with the Pope, who had now excommunicated him, declaring that his marriage to her was annulled. Yet, he was, in fact, only too well aware of the feeling in the country, of the slanders and dire prophecies of such influential soothsayers as Elizabeth Barton, a psychic and epileptic nun from Kent, whom he was driven to have arrested and eventually executed. Foreign envoys also noticed that, attentive as he still was to her, the King was on occasions exasperated by Queen Anne's demanding moods, her caustic comments, her outbursts of rage. There were rumors that – as Queen Anne withdrew into her private chambers at Greenwich Palace to await the birth of her child in the splendid bed of state that her husband had provided for her – he had already found another mistress. He was forty-two; he had reached an age, so he said himself, when "the lust of man is not so quick as in lusty youth"; yet it was not to be supposed that his days of promiscuity were over.

Such marital squabbles as there were were soon patched up, however. Eustace Chapuys reported that there had been a serious quarrel during which the King had angrily told the Queen that she "must shut her eyes and endure as those better than herself had done" and after which he had refused to speak to her for two days. The ambassador learned later, though, that he had been misled. Certainly there were differences; but just as certainly they usually resulted in an attachment more fond than ever.

At the beginning of September it was announced at Greenwich Palace that the Queen was in labor. The courtiers gathered in the chamber next to hers to await the birth of the baby whom the King had already decided to call Henry or Edward. Inside the Queen's privy chamber the doors and windows were hung with heavy curtains to keep out draughts, despite the summer heat; an oratory was prepared should the baby need instant baptism.

It was, however, a quick and easy delivery: a healthy, perfect child appeared between three and four o'clock on the afternoon of Sunday 7 September 1533. The herald entered the room where the courtiers were waiting to make the expected announcement: the Queen, he declared, had been delivered of a princess.

The King, who had abandoned his usual summer progress that year, contrived to hide his bitter disappointment. Orders were given for the birth to be celebrated with bonfires and the pealing of church bells, with services of thanksgiving and festivities at court. The child was to be christened Elizabeth with all the pomp due to the heir to the throne. Her father asked his former wife for the shawl in which their daughter Mary had been baptized; but Catherine refused to hand it over.

The ceremony of baptism took place on 10 September, three days after the birth, in the tapestry-hung Church of the Observant Friars at Greenwich. The service was conducted by John Stokesley, Bishop of London; Henry Courtenay, Marquess of Exeter, carried "the taper of virgin wax"; the Duke of Suffolk escorted the baby; the godfather was Archbishop Cranmer; the godmothers were the Lady Marquess of Dorset, the Dowager Duchess of Norfolk, who held the baby beside the silver font beneath a crimson canopy, and the Marchioness of Exeter, who happened to be a friend of the former Queen, and who was consequently not at all pleased to be so honored, particularly as she was required to provide an expensive christening present of three silver-gilt bowls with covers.

A fire had been lit in the church and "divers gentlemen, with aprons and towels about their necks, gave attendance about [the font] so that no filth should come" to it. The service over, the herald, Garter King of Arms, cried out, "God of His infinite goodness, send prosperous life and long to the high and mighty Princess of England, Elizabeth." The congregation, walking down a path strewn with green rushes, was escorted by torchlight back to the palace where the Lord Mayor and forty prominent citizens, who had been rowed down river from the city, were awaiting its return. They were taken to the cellars for refreshment before being rowed back to London in their great state barge. The French ambassador reported that "the whole occasion was so perfect that nothing was lacking." But it was remarked that the King had not attended the ceremony nor the subsequent reception.

It seemed at that time that the marriage would survive its early difficulties. The Queen's maids of honor reported that the King had declared that he loved her so much he would go begging from door to door rather than give her up. He continued to behave towards her with his accustomed lavish generosity, buying her presents, having silver and gilt vessels engraved with their joint initials, expressing confidence that her next child would be a son. Yet close observers detected signs that he was growing tired of her, impatient of her histrionic tantrums, of her constant remonstrations. She complained that her baby was rudely spoken of as the "Little Whore," daughter of the "Great Whore," that her ladies were insufficiently respectful, that her stepdaughter Mary continued to act as if she were still heir to the throne, though Parliament had passed an Act declaring her to be a bastard.

Mary was now eighteen. She had been obliged to give up her own household and to go to live in most modest quarters in the household of the Princess Elizabeth, to whom she was appointed a maid of honor and whom she was instructed to address by a title she considered her own. She refused to submit to such indignities, refused to acknowledge that the woman she still called the King's mistress could possibly be the Queen of England while her mother was still alive, trusting in God and in her constancy to her mother's faith to support her in her adversity. She declined to sit at the same table at which her half-sister was fed; she refused to accompany her when she was carried about the grounds at Hatfield. Their father, determined to bring her to heel, remonstrated with her; but her stepmother, so it was said, protested that he was not nearly firm enough with the girl. Anne herself gave orders to the recalcitrant young woman's governess to bring her to heel by force, to beat her if necessary, to remind her that she was only a bastard. So virulent was Anne's animosity towards Mary that it was feared she might try to have her poisoned. Eustace Chapuys, the Imperial ambassador, certainly thought her capable of such a plot; and her former suitor, Henry Percy, now Earl of Northumberland, was "certain that Anne had been thinking of having" her murdered. "She is my death," Anne said, "and I am hers."

Before Princess Elizabeth was a year old, her mother became pregnant again. This time surely, she hoped, she would have a boy. The King ordered a silver cradle complete with jewels, Tudor roses and cloth-of-gold baby clothes from his goldsmith, Cornelius Hayes. By June the Queen had "as fair a belly" as Sir William Kingston, Constable of the Tower, had ever seen; and, as the unborn baby grew, so did rumors of her husband's infidelities. The baby, however, did not appear. Perhaps there was a miscarriage; perhaps there had never been a pregnancy at all. No one knew for sure. Yet everyone knew that the days of Queen Anne's dominance were over; and she seemed to sense this herself. No longer the witty audacious woman confident of her powers, she appeared tamed, even servile, following her husband about "like a dog its master," aware that even those who had once befriended her were deserting her in her decline, that foreign envoys were turning their backs on her. As her little red-haired baby girl was nursed and fondled in the country, she longed for the King to allow her another chance to give him the male heir he so badly wanted.

She was softer and gentler in her approach to him, as she was also to Mary. She still took care, so Chapuys said, to remind the King that it was she who, by marrying him, had extricated him from the state of sin he had formerly been living in with Catherine, that "moreover, he came out of it the richest prince that ever was in England and that without her he would not have reformed the church to his own great profit and that of all the people." She still spoke against Catherine and Mary, putting into the King's suggestible mind the idea, supported by a person who had had "a revelation from God," that they were responsible for her present failure to give him a son. If they were to be removed all would be well. Men were already dying because of their refusal to accept the King's reforms of the church. John Fisher, Bishop of Rochester, had been beheaded on 22 June 1535 for denying the King's right to his assumed title of Supreme Head of the Church of England; Thomas More, the humanist scholar and former friend of the King, had been executed a fortnight later. Were not Catherine and Mary also refusing to accept the King's commands and rightful honors?

Anne did not nag the King, though. She was still capable of lambasting everyone else; yet with him she was as quiet as she could bring herself to be. It was said that after the storms of the past the seas were calmer now that husband and wife were sleeping together again. Soon she was pregnant once more. And then on 17 January 1536 at Kimbolton, a large, dark house near Huntingdon, Catherine of Aragon died of cancer.

The King did not trouble to disguise his relief. There was now no likelihood that the feared invasion of England by the forces of the Emperor Charles V would take place. If Henry were to get rid of Anne he would not now be pressed to take Catherine back. If Anne failed him yet again, he would consider himself free to marry anyone he chose. And his eye had fallen upon Jane Seymour. The eldest of the eight children of Sir John Seymour of Wolf Hall, Savernake, Wiltshire, she was one of Queen Anne's maids of honor, a rather plain, pale, quiet girl, by no means clever or in any way remarkable, but amenable and accommodating. Jane Seymour's family and supporters joined forces with other factions at court, with friends of Catherine of Aragon, with the Imperial ambassador and with various ambitious and conservative peers and courtiers to encourage the King in his new interest and to poison his mind against his present wife.

Soon after learning of Catherine's death, the King burst into court clothed in yellow silk "for mourning." "God be praised!" he said. "Now we are free from all suspicion of war." And, catching sight of the Princess Elizabeth, then just over two years old, he snatched her up into his arms and in the candlelight danced about with her from room to room.

The child's mother could not share his excitement. Her new baby was due in five months, and she dared not think what might happen if it were another girl. Jane Seymour was taking her place as surely as she herself had taken the place of Catherine of Aragon, and the King, she knew, would not hesitate to rid himself of a second unwanted wife as ruthlessly as he had discarded the first. Even Anne's enemies found it in their hearts to pity her now that she looked, with her sunken cheeks, her apprehensive eyes, her long hair concealed within the folds of her cap, so much changed from that vital young woman who had once bewitched the King. When she miscarried a dead child which, so the midwives said, had "the appearance of a male about three and a half months," everyone knew that her life as

Queen would soon be over. There were rumors that the fetus was deformed and that the King took this as evidence of her sinful life and of God's displeasure at their marriage. He was reported to have gone to see her in her bedchamber where she lay recovering from her ordeal. He eyed her coldly. "I see that God will not give me male children," he said. "When you are up I will come and speak to you." He then strode abruptly from the room.

Thomas Cromwell, a blacksmith's son, once Wolsey's secretary and now the King's chief agent in the reformation of the Church and the dissolution of the monasteries, was put to the task of finding proof of her sin and reasons for getting rid of her. Cromwell had formerly been one of Anne's leading and most astute supporters, seeing in her a valuable ally in his plans for the country, the Church and the furtherance of his career; but he had his future and that of the kingdom to consider now. Besides, his appointed task would give him the opportunity to entangle the whole Boleyn faction in her fall, filling their offices with his own friends and colleagues. Within a week of the appointment of a commission of inquiry, the case against Anne had been made out. She was accused of "using fornication" with various men over a period of three years and of incest with her brother, George, now Lord Rochford, whom she had enticed with "her tongue in the said George's mouth and the said George's tongue in hers." All the accused men denied the charges except for one, Mark Smeaton, a musician and "one of the deftest dancers in the world," whom, so it was alleged, a servant had brought into Queen Anne's apartments and concealed in a cupboard used for the storage of dried and candied fruits. Smeaton had also at first denied the charge, but when a rope was knotted around his head and tightened with a stick, he confessed that he had "violated" the Queen three times. After other witnesses had accused her of uttering threats against the King and maintaining that he was impotent, of plotting to poison the Lady Mary as well as the King's illegitimate son, Henry Fitzroy, Duke of Richmond, Anne Boleyn's guilt was held not to be in doubt. But Anne herself as Chapuys was told "in great secrecy" by the "lady who had charge of her" affirmed on the damnation of her soul that she had never been unfaithful to the King.

She was taken to the Tower and handed over to Sir William Kingston of whom she asked, "Shall I go into a dungeon?" She then burst into tears before falling into "a great laughter." The next day, too, her shrieks of inexplicable laughter echoed chillingly around the grey stone walls.

She could see the scaffold on Tower Green from the window of her room. She was to mount it on the morning of 19 May 1536. Towards

twelve o'clock that day, when no summons had come, she sent for Sir
William and said to him, "Mr Kingston, I hear say I shall not die before
noon and I am very sorry therefore, for I thought to be dead now and past
my pain." "I told her it would be no pain, it was so subtle," Sir William
reported to Cromwell. "Then she said, 'I have heard say that the executioner [a swordsman specially brought over from France] is very good and I
have a very little neck'; and putting her hands about it laughed heartily."

There was no more laughter. From that moment on she seemed quietly
resigned to her death, even to welcome it. She wrote to her husband, once
again protesting her innocence and acknowledging the many favors she
had received at his hands. She begged him to take her baby daughter, the
Princess Elizabeth, into his paternal care.

In later life Elizabeth was heard to mention her mother's name upon only
two occasions; yet it was clear that, while she chose to be associated in the
public mind with her father, often proudly referring to herself as King
Henry's daughter, she was not ashamed to be a Boleyn. Whenever she
could she singled out her Boleyn relations for friendship and advancement;
she carefully preserved a ring that contained a miniature of Anne Boleyn;
and on occasions she chose as her badge her mother's symbol, the falcon,
the bird of prey of which the female is the larger bird.

2

The King's Daughter

"How haps it, Governor: yesterday
my Lady Princess, and today but
my Lady Elizabeth?"

At the time of the execution of her mother, Princess Elizabeth was two years and eight months old. She was a pretty child, far more closely resembling her father than her mother, who might have been taken for a Spaniard. Her hair was much the color of her father's, her skin as pale as his had been as a boy, her eyebrows and lashes faint, her eyes variously reported as grey, black and brown but certainly dark and lively. There was a bright alertness about her which her governess, her mother's cousin, Lady Bryan, found endearing; and although she could be willful and pertinacious, on occasions displaying her mother's flashes of ill temper, she was generally well-behaved and amenable. Yet Lady Bryan was concerned that the owner of the house where they were staying, Sir John Shelton, "would have Lady Elizabeth to dine and sup every day at the high table." It was "not meet for a child of her age to keep such rule yet," she wrote to the King's minister, Thomas Cromwell. Besides the little girl would see "divers meats, and fruits, and wine" which it would be very hard "to restrain her Grace from." She was, after all, "too young to correct greatly," and "God knoweth, my Lady hath pain with her great teeth, and they come very slowly forth, which causeth me to suffer her Grace to have her will more than I would." Then there was the matter of the child's lack of decent clothes. Her mother had taken great care to see her well supplied with all that a royal princess might expect, with dresses of yellow satin and white damask, with little shoes and ribbons and taffeta caps. But these she had outgrown: "She hath neither gown, nor kirtle [skirt] nor petticoat, nor no manner of linen nor smocks, nor kerchiefs, nor rails [nightdresses], nor body-stitchets [corsets], nor handkerchiefs, nor sleeves, nor mufflers [scarves], nor biggens [night-caps]." Lady Bryan had "driven off" as long as she could, but "by my troth," she pleaded, "I can drive it off no longer. Beseeching you, my Lord, that ye will see that her Grace hath that which is needful for her."

The plea was likely to be received indulgently. The King was in a contented mood. He had been out hunting when his wife had been beheaded.
He had reined in his horse to listen to the firing of the guns and had
married Jane Seymour a few days later. To be sure, as a consequence of
Archbishop Cranmer's obliging declaration that her mother's marriage to
the King had been null because of her previous relationship with Lord
Henry Percy, Princess Elizabeth would have to be declared illegitimate, as
the Lady Mary had already been. But she was still the King's daughter and
could expect to be treated with honor. So could Mary, even though, in
obedience to the faith that she held so dear, she still refused to acknowledge her father as Supreme Head of the Church. When the new Queen
became pregnant at the beginning of the next year, she asked if Mary
could be brought back to court as a companion for her. Queen Jane was
twenty-seven, Mary twenty-one. "Now it hath pleased your Grace to
make me your wife, there are none but my inferiors to make merry
withal," Jane explained to her husband, "unless it would please your Grace
that we might enjoy the company of the Lady Mary's grace at court. I
would make merry with her."

"We will have her here, darling," the King readily assented, "if she will
make thee merry."

Once Mary was back at court in attendance upon the Queen it was
agreed that she should be accorded her previous rank and that Princess
Elizabeth must be deprived of hers. When the governor of her household,
Sir Thomas Bryan, broke this news to Elizabeth, the child, not yet four
years old, gravely asked, "How haps it, Governor: yesterday my Lady
Princess, and today but my Lady Elizabeth?"

Yet despite the sudden change in her title, the Lady Elizabeth was not
forgotten when arrangements had to be made for the important ceremonies of the court. And on 15 October 1537 she was called upon to play her
part when the baby son, whom Jane Seymour had triumphantly presented
to the King three days before, was christened in the chapel of Hampton
Court Palace.

Because of the plague, which had been exceptionally virulent of late,
the numbers of those summoned to the ceremony were to be severely
limited and those living in certain areas were not to be asked at all. Dukes
were to be permitted a retinue of no more than six persons; marquesses
had to be content with five and bishops with three. Even so, there were
well over three hundred people in the procession that wound its way from
the ante-room adjoining the Queen's bedchamber to the chapel. In obedience to the ordinances laid down by Lady Margaret Beaufort, the baby's

great-grandmother and the mother of Henry VII, the gentlemen of the household led the procession carrying torches, then came the choir and various prelates with their chaplains, the privy councilors and noblemen, foreign ambassadors escorted by the Controller of the Household, and the great officers of state, the Lord Treasurer, the Lord Chancellor and Thomas Cromwell, Thomas Boleyn's successor as Lord Privy Seal. Behind them walked the three godfathers, Thomas Cranmer, Archbishop of Canterbury, Charles Brandon, Duke of Suffolk, and Thomas Howard, Duke of Norfolk, followed by the Earl of Sussex and Lord Montagu both carrying silver basins, the Earl of Wiltshire, bearing a wax taper and Henry Bourchier, Earl of Essex, a gold salt-cellar. Between these four nobles and the royal baby, who was in the arms of the Marchioness of Exeter, came the Lady Elizabeth carried by Edward Seymour, the Queen's elder brother, recently created Viscount Beauchamp, and soon to be Earl of Hertford and later Duke of Somerset. Clutched in the Lady Elizabeth's own arms was the chrysom, the robe put on a child at baptism as a symbol of the cleansing of its sins, and to be used as a shroud should it die within a month. Bringing up the end of the procession, behind the canopy that was held over the baby's head by three marchionesses, were the wetnurse, the midwife and the Princess Mary with her ladies.

After a fanfare of trumpets the baby was baptized in a silver font by the Archbishop of Canterbury and washed in the perfumed water kept warm in pans standing on glowing coals. The blessing was pronounced; the trumpets sounded; and Garter King of Arms came forward to proclaim, "God of His almighty and infinite grace give and grant good life and long to the right high, right excellent and noble Prince, Prince Edward, Duke of Cornwall and Earl of Chester, most dear and most beloved son to our most dread and gracious lord, King Henry VIII. Largesse, largesse, largesse!"

The ceremony over, the congregation filed out of the chapel as it had entered, the Princess Mary, as though dissatisfied with her former position at the rear of the procession, going forward to take the hand of her little sister as she carried the baby Prince's train. The Prince's parents, as Lady Margaret Beaufort's ordinance required, had not taken part in the procession but had remained in the state apartments where they now received the baptized Prince. The King took his son into his arms and, as he held him, he was seen to be in tears.

As the years passed the Lady Elizabeth grew increasingly fond of her brother, whose mother died of puerperal fever within three weeks of his birth. She gave him presents that she had made herself, more than once a cambric shirt most neatly sewn; she received in return a necklace or a pair of stockings; and when old enough to write them, she sent him letters, often sententiously phrased as though under the eyes of a tutor but expressive of her love for him. They were not often in each other's company, though, for they had separate households and both were as peripatetic as the King's, moving from palace to palace and country house to country house as the need for fresher air and cleaner stables drove them to leave one too-long inhabited place for another cleansed and purified against their arrival.

In her own household, which moved at irregular intervals from Windsor to Enfield, from Richmond to Greenwich, Hatfield to Eltham, Hunsdon to Hertford or Rickmansworth, Ashridge or Havering, the Lady Elizabeth seemed perfectly content. Lady Bryan, her governess, was a competent and kindly woman who shielded her as much as she could from the realities of her motherless state. The governess who took over from Lady Bryan when she was four years old, Katherine Champernowne – later the wife of Elizabeth's cousin and senior gentleman attendant, John Ashley – was less sensible and discreet, but she was devoted to her charge and, as a well-educated woman herself, exceedingly proud of her precocious accomplishments. The Lady Elizabeth in return loved Kat as she called her and remained closely attached to her throughout her childhood. Her father the little girl rarely saw, but she was thought to be proud of him and was obviously excited by the attention he paid to her in his bluff and genial way on the infrequent occasions when he came to inquire about her progress. From time to time he sent a courtier to bring him news of her. In December 1539, when she was six, he sent Sir Thomas Wriothesley, later Earl of Southampton, to see her at Hertford Castle and to wish her and her household a happy Christmas. "She gave humble thanks," Wriothesley reported, "inquiring again of his Majesty's welfare, and that with as great a gravity as she had been forty years old. If she be no worse educated than she now appeareth to me, she will prove of no less honour to womanhood than shall beseem her father's daughter."

Not long after the death of Jane Seymour, the King had been persuaded for political reasons to marry his fourth wife, the exceptionally plain Lutheran Princess, Anne of Cleves; but that marriage had predictably lasted a few months only, the King admitting that if the woman had "brought maidenhead with her" he had never taken "any from her by true carnal copulation." He had not since his youth, it seems, been the masterful lover he would have liked to appear, and he may well have been occasionally impotent. At George Boleyn's trial the accused had been asked if it were true that Anne Boleyn had told his wife that the King did not have the "*puissance . . . [de] copuler avec femme.*" The embarrassing question was put to him in writing; but Boleyn read it out and by doing so, it was said, he had made his execution inevitable. "Am I not a man like other men?" the King had asked Eustace Chapuys some years before when the ambassador had observed that by taking a new wife he was not necessarily guaranteeing the birth of children, and Henry had vehemently repeated the question twice, as though anxious for reassurance.

At least the annulment of his marriage to Anne of Cleves enabled the King to marry a plump, vivacious, nineteen-year-old girl much more to his liking, Catherine Howard, who, while living in the household of her step-grandmother, the Dowager Duchess of Norfolk, had had an affair with a rich young gentleman, Francis Dereham, with whom she was reported to have been "so far in love" that they clung to each other "after a wonderful manner, for they would kiss and hang by their bellies together as they were two sparrows." This behavior had so annoyed the Dowager Duchess that, when she had caught them thus in her great gallery, she had slapped them both and asked them indignantly where they supposed they were. They were at Norfolk House, she reminded them, not at the court of the King. Catherine Howard had also, it seems, made love with another gentleman, Henry Manox, who taught her to play on the virginals and who confessed that he had "commonly used to feel the secrets and other parts of the Queen's body." When the King heard of this confession and learned that Dereham admitted to having known the Queen "carnally many times, both in his doublet and hose between the sheets and in naked bed," he could not at first believe the reports. Nor could he believe that his young wife, whom he had supposed to be "a jewel of womanhood," had since her marriage spent many hours alone in her room at night with her cousin, Thomas Culpepper. But when the evidence seemed incontrovertible his rage and self-pity were boundless. Appalled by the realization that he had been shamefully cuckolded, he shouted for a sword so that he could kill the girl who had thus insulted his pride, swearing that she would never have "such delight in her incontinency as she would have torture in her death." Then, blaming his Council for this "last mischief," he burst into tears.

The Lady Elizabeth had good cause to feel distressed at the young Queen's fall from grace and her inevitable execution. Her own grandmother was a Howard, and she was always well disposed towards members of her mother's family. She had taken a liking to Catherine who in her friendly, good-natured way had always been kind to her, giving her the place of honor immediately opposite her when the Queen had first dined in public in the hall at Hampton Court. Elizabeth had been seven years old then; she was not yet eight and a half when Queen Catherine was beheaded; and when her father married his sixth and last wife, Catherine Parr, in 1543 she was nine.

Catherine Parr, the daughter of a north-country landowner who had been Controller of the King's Household, had been married twice before and was very rich. She was thirty-one at the time of her marriage to the King, an affectionate and understanding woman, good-looking and good-tempered, pious and learned enough to have written a book, *The Lamentation or Complaint of a Sinner,* though extremely romantic and susceptible. When the King's intentions towards her became known she was said to have been at once excited, alarmed and dismayed. She had hoped to marry Sir Thomas Seymour, Jane Seymour's elder brother, but he had diplomatically withdrawn his suit when she, as she put it, was "overruled by a higher power." She was the perfect wife for the King. He was more than twenty years older than she was, and looked even older than that. He was still a commanding and, on occasions, overpoweringly intimidating figure, grimly masterful and inordinately selfish. But he suffered increasingly from feverish headaches and depression; his frequent falls when jousting had probably led to inflammation of the marrow of the bone and possibly to some brain damage; he had a varicose ulcer on his thigh which broke out spasmodically, causing such pain that at times he was speechless and his face grew black; he may have been suffering from scurvy brought on by an unhealthy diet; he had also, perhaps through some glandular maladjustment, become immensely fat. "He had a body and a half," so it was reported, "very abdominous and unwieldy with fat. It was death for him to be dieted, so great his appetite, and death to him not to be dieted, so great his corpulency." In five years, if his armor provides an accurate guide, he had added seventeen inches to his waist measurements. Machines and ropes had to be provided for him in all his palaces, as he could no longer unaided mount the stairs. Yet the King did not want it to be supposed that he was marrying a mere kindly nurse. He made a new will, stipulating that any children of the marriage, or indeed of any future marriage, were to take precedence over Mary and Elizabeth. His natural son, Henry Fitzroy, Duke of Richmond, had no longer to be considered, for the boy had died of consumption aged seventeen some years before.

It was as a nurse and companion, however, that Catherine Parr's duties were fulfilled. She soothed her husband in his rages; she sat with his painful leg on her knee; she listened to him patiently when he elaborated upon the difficult and usually petty theological problems of the day, once disagreeing with one of his propositions, a daring presumption which predictably drew from him the heated observation that it was a fine time "when women were becoming such clerks." "It is a thing much to my comfort," he added sarcastically, "to come in mine old days to be taught by my wife." Above all, Catherine Parr was an ideal stepmother to the King's children, interceding with their father whenever they happened to offend him, as the Lady Elizabeth seems to have done for some unknown reason when she was twelve. The King was apparently so angry with the child he banished her from court for this offense; but his wife gradually brought him round and she was soon allowed to return. Deeply grateful to her stepmother, she translated "out of French rhyme into English prose" a poem which she rendered as *The Mirror or Glasse of the Synneful Soule,* writing it out in her neat, well-formed though still childish hand, binding it in a cover which she embroidered in blue silk and silver thread with yellow and purple wild pansies, and submitting it for correction to "Our most noble and vertuous Queen Katherine [to whom] Elizabeth her humble daughter wisheth perpetual felicity and everlasting joy."

As a friend of such reformers as Hugh Latimer, Bishop of Worcester, Miles Coverdale, the biblical scholar, and John Parkhurst, who was her chaplain, Catherine Parr always kept a careful eye upon Elizabeth's religious instruction as well as upon her general education. The Queen spoke to her of the teachings of the reformed Church, noting with approval that Elizabeth was drawn neither to the kind of strict Protestantism favored by her brother nor to the old religion to which her sister Mary remained so steadfastly true. It was clear that Elizabeth's faith was sincere but it was not, nor ever was to be, darkened by prejudice or bound by dogma: she had no interest in the pettifogging quibbles with which her father concerned himself. It was also clear that Elizabeth was a natural scholar: she appeared actually to enjoy her lessons, which were not attended by the physical punishments recommended in the case of her sister, Mary, by her Spanish preceptor, Juan Luis Vives, a firm believer in the efficacy of flogging for both boys and girls, indeed particularly for girls. "Never have the rod off a boy's back," advised Vives in one of his works on education. "And the daughter especially should be handled without cherishing. For cherishing marreth sons, but it utterly destroyeth daughters."

Under the general supervision of her kindly governess, Kat Ashley, Elizabeth had lessons in mathematics, history and geography, sewing, dancing,

deportment and riding; she was taught the principles of architecture and
the fundamentals of astronomy; she learned French, Italian, Spanish and
Flemish and acquired in addition, some Welsh, presumably from Blanche
Parry, a Welshwoman who had been one of her attendants since she was a
baby and who remained with her until she died, unmarried and blind, in
1596. The greatest attention was paid to Latin and Greek in which her
masters were Richard Cox, headmaster of Eton and later Bishop of Ely,
and William Grindal, a Fellow of St. John's College, Cambridge, where, as
a poor student from the north of England, he had come to the attention of
Roger Ascham, a Yorkshireman and senior Fellow of the College, in whose
rooms he had lived.

Through Grindal, as well as the Ashleys who were also friends of his –
and through John Cheke, another Fellow of St. John's, Cambridge, who,
together with Anthony Cooke, was appointed tutor to Prince Edward –
Ascham himself had come to take an interest in the Lady Elizabeth's education. It was a subject upon which he was an acknowledged expert. His
*Scholemaster, a plaine and perfite way of teachying children to understand,
write and speake in Latin tong* was frequently reprinted and had widespread influence. Yet Ascham's interests extended far beyond education
and the classics. He was an authority on archery, which he practiced almost daily and upon which he wrote an authoritative work, *Toxophilus;*
he enjoyed chess and music; he was a dedicated gambler and frequenter of
cockfights; he traveled widely; he hunted with enthusiasm.

From 1545 Ascham wrote to the Lady Elizabeth and Kat Ashley often,
encouraging the girl in her studies and pursuits, occasionally giving or
lending her books, and once mending her pen. When Grindal died of the
plague in the summer of 1548, Ascham made it plain to Cheke that he
would like to be appointed the Princess's tutor himself and in a letter of
condolence to the bright little pupil he hinted that his services would be
readily available were she to require them. His wishes were soon granted
and, within weeks of Grindal's death, he was living in the Lady Elizabeth's
household at Cheshunt, the Hertfordshire home of the King's friend, Sir
Anthony Denny, who had known Ascham when they were undergraduates
together at St. John's.

He found Elizabeth an even more adept pupil than he had expected. By
the time she was fourteen her French was fluent, though she spoke it with
an accent, which a French envoy was to imitate, parodying the way she
drew out her a's; *"Paar ma foi!"* she would say, *"paar dieu!"* Her Italian
was also fluent; and this accomplishment was to prove extremely useful to
her, since Italian was replacing Latin in western Europe as the language of

international diplomacy. She could also speak Latin well. Indeed, in later life, when responding to a speech from a foreign ambassador who she felt had been impertinent, she brought forth as fluent an outburst of angry Latin as the English ministers who were present had ever heard. "God's death, my Lords," she congratulated herself when she had finished, "I have been forced this day to scour up my old Latin that hath long been a-rusting."

She also spoke Greek more than adequately. "She readeth more Greek every day," Ascham wrote, "than some Prebendaries of this Church do in a whole week." He had come across other learned ladies in his time. The daughters of his Cambridge colleague, Anthony Cooke, whom their father had taught, were said to be the two cleverest women in England. But among them all, the "brightest star" was his "illustrious Lady Elizabeth." They read Cicero together and Livy, Sophocles and Isocrates as well as the Greek Testament and even Cyprian and Melanchthon. They listened to music in which she as well as he delighted; and he encouraged her in practicing her handwriting, both the elegant, delicate script in which she was instructed by her Italian master, Battisti Castiglioni, and her normal hand which acquired its own precision and characteristic beauty, except when she wrote in a great hurry and then it became almost indecipherable. She could talk intelligently on almost any intellectual topic and liked to spend three hours a day reading history. Even when out walking she would take a book from the pouch she wore hanging from her girdle. Indeed, Ascham seems to have been concerned that she might work too hard and be pushed too fast. "If you pour much drink into a goblet, the most part will dash out and run over," he told Mrs. Ashley. "If ye pour it softly you may fill it even to the top, and so her Grace, I doubt not, by little and little may be increased in learning, that at length greater cannot be required."

In schools at that time the day was arduous and long, beginning as early as six o'clock in the morning or in the summer even at five, the pupils being kept to their books by the constant threat of the regularly wielded birch. But, as he explained in *The Scholemaster,* this was not Ascham's way. Children should be encouraged rather than coerced. He agreed with Sir Thomas Elyot who, in *The Boke called Governour* which was dedicated to Henry VIII, had suggested that young pupils should not be "inforced by violence to lerne but . . . swetely allured with praises and such praty gyftes as [they] delite in." As Ascham himself told Mrs. Ashley, the younger, the more tender a child's mind was, the "quicker, the easier to break."

Interesting as he found his pupil, though, Ascham was not happy in royal service. Obliged to attend the court, he found its atmosphere wholly uncongenial, its denizens either trivial or corrupt, a sad contrast with Cambridge, which he was able to visit all too infrequently. Frustrated and unhappy, he quarreled with the steward of the Lady Elizabeth's household and then, as his biographer recorded, since "a coolness sprang up between himself and his mistress, he hastily resigned his post to resume his own studies, and his official duties as Public Orator at Cambridge."

After his departure the Lady Elizabeth's education continued much as before. She was growing from childhood now into an attractive young woman, polite, well-mannered and composed, "a very witty and gentyll young lady," in the description of William Thomas, Clerk of the Closet. On a visit to John Cheke at Ampthill, the antiquary John Leland was presented first to Prince Edward, then to the Lady Elizabeth who, besides impressing him with her excellent Latin, captivated him by her grave charm. Children of her own age, however, were inclined to regard her as rather withdrawn, sometimes even haughty. Jane Dormer, the granddaughter of Prince Edward's Chamberlain, Sir William Sidney, described her as "proud and disdainful," so much so that these unpleasant traits in her character "much blemished the handsomeness and beauty of her person." Elizabeth was certainly most striking in appearance with her reddish golden hair, her white skin, her long, slightly hooked nose, her extraordinarily long-fingered hands of which she was already so proud that she displayed them against her bodice or skirt in gestures that were to become instinctive.

She was growing too old now to find Prince Edward's companionship interesting. They still gave each other presents; they still exchanged letters, usually in Latin, when their households were in different palaces. "Change of place did not vex me so much, dearest sister, as your going from me," Edward wrote to her at the beginning of 1546 in reply to a letter regretting that he had had to go to Hertford when her household had been directed to Enfield. "Now there can be nothing pleasanter than a letter from you . . . It is some comfort in my grief that my chamberlain tells me I may hope to visit you soon (if nothing happens to either of us in the meantime). Farewell dearest sister." Yet the days of their close intimacy were past. Jane Dormer thought that the Prince preferred the company of Princess Mary to that of Elizabeth, even though he was over twenty years younger than his elder sister.

When Edward was nine his father died. He was not told immediately. He was at Ashridge at the time, and it was supposed that he would be easier to deal with if he were with his sister when the news was broken to him. So he was brought to Enfield and in the Presence Chamber there, with Elizabeth standing by, Edward Seymour, Lord Hertford, knelt down before him to tell his nephew that he was King of England. The boy burst into tears; so did his sister; they clung to each other sobbing uncontrollably. It was the last time they were to be so close. Soon afterwards Edward was taken away to London to begin his unhappy reign under the influence of Lord Hertford, who had himself appointed Protector and then created Duke of Somerset.

Elizabeth continued to write to her brother regularly but she saw him infrequently and their meetings could never now be marked by that easy affection which they had shown towards each other as children. Elizabeth was entering another world as Edward was; and in her new world loomed the fascinating, charming presence of the Protector's younger brother, Thomas Seymour, Lord Seymour of Sudeley, the red-bearded Lord High Admiral of England who had acquired huge estates in Wiltshire and along the Welsh Marches when his brother had seized power.

Thomas Seymour was an extremely good-looking man, lively, forceful, aggressively masculine, utterly selfish and, to most women, irresistible. The widowed Queen, Catherine Parr, certainly found him so; and having been in love with him before her marriage to King Henry, had no hesitation in accepting him as her husband now, after his previous suggestion that he should marry the Lady Elizabeth had been quickly rejected by the horrified members of the Council. Convinced that he should have been appointed Protector jointly with his elder brother, Seymour accepted his role as husband of the Queen Dowager as a kind of compensation, knowing that, since Elizabeth had been entrusted to her stepmother's care, he would find ways of gaining the political influence to which he aspired. He married Queen Catherine secretly and became a frequent visitor to her home in Chelsea, bursting upon the household there with the unselfconscious animation of a genial buccaneer.

Elizabeth's governess, Kat Ashley, seemed to be as taken with him as was the Queen Dowager; but John Ashley recognized the danger which the incursions of Thomas Seymour presented to her charge, an inexperienced fourteen-year-old girl, who seemed more than a little attracted by him, who seemed to listen intently when he was spoken of and to blush when drawn into conversations about him. Ashley told his wife that she ought to "take heed, for he did fear that the Lady Elizabeth did bear some affection to my Lord Admiral."

Seymour did all he could to intrigue and excite her. He romped with her and her ladies in that boisterous way which allows lasciviousness to

pass for foolery; he sent her and Kat Ashley saucy messages such as one
that demanded to know whether Kat Ashley's "great buttocks" had grown
"any less or not." He would tease Elizabeth and buffet her, striking her
"on the back or on the buttocks familiarly." He would come into her
bedchamber, having left the Queen Dowager's in his nightgown and slippers, and either cautiously lift or snatch back the curtains and make as if
to jump at her, while she would crawl further down into the bedclothes.
On one morning at least he tried to kiss her in bed; and to this Kat Ashley
did object, though not it seems very sternly, protesting that it was shameful to see a man come so "bare-legged to a maid's chamber." The Queen
Dowager knew of his behavior, and, as though to show she thought nothing of it, she joined in the romps herself.

> They both tickled my Lady Elizabeth in bed [Kat Ashley later deposed]. And
> another time at Hanworth he romped with her in the garden, and cut her
> gown, being black cloth, into a hundred pieces and when [I] came up and
> chid Lady Elizabeth, she assured me she could not strive withal, for the
> Queen held her while the Lord Admiral cut the dress.

The horseplay was now getting out of hand. Seymour, having obtained a
master-key of the Lady Elizabeth's apartments, would unlock her door
and let himself in unexpectedly; and she would fly from her book to her
ladies and hide behind the curtains while he "tarried a long time in hopes
she would come out."

Then one day, so it appears, the Queen, on going to see Elizabeth in her
apartment, found her husband holding the girl in his arms. She evidently
decided now that the games had gone too far; and she thought it best that
Elizabeth and her household should be sent away, particularly as she herself was pregnant at last at the age of thirty-six. It was arranged that
Elizabeth should move to Sir Anthony Denny's house at Cheshunt. There
was no open quarrel and Elizabeth was soon writing to her stepmother in
the same affectionate way as before, signing herself "your humble daughter
Elizabeth."

Both the Queen and Elizabeth were in poor health. The Queen's pregnancy was not an easy one: Elizabeth wrote to her to commiserate with
her on her being "so big with child and so sickly." On 30 August 1548 at
Sudeley Castle the baby – to the father's disappointment, a girl – was born;
and a week later the mother died of puerperal fever. It was suggested to
Elizabeth by Mrs. Ashley that she should write a letter of condolence to
the bereaved husband; but she, declining to believe that he could be much

distressed, refused to do so. "I said I would not do it," she later recalled, "for he needed it not."

Her own ill health showed little sign of improvement. Whether or not as a result of the recent emotional turmoil she had undergone, she was suffering from violent headaches and pain behind the eyes. From time to time, so Mrs. Ashley said, "she was sick in her bed"; and, when she reached the age of menstruation, her periods were highly irregular or, as some reported, non-existent, as in cases of amenorrhoea.

She was, however, as bright and astute as ever, displaying all her familiar spirit when, soon after the Queen Dowager's death, her cofferer, or financial comptroller, Blanche Parry's brother, Thomas Parry, approached her with a message from the Lord High Admiral, Lord Seymour.

Parry, an ingratiating though often irascible Welshman, had been on a visit to London where he had met Lord Seymour, who had offered to lend Parry's young mistress his London house, Seymour Place, as a town house for herself and her household. By her father's will, Lady Elizabeth had inherited Durham House, a "stately and high" mansion "supported with lofty marble pillars" in the Strand, which once had belonged to Cardinal Wolsey as Bishop of Durham and which Wolsey's successor had been obliged to exchange for a less desirable mansion known as Coldharbour in Thames Street. But Durham House had been taken over by the Protector, and the Lady Elizabeth was consequently without a house of her own in London. She accepted with pleasure when Parry conveyed Lord Seymour's offer to her; but when he went on to suggest that she might consider marrying the widowed Seymour and exchanging the estates she owned in the west country for other land close to the Seymour estates there, she grew cautious and reserved. Once the time for marriage came, she said, she would do as God put her in mind to do. As for Lord Seymour's additional proposal that she ingratiate herself with his sister-in-law, the Duchess of Somerset, she would have nothing to do with it. The Duchess was the daughter of Sir Edward Stanhope of Sudbury, Suffolk and, on her mother's side, a direct descendant of Edward III. An excessively proud and vain woman, she had been constantly in dispute over precedence with Catherine Parr – whose ancestry was undistinguished in comparison with hers – and she had once haughtily reprimanded Mrs. Ashley for allowing her charge to go to a party held on the river after dark, informing the governess in her imperious way that she was not fit to be looking after a king's daughter. The Lady Elizabeth told Parry that she would not dream of paying court to such a woman, desiring him to inform the Lord High Admiral that she had no intention

of doing so. She then prudently asked Parry to tell Mrs. Ashley all that
had passed between them.

So Parry left to seek out the governess, who expressed herself delighted
that so attractive a man should have proposed marriage to her charge. "I
would," she said, "wish her his wife before all men living." Parry himself
was not so sure that the marriage was a good idea; he believed the Lord
High Admiral had not treated his late wife very well. "Tush! Tush!" replied
Mrs. Ashley. "I know him better than you do." He would make a great
fuss of Elizabeth. She went on to reveal why her household had been sent
away to Cheshunt, a revelation that astonished Parry. Seeing his amazement, she sighed and added, "I will tell you more another time." Soon
after this interview both Mrs. Ashley and Thomas Parry were removed
from Elizabeth's household.

The Lord High Admiral had overplayed his hand. Having beguiled Kat
Ashley, he had set about trying to win the affection and confidence of
Elizabeth's brother, King Edward VI. He had given him pocket-money,
which was doled out to him scantily by the Lord Admiral's brother, the
Duke of Somerset who was now "Protector of all the realms and domains
of the King's majesty and Governor of his most royal person." He had
made overtures to the King's attendants; he had endeavored to arrange a
marriage between Edward and his cousin, Lady Jane Grey, a daughter of
Henry Grey, Marquess of Dorset, and granddaughter of Henry VIII's
younger sister, Mary, who was then living in the Lord High Admiral's
household. He had tried to foster a dislike and distrust of the Lord Protector in Edward's mind; and, believing that he had succeeded in doing so, he
had made an attempt to abduct him and to bring him under his own
personal control. He had planned to finance his rebellion by blackmailing
the vice-treasurer of the Bristol mint, who had defrauded the Crown of
vast amounts of money, and by entering into negotiations with pirates
whom, as Lord High Admiral, it was his responsibility to bring to justice.
His conspiracy had been discovered and he had been taken to the Tower,
precipitating the arrest of Mrs. Ashley and Thomas Parry, his supposed
accomplices in his designs upon the Lady Elizabeth.

After these two former members of her household had been escorted to
London, the Protector sent down a special commissioner, Sir Robert
Tyrwhit, to interrogate Elizabeth herself and to discover how deeply, if at
all, she was implicated in the Lord High Admiral's seditious plans. Tyrwhit
told her that Mrs. Ashley and Parry had both been taken to the Tower, at
which she was "marvellously abashed, and did weep tenderly a long time."
She knew she herself was in grave danger – Tyrwhit had pointedly re-

minded her that "she was but a subject." She was well aware, too, that she must not refuse to answer Tyrwhit's questions, for she might thus be suspected of complicity, or accused of being in contempt of the King, the Lord Protector and the Council. Yet she must not, by her answers, incriminate either the Lord High Admiral or Kat Ashley or Thomas Parry; she must not even hint that the blame for any indiscretion of which she might have been guilty through her association with Lord Seymour lay with any members of her household. Tyrwhit did his best to persuade her to escape from her predicament by pleading her youth and inexperience and by acknowledging her elders as culprits. But she steadfastly declined to do so, realizing that their guilt might imply her own; and Tyrwhit was eventually obliged to report that in no way could she be brought to confess to "any practice by Mistress Ashley or the cofferer [Thomas Parry] concerning my Lord Admiral." "And yet," Tyrwhit added, "I do see it in her face that she is guilty, and do perceive as yet she will abide more storms ere she accuse Mistress Ashley."

After Mrs. Ashley had been released from the Tower to be confined under house arrest in Westminster, Tyrwhit examined the Lady Elizabeth again, endeavoring to wring from her by "gentle persuasion" the confession that threats had failed to elicit, recognizing that she had "a very good wit" and that nothing could be got from her except by "great policy." But his new methods were scarcely more effective than those he had tried first; and, even after he had shown her depositions signed by Parry and Mrs. Ashley retailing all that had happened in the Queen Dowager's household between her and the Lord High Admiral – the sight of which made her catch her breath – he had to content himself with her own signature to a document in which she admitted merely that she had been told that Lord Seymour wished to marry her and that she knew that people were talking of their relationship. She insisted, though, that the latest stories which were spread about her were false, that outrageous rumors that she was with child by Seymour and being held in the Tower as a prisoner ought to be publicly contradicted. She wrote to the Lord Protector to say so, asking him to deny them openly since "no such rumours should be spread [about] any of the King's Majesty's sisters, as I am, though unworthy." "My lord, these are shameful slanders," she told him in one of several subsequent letters which showed that she was fully aware of what was at stake and how best to deal with the problem, "for which, besides the great desire I have to see the King's Majesty, I shall most heartily desire your Lordship, that I may come to the court . . . that I may show myself there as I am."

So far as the Lady Elizabeth was concerned, the matter was allowed to rest. But it was clear that her household could not remain as it was. Tyrwhit had discovered that Parry was quite unfit to be a treasurer: on looking into his account books, he had found them "so indiscreetly made" that the man had evidently "little understanding to execute his office." Mrs. Ashley, it was also considered, was not to be trusted to execute hers. She was replaced by a most unwilling Lady Tyrwhit. Elizabeth, who remained devoted to Kat Ashley, was extremely grumpy when her new governess arrived. She was Mrs. Ashley's pupil, she complained, and had done nothing to deserve the rebuke that her replacement implied. She did not want any more governesses: she would rather have none. Trywhit replied that in his opinion she ought to have two. She spent most of that night in tears, and the next day was gloomy and petulant. She wrote again to the Protector to express her grievances, to complain that people would say that she had been sent a new governess because of her "lewd behaviour." Intensely anxious always to appear before the public in a favorable light, she was deeply concerned that the whole affair might lose her the good opinion of the people. She could name some of those who were spreading abroad the slanders about her, but she did not care to do so as this might suggest she was eager to see them punished. Such revelations, however justified, might bring upon her the ill-will of her brother's subjects which she would be "loth to have." She asked the Council to "send forth a proclamation into the counties, that they refrain their tongues, declaring how the tales be but lies." The Council considered this plea and found it unobjectionable. A proclamation was accordingly drafted – though never issued – forbidding the issue of slanders about the sisters of the King.

The Lady Elizabeth wrote also to the Protector on behalf of Mrs. Ashley, pointing out that so long as her former governess remained in custody, people would have grounds for saying that Elizabeth too must be guilty of the crime with which she stood accused, and had been pardoned only on account of her youth. This plea also was accepted, and Mrs. Ashley was released. But for the Lord High Admiral there was to be no pardon. Accused, amongst many other charges, of plotting to marry Elizabeth "by secret and crafty means . . . to the danger of the King's Majesty's person," he was condemned to death as a traitor; and on the morning of 20 March 1549 he was beheaded on Tower Hill. Referring later to his fate, Elizabeth is reported to have remarked with a laconism which reflected her anxiety to show to the world how little Lord Seymour had meant to her, "This day died a man with much wit and very little judgement."

She had still not recovered from the illness from which she had been suffering intermittently ever since the middle of the previous summer. Indeed, she grew worse, having to spend whole days in bed where she was attended by Dr. Thomas Bill of St. Bartholomew's Hospital, her brother's physician. Under his care she began to get better, and as soon as she was up and about again she wrote to him to thank him for his skillful treatment.

That summer of 1549 she was much more content. The Seymour affair, though having effects upon her development which no one could gauge, was receding into the past; Mrs. Ashley had been allowed to come back to her; and in September she was permitted to have Thomas Parry back as well, though she sensibly appointed a more exact official to help him with his sums and thereafter took the trouble to supervise the accounts herself, checking the figures carefully, signing the columns only when she was satisfied as to their accuracy, revealing that deep concern for strict economy which was to characterize her rule.

She still suffered from headaches and what no doubt was migraine, an affliction which, so she regretted in one of her letters, prevented her from writing to her brother as often as she would otherwise have done. She wished, too, she said, that she could see him more often. She sent him her portrait in response to his request; assured him always of her love; and on 17 March 1550, six months after her sixteenth birthday, when it was considered that she had outlived her disgrace over the Seymour affair, she rode into London with a large retinue to visit him. Thereafter she was usually accompanied by impressive entourages. On important outings she was escorted by as many as two hundred horsemen; and when she had guests in her own household they were entertained by minstrels, lute-players, harpists and pipers. "She was most honourably received by the Council," reported the Emperor's ambassador one day in January 1551, "to show the people how much glory belongs to her who has embraced the new religion and has become a very great lady."

She was watched with the closest interest. She did not often appear in public and when she did so people were curious to see her and to form impressions about her. She was undeniably a striking figure, upright, pale, dignified, controlled, rather taller than the average. "She greatly prefers a simple elegance to show and splendour," Roger Ascham noted approvingly, "despising the outward adorning of plaiting the hair and wearing of gold." At St. James's Palace her fine, straight hair and modest, even somber dress seemed strangely out of place among the other ladies whose clothes were so much brighter and whose hair was tightly curled, brightly jeweled and heavily scented. Renaissance ideals of beauty required a white skin and fair hair, a high smooth forehead and barely perceptible eyebrows and lashes. The Lady Elizabeth enjoyed these attributes as given by nature; but those less favored had to bleach their hair by sitting in the sun, protecting their faces from its rays by wearing masks which they kept in position by a button held between the teeth. They felt obliged to whiten their skin by applications of powder made of ground alabaster, and a variety of lotions and ointments containing all manner of ingredients, including beeswax, asses' milk and the ground jawbones of hogs. Such preparations were harmless enough, but others used for more dramatic results were highly dangerous. In order to obtain the desired pallor some ladies resorted to white lead mixed with vinegar or with borax and sulphur; and, to make their lips a vivid red in contrast, they used madder, red ocher and red crystalline mercuric sulphide as well as cochineal. For the treatment of spots and freckles they applied birch-tree sap, ground brimstone, oil of turpentine and sublimate of mercury, which in time led to a skin as ravaged as white lead left it mummified. It was then necessary to apply a glaze of white of egg to the skin so that it resembled polished marble, particularly if attempts had to be made to disguise the effects of smallpox. The impression of artificiality was emphasized by hairs being plucked out, if not dyed or bleached, by lines representing thin veins being drawn upon the bosom, which unmarried women left largely exposed, by the application of kohl around the eyes, the pupils of which were much enlarged by belladonna, and by the teeth being rendered unnaturally white by vigorous rubbing with aqua fortis or a mixture of powdered pumice-stone, brick and coral.

As yet, the Lady Elizabeth felt no need of these aids to beauty to which other ladies resorted and of which she herself was to make use in time. Her appearance seemed quite unspoiled by artifice. In later life she scented herself with marjoram, but she much disliked those heavy scents favored by some men and women at court, scents containing aloes, nutmeg and storax, or, like the one said to have been invented by her father, comprising musk, rose-water, ambergris and civet.

Her demure behavior and the modest clothes she wore on her visits to court appeared to some observers almost prudish. One remarked that she must still be trying to live down her scandalous behavior with the Lord High Admiral. John Aylmer, who had known her since she was a child and was later to become Bishop of London, praised the plainness of her hairstyle and her "pure hands"; while the Prostestant propagandist, John Foxe, wrote approvingly of her disregard of the newly fashionable clothes worn by some of the other ladies at court. They "flourished in their bravery, with their hair frowsened and curled, and double curled, yet she altered

nothing, but to the shame of them all, kept her old maidenly shamefast-
ness." Her brother, the King, referred to her as his "sweet sister Temper-
ance."

She treated him with affection but with the utmost respect, sitting politely upright in his presence, kneeling before him when he sat in state
beneath the royal canopy, concluding her letters to him as from "Your
Majesty's most humble sister and servant." "I have seen the Lady Elizabeth kneel before her brother five times before she sat down," reported an
Italian visitor to court of the ceremonial meal times, "and then so far from
the head of the table . . . that the canopy did not hang over her." No one
could doubt, though, that just as she was being watched, so she was
keeping her alert eyes upon those around her, upon the shifts of friendship
and changes of allegiances, the politics of power.

The King's uncle, the good-natured but overbearing Protector, the
Duke of Somerset, was losing his influence and gradually being supplanted
by John Dudley, Earl of Warwick, who, recognizing that the King was not
likely to live long, determined to obtain the crown for his own family. So,
after Somerset had been brought to trial and execution, Warwick, who
had himself created Duke of Northumberland, persuaded the King to sign
letters patent by which both Edward's sisters were set aside in favor of any
male heir that might be born during the King's lifetime to his aunt the
Duchess of Suffolk. Failing that, the crown was to pass to the heirs of the
Duchess's granddaughter, the Lady Jane Grey, who was to be married,
most unwillingly, to one of Northumberland's sons, Lord Guildford Dudley. The King had been reluctant at first to agree to Northumberland's
proposals, to lay aside the will of a father whom he had held in such awe.
But Northumberland had put it into his mind that if Mary were to become
Queen she would immediately force Popery upon the nation and that it
was "the part of a religious and good prince to set aside all respects of
blood where God's glory and the subjects' weal may be endangered."
"That your Majesty should do otherwise," he added darkly, "were, after
this life, to expect revenge at God's dreadful tribunal." As for the Lady
Elizabeth, to set her aside too was inevitable, for the Lady Mary "could
not be put by unless the Lady Elizabeth were put by also." Besides, if
either of them married, their inevitably foreign husbands would abolish all
the country's ancient rights and immunities "until they had extinguished at
last the very name of England." The King needed little inducement. He
appeared convinced that Mary must not succeed him and that, if she did
not, Elizabeth must not do so either. He decided that the succession
should pass not to the heirs male of Lady Jane Grey but to Lady Jane

herself; and, with "sharp words and angry countenance," he told the reluctant Lord Chief Justice to draw up a will along these lines, superseding his father's. Edward, with a precociously confident authority, then commanded the Privy Councilors from his sickbed to endorse the deed.

Once it had been decided to divert the succession of the crown, it was considered essential to keep Elizabeth away from further contact with her brother. There was no fear that the boy would change his mind in favor of his Roman Catholic sister Mary, because his Protestantism was firm and unshakable; but there was still the chance that he might be induced to bequeath his crown to Elizabeth, a good Protestant as he knew her to be and an apparently devoted sister of whom he was evidently fond. Northumberland, therefore, saw to it that brother and sister did not meet; her letters to him were not delivered; and when she set out upon a visit to him she was intercepted and sent back to Hatfield. She wrote to him from there expressing her concern for his health and her desire to see him again. This letter, like others, did not reach him.

Soon after the King's "Devise for the Succession" had been signed it was rumored that he was dying. One of his doctors told the Spanish ambassador that he would be gone by June. In the past he had not been a sickly child, and great care had been taken to ensure that he did not become one. But of late he had contracted one illness after another, and was now covered with ulcers and bedsores; his stomach was swollen; his cough was constant; he vomited frequently; he was feverish and in much pain; there was a "suppurating tumour" on his lung. The doctors prescribed the stimulants and medicines that were commonly used in such cases as his, one of these being nine spoonfuls of a liquid distilled from spearmint and red fennel, liverwort and turnip, dates and raisins, an ounce of mace, two sticks of celery, and the quarters of a sow nine days old. On being told what his doctors were doing to their patient, William Cecil, one of the Secretaries of State, wrote to a friend who was also ill, "God deliver you from the physicians." Finally, poisoned by the medicines that had at first stimulated him, with grotesquely swollen legs and arms and darkened skin, with fingers and toes touched by gangrene, Edward's hair and nails began to fall out; and on 6 July 1553 he died, too weak to cough, murmuring a prayer.

3

The Queen's Sister

*"I have been kept a great while from
you, desolately alone."*

The Lady Elizabeth was at Hatfield Palace, one of her favorite residences, when news was brought to her of her brother's death. With the caution already characteristic of her nature she remained there while the Duke of Northumberland proclaimed Lady Jane Grey Queen of England, letting it be known that she was ill, heeding advice not to obey the Duke's summons to come immediately to London, waiting upon events and, in the meantime, informing Northumberland that if he had anything to say to her he must first consult her sister.

The Lady Mary herself set off for Framlingham Castle in Norfolk. Here she was soon joined by over forty thousand adherents including mutineers from a ship that had been dispatched by Northumberland to prevent her escaping to rally support for her cause on the Continent. Mary had no need of such support. Her cousin, the Emperor Charles V, whom she regarded as a kind of father-figure, advised her to submit, convinced that her force would be overwhelmed in any struggle for power. But the people, Protestants and Roman Catholics alike, showed themselves determined to thwart Northumberland's *coup d'état*. A quatrain from the *Legend of Sir Nicholas Throckmorton* expresses the views of many Protestants such as Throckmorton himself:

> And though I liked not the religion
> Which all her life Queen Mary had professed
> Yet in my mind that wicked notion
> Right heirs for to displace, I did detest.

John Hooper, Bishop of Gloucester and Worcester, and one of the most advanced of the Protestant reformers, also strongly opposed the attempt to set aside Mary, insisting that, whatever her faith, she was the rightful Queen; and when Nicholas Ridley, Bishop of London, forcefully denounced Mary's religious beliefs and declared both her and her sister to be illegitimate in a sermon delivered at St. Paul's Cross before the Lord Mayor and Corporation, he was shouted down by the congregation. Within a fortnight the whole affair was resolved: the Duke of Northumberland was brought a prisoner to the Tower, through streets crowded with people reviling him as a traitor, having vainly tried to save himself by abandoning Lady Jane and, with the tears running down his cheeks, proclaiming Mary Queen. Arraigned for high treason and condemned, he was executed on Tower Hill. Lady Jane was also arrested and six months later she too was beheaded, together with the man she had so unwillingly married.

Londoners greeted the defeat of Northumberland's *coup* with delight. "There was such a shout of the people, with casting of caps and crying, 'God save Queen Mary!'" wrote one of them in his diary, "that the style of the proclamation could not be heard . . . Great and many fires [were made] through all the streets and lanes within the city, with setting tables in the streets and banqueting also, with all bells ringing in every parish church, till ten of the clock at night, that the inestimable joys and rejoicing of the people cannot be reported."

As soon as the crisis was past, the Lady Elizabeth traveled to London with a large escort of horsemen to acknowledge her sister as Queen. From Somerset Place in the Strand, where she spent the night of 29 July, she rode down the Strand to the city and out through Aldgate, one of London's six gates originally built by the Romans, and here, beside the road which led to Colchester, she waited to welcome Queen Mary. The Queen's entourage was seen approaching the city on 3 August. The sisters greeted each other with apparent affection, the Queen holding the Lady Elizabeth's hand as she spoke to her. Then, accompanied by an immense retinue of ladies and gentlemen, city dignitaries and foreign ambassadors, they rode back together through Aldgate, into a city bedecked in the Queen's honor, the crowds cheering them through the pealing church bells, Mary looking tired but happy, so one spectator noticed, Elizabeth smiling as she rode along behind her, sharing her triumph. They passed the Tower where the Queen formally released from captivity several of its inmates, including Stephen Gardiner, Bishop of Winchester, who had been imprisoned in the previous reign because of his opposition to doctrinal reformation and who was now appointed Lord Chancellor.

Anxious as she was to reward those who had remained steadfast in their loyalty to the old faith, the Queen had no wish to behave unmercifully to those who had abandoned it, but were now prepared to return outwardly to the fold. Elizabeth showed herself to be one of these. At first she had declined to attend Mass at court, declaring that she could not do so while she remained a Protestant. At that time her sister's intentions were not yet as clear as they were later to become. A cautious approach had been urged upon Mary by Charles V's ambassador, Simon Renard, who had come to England to arrange a marriage between the Queen and the Emperor's only and dutiful son, Philip, soon to become King of Spain. Fearing that Spain would be blamed if the Queen tried to force anti-Protestant measures upon her subjects and that a Spanish match might then be difficult to bring off, Renard had warned Mary of the danger of proceeding too precipitately against the established religion. As though in accord with this advice a proclamation was issued on 12 August announcing that, while the Queen hoped that her people would become good Catholics, they would not be coerced against their consciences. Not long afterwards, however, there were anti-Catholic demonstrations in London and, in consequence, arrests of leading Protestants. Both Hugh Latimer, the former Bishop of Worcester, by then sixty-seven years old, a most assiduous preacher against what he took to be the abuses of Papacy, and Thomas Cranmer, Archbishop of Canterbury, a firm opponent of the celebration of Mass, had been sent to the Tower. Simon Renard considered that it might be as well if the Lady Elizabeth, with her known Protestant sympathies, were sent there too. She could be highly dangerous to Mary as the figurehead of Catholicism's enemies. "She seems to be clinging to the new religion out of policy to attract and win the support of those who are of this religion," he warned Mary. "We may be mistaken in suspecting her of this, but at this early stage it is safer to forestall than be forestalled."

Conscious of the perilous position into which she might be maneuvered, and determined not to follow Cranmer to the Tower, Elizabeth requested an audience with her sister. After a delay of two days this was granted her in one of the long galleries of Richmond Palace, their grandfather's favorite palace where their father had spent much of his boyhood; and here, kneeling before the Queen, with tears in her eyes, and, so Mary said, "very timid' and trembling, Elizabeth pleaded once again that she had been brought up as a Protestant and had "never been taught the doctrines of the ancient religion." She asked for Catholic books to guide her into the path of truth. Her sister replied that she hoped she would attend Mass in the Chapel Royal when the court returned to Whitehall, mentioning 8 September, the Feast of the Nativity of the Blessed Virgin, as a suitable day. Elizabeth said that she had not yet recovered from her recent illness and was still suffering from stomach pains; but in the end she decided it would be prudent to go. She did go, on the way complaining of severe pain, "wearing a suffering air," and asking – some said pointedly asking – one of the Queen's ladies to rub her stomach for her.

Neither Renard nor the Lord Chancellor, Gardiner, believed Elizabeth to be sincere in asking for instruction in the Catholic faith, which they believed she rejected out of hand. She was dissembling, Renard thought, "the better to play her game"; while the French ambassador, Antoine de Noailles, reported to Henri II that it was widely supposed she had attended Mass not so much from good devotion as "for fear of the danger and peril which were facing her." Mary herself suspected that when she had asked for Catholic books she had done so "only out of hypocrisy," that she would stay away from Mass as often as she could, that her words were never to be fully trusted when her own interests were threatened. Certainly Elizabeth stayed away from Mass the Sunday after the Feast of the Nativity. She did attend the following Sunday, however, and thereafter went quite regularly, though she wore round her waist a little gold ornament in the shape of a book which was inscribed with the words: "The Prayer of King Edward VI which he made the 6th day of July 1553, and the 6th year of his reign, 3 hours before his death, to himself, his eyes being closed, and thinking none heard him, the 16th year of his age." When, inappropriately, a requiem Mass was said for her brother, Elizabeth did not attend it. The Queen, however, was grateful that her sister had publicly attended Mass as often as she had done. She presented her with a diamond and ruby brooch as well as a rosary of white coral, happy in the knowledge that Elizabeth's submission would make it so much less difficult to induce Parliament to vote for the re-establishment of Roman Catholicism in England.

At Mary's coronation, which took place in Westminster Abbey on 1 October 1553, Elizabeth was allowed to take a prominent place. She was the first to take the oath of allegiance, and her coach followed immediately behind that of the Queen in the subsequent procession. Although she remained officially a bastard when an Act of Parliament declared her sister to be the legitimate daughter of their father's marriage to Catherine of Aragon, she nevertheless retained her rights as successor to the throne under King Henry's will; and she was granted equal precedence with Anne of Cleves, with whom she was seated at the coronation banquet. She still lived in considerable state, and was in regular receipt of presents from her sister, particularly of clothes and jewelry. It was believed that these gifts were a hint from the Queen to her sister that she ought to wear more colorful clothes, instead of the plain and simple dresses that she so pointedly affected and which seemed to proclaim her Protestant sympathies.

This did not go unremarked by Simon Renard, who continued to insist that the Lady Elizabeth should be excluded from the succession and sent to the Tower for questioning. Such drastic measures were, however, opposed by a majority of the Queen's Privy Council, who considered that her attendance at Mass should be accepted as sincere and that any future displays of independence might best be checked by a husband who could be trusted to take her in hand or, even better, one who might take her out of the country. Several bridegrooms had already been proposed, among them Emmanuel Philibert, Duke of Savoy, one of the Emperor's most successful generals; Philip of Spain's son, Don Carlos, a child twelve years younger than herself; a slightly older boy, a member of the Medici family of Florence; a son of Hans Frederick of Saxony; a son of the Earl of Arran; a brother of the King of Denmark; the Dukes of Enghien and Aumale; and both a brother of the Duke of Ferrara and the Duke's son, "one of the goodliest young men of all Italy." For a time interest centered upon Edward Courtenay, son of the Marquess of Exeter and Edward IV's great-great-grandson, who had been imprisoned with his parents in the Tower when he was twelve years old and had been held there for almost fifteen years until Queen Mary had released him. His father, who had been in correspondence with Cardinal Reginald Pole, had been executed in 1538; his mother, godmother to the Lady Elizabeth and a most devout Catholic, had been pardoned and released two and a half years later and had since become a lady-in-waiting to Queen Mary. Courtenay himself was a pale, fair young man with a rather vacant expression and a strong desire to indulge in all those pleasures of which his long incarceration had deprived him. There had been talk of his being married to the Queen herself before the match with Philip of Spain had seemed to her more desirable, and then it had been suggested to her that, since he was a confirmed Catholic like his mother, it might be a more satisfactory arrangement for him to be married to Elizabeth, or even, perhaps, for him to be designated heir to the throne in Elizabeth's place.

The idea of marriage to Edward Courtenay was evidently not unattractive to Elizabeth herself. It was noticed at court that she looked upon him with favor; it was even suggested later by a court official that she was in love with him, that her disappointment at not becoming his wife was a principal reason why she declined to become the wife of anyone else. Courtenay himself seems to have had no desire to be her husband. She was "too proud," he is supposed to have told the Queen; he would much rather marry "some simple girl." Perhaps he was a little frightened of her, as people were already inclined to be; she was, indeed, in Simon Renard's opinion, already "greatly to be feared"; she had "a spirit full of incantation."

Even so, she and Courtenay were often to be seen together, and Mary's advisers began to believe that they might be plotting some mischief. After all they would, if married, represent a real threat to Mary because of their joint claims to the throne and the support they would command in the country, particularly in the west where Courtenay held large estates as Earl of Devonshire, and in London and the south-east where Elizabeth was so popular. Certainly their marriage would be regarded in quite a different light from the impending union of Mary and Philip of Spain, which was causing so much disquiet, even disgust, in the country. Renard warned Mary constantly not to trust Elizabeth; she was "too clever" and "too sly." The Queen replied that she did not trust her, but that she would soon learn if she were indiscreet enough to intrigue against her, since Courtenay would certainly tell his mother, and his mother would just as certainly tell the Queen. In any case, so Mary said, she would do all she could to prevent her sister succeeding to the throne. Her affection for her, never warm for long, was gradually being dissipated; the girl's religion was suspect, her popularity galling and dangerous. She had been kind to her up till now; she would continue to give her presents, but it was as well that she should not be allowed to become presumptuous. She was to be required to yield precedence at court to the Duchess of Suffolk and to Lady Margaret Douglas, Countess of Lennox, daughter of her aunt, Margaret Tudor, eldest child of Henry VII.

Feeling slighted by this requirement, Elizabeth asked to be allowed to leave court and to go to her house at Ashridge in Hertfordshire. Permission was granted her; but, before she left, two of her friends in the Council, Lord Paget, who had been a Secretary of State in the reign of Henry VIII, and Henry Fitzalan, Earl of Arundel, Lord Steward of the Household, came to advise her not to become involved in any conspiracies. Already Paget had been warned by two of her servants that Elizabeth was implicated in some sort of plot with the French ambassador, Antoine de Noailles, who was doing his best to undermine the Queen's marriage to Philip of Spain; and although Elizabeth's complicity in this plot could not be established, there could be no doubt that she would be closely watched at Ashridge and any indiscretion would be reported. She assured Paget and Arundel that she would never be so foolish as to conspire against her sister, that her adherence to the Catholic faith was sincere, and that she would take Catholic priests with her to Ashridge so that Mass could be celebrated there in the proper form. She reported these assurances to the

Queen, begging her not to believe any stories she might be told about her until she had been given an opportunity to explain her conduct personally. Mary agreed to this, made her a present of pearls and a sable fur and, after Elizabeth's return to Ashridge, was gratified to receive a request for chasubles, copes, patens and crucifixes.

While Elizabeth was in Hertfordshire, the long-expected revolt against the Spanish match broke out in Kent. A far more wide-ranging rebellion had been planned, but this had come to the ears of the government and the risings elsewhere were either abortive or were soon suppressed. The leader of the rising in Kent was Thomas Wyatt, son of the poet who had been the lover of Anne Boleyn. A brave and personable man, described by a French diplomat who met him in London as a *"gentil chevallier et fort estimé parmy ceste nation,"* Wyatt wrote to Elizabeth and Courtenay to tell them that he intended to overthrow the present government and to place them on the throne. He would raise the standard of revolt in Kent and march upon London. His letters were intercepted as was a letter from Antoine de Noailles to the King of France which implied that Elizabeth knew of the plot and repeated unfounded stories that she had moved from Ashridge to another of her houses where she had "already assembled her supporters." Although the Privy Council could discover no proof of Elizabeth's involvement, they thought it advisable to have her brought to court where they could keep an eye on her. She was accordingly summoned to London; and, when her household replied that she was too ill to travel, that, in her own words, she had "such a cold and headache" as she "had never felt the like," two of the Queen's physicians, Dr. Thomas Wendy and Dr. George Owen, were sent to examine her and to bring her to court in the Queen's litter if they considered she could be moved. Hearing of her excuses, Renard jumped to the conclusion that she was pregnant, probably by Courtenay; de Noailles suggested that the Queen had arranged for her to be poisoned. But after examining her and consulting with each other, the Queen's physicians came to the conclusion that she was suffering from what they described as "watery humours" and what seems to have been inflammation of the kidneys. Her sickness was not feigned, but she was not so ill that her life would be endangered by a journey of scarcely more than thirty miles in a comfortable litter. So three members of the Council, Lord William Howard, Sir Edward Hastings and Sir Thomas Cornwallis, were sent to escort her to London. All three were sympathetic towards Elizabeth and consequently rode very slowly back from Ashridge, covering no more than about six or seven miles a day. By the time they arrived in London, Wyatt's brief rebellion had been suppressed. After a skirmish between the Queen's troops and his dwindling band of supporters – who were dismayed by the lack of enthusiasm for their cause following a disingenuous announcement by the Queen that she would not marry "out of the realm" without the advice of her Council and the consent of Parliament – Wyatt had surrendered near Temple Bar and been taken prisoner to the Tower.

Elizabeth had been sick in the litter, and looked nervous and as pale as her white dress. She had the curtains pulled back so the crowds in the street could see how ill she was. For once she did not smile upon them. Renard said her appearance was "proud, lofty, defiant." She had cause to be frightened, for the evidence pointed to her knowledge of the plot if not to her encouragement of it. The heads and corpses of several of Wyatt's supporters were displayed upon spikes and gibbets. When she arrived at Whitehall most of her household were dismissed; and she was told that her request to see the Queen would not yet be granted: she must first undergo close examination as to the nature of her involvement with Sir Thomas Wyatt. Under questioning by Stephen Gardiner she strongly denied she had had any connection with Wyatt at all, steadfastly refusing to admit that she had done anything for which she could be reproached. Again she asked to see the Queen; again an audience was denied her. The Queen, she was told, would be leaving London soon to hold a Parliament at Oxford; she herself would have to leave Whitehall for closer supervision elsewhere. At first it was proposed that she might be held in house arrest by some member of the Council; but since no Councilor was prepared to undertake so unpleasant and possibly dangerous a responsibility, it was decided that she must be taken to the Tower as Renard and Gardiner had both already advised. So two leading Councilors, one of them, Thomas Radcliffe, Earl of Sussex, who had taken a prominent part in the suppression of Wyatt's rebellion, were sent to the Lady Elizabeth to inform her of this decision.

She listened to Sussex with obvious alarm, and when he had finished speaking she begged to be allowed to write to her sister before she was taken away. Sussex's colleague, the Marquess of Winchester, was reluctant to allow this, but Sussex himself relented: pen and paper were brought into the room and she sat down to her task, writing in her familiar well-formed hand, the occasional repetitions, omissions and erasures in her wordy sentences towards the end of her letter betraying her anxiety:

> I have heard in my time of many cast away for want of coming to the presence of their Prince . . . Therefore once again kneeling with humbleness

of my heart, because I am not suffered to bow the knees of my body, I humbly crave to speak with your Highness, which I would not be so bold to desire if I knew not myself most clear as I know myself most true. And as for the traitor Wyatt, he might peradventure write me a letter but on my faith I never received any from him; and as for the copy of my letter sent to the French King, I pray God confound me eternally if ever I sent him word, message, token or letter by any means, and to this truth I will stand it to my death.

Anxious as always about her reputation with the English people, she asked again for permission to see the Queen,

for that thus shamefully I may not be cried out on, as now I shall be, yea, and without cause. Let conscience move your Highness to take some better way with me than to make me be condemned in all men's sight afore my desert known.

As she drew to the close of the letter she began to write more slowly, hoping, so it was afterwards suggested, that if she spun out the composition long enough, the tide would have gone down so low that it would be impossible for the barge which was to take her to the Tower to shoot between the piers of London Bridge. Having dotted in her last full stop, she drew thick lines diagonally across the sheet so that no forger could make use of the blank space, and wrote at the bottom of the page, "I humbly crave but one word of answer from yourself. Your Highness's most faithful subject that hath been from the beginning and will be [to] my end, Elizabeth."

She had been long enough: they had missed the tide, and would not be able to leave now until long after dark. But a nighttime journey, the Councilors decided, would be risky: an attempt might be made to rescue her under cover of darkness. It would be wiser to wait until the following morning, a Sunday, fortunately Palm Sunday, when the streets would be quiet and the people in church. In the meantime they sent her letter to the Queen, who was angry to receive it and to see how long it must have taken to write. She refused to read it all. Such a thing, she said, would never have been allowed in her father's time; she wished he could come back for a day and give her Councilors the rebuke they richly deserved.

The next morning, 17 March 1554, the rain fell drearily from a grey sky. At nine o'clock the Lady Elizabeth was escorted from her apartments, through the door into the garden, out of the gate and down to the river steps. The barge splashed past the Savoy Stairs and Somerset Water Gate,

by Temple stairs and Paul's Wharf, past Old Swan Stairs and under London
Bridge towards Billingsgate Dock and the Tower. With six of her ladies
and two gentlemen attendants, Elizabeth sat in the barge's cabin sheltering
from the rain; and, when the boatmen began to slow the craft, she came out
to see that she was to be taken into the fortress through the entrance now
known as Traitor's Gate, the one beneath St. Thomas's Tower, a tower of
uncompromising starkness beneath whose grey walls state prisoners were
returned to their cells after their trials in Westminster Hall. Looking up at
the iron grating by which Sir Thomas Wyatt had so recently passed to await
his execution, she begged to be allowed to enter the Tower by any gate but
this. When her request was refused, her misery turned into angry indignation. One of the lords in attendance offered her his cloak to protect her
from the rain, but she scornfully rejected his offer, pushing the cloak away
from her "with a good dash." As soon as she stepped ashore on the landing
steps, she exclaimed, "Here landeth as true a subject, being prisoner, as ever
landed at these stairs. Before Thee, O God, do I speak it, having no other
friend than Thee alone." "Oh Lord!" she added, for the benefit of the
yeoman warders lined up to receive her on the other side of the gate, "I
never thought to have come in here as a prisoner, and I pray you all bear me
witness that I come in as no traitor but as true a woman to the Queen's
Majesty as any as is now living." Several of the warders stepped forward at
these words and knelt down before her. One of them called out, as though
speaking for the rest, "God preserve your Grace!"

   She then sat down on a stone, refusing to go further. The recently
appointed Lieutenant of the Tower, Sir John Brydges, soon to be created
Lord Chandos of Sudeley, a devout Roman Catholic and a kindly man,
said to her gently, "You had best come in, Madam, for here you sit un-
wholsomely."

   "Better sit here," she replied tartly, "than in a worse place, for God
knoweth where you will bring me." And there she sat until one of her
gentleman attendants suddenly burst into tears. This provoked her. She
stood up, upbraided the man for showing such weakness when he ought to
be supporting her by his strength, and thanked God that in her innocence
no one had cause to weep for her. She then allowed herself to be taken
away to the Bell Tower, a corner tower beside the Lieutenant's Lodgings,
so called because it housed the great bell which summoned the garrison to
arms. Here she was taken up to the first floor, to a big, vaulted chamber
with a huge fireplace and three narrow windows in the thick walls. Opposite the door, a passageway led to three latrines set in high niches over-
hanging the moat. As the door clanged shut and was bolted upon the

prisoner and her ladies, the Earl of Sussex said to his companions, "Let us take heed, my Lords, that we go not beyond our commission, for she was our King's daughter." He had already told the Lieutenant of the Tower to treat her well: "Let us use such dealing that we may answer it thereafter, if it shall so happen; for just dealing is always answerable."

Sir John Brydges certainly treated her as the King's daughter. She was allowed to have her meals in his timber-framed lodgings, which had been completed but a short time before; she was permitted to walk with five attendants along the battlements as far as Beauchamp Tower, named after Thomas Beauchamp, Earl of Warwick, a prisoner of King Richard II. She was, indeed, so much indulged that the Constable of the Tower, Sir John Gage, as zealous a Roman Catholic as Brydges but a less kindhearted man, put a stop to her privileges and forbade her servants to bring her extra provisions, requiring instead that they hand them over at the gates, even though the "common rascal soldiers" commandeered and ate what they fancied before allowing the rest through for the prisoners. "More for love of the Pope than for hate of her person," Gage also put a stop to her walks across the battlements; and, when her health began to suffer from this lack of fresh air and exercise and she was consequently permitted to resume her walks and to stroll in the Tower's walled garden, he ordered that she was always to be accompanied by an armed guard. Even a four-year-old boy, the son of one of the warders, who approached the prisoner with a present of a posy of flowers, was closely questioned in case he were the bearer of a secret message and warned that he would be whipped if he spoke to her again. Despite this warning the boy crept through the gate to tell her he would not be able to come to her any more. She smiled in reply, but said nothing.

She herself was also closely examined by Stephen Gardiner and several Councilors still anxious to discover whether or not she had been in Wyatt's confidence. Why, she was asked, had she made arrangements to move from Ashridge to her fortified castle at Donnington in Berkshire, the very place to which Wyatt had wanted her to go? For a moment she lost her nerve and went so far as to suggest that she did not even know where Donnington was; but she soon recovered herself, repeated her denial that she had ever received a letter from Wyatt, and demanded to know why she should not go to one of her own houses whenever she had mind to do so. The questioning continued, but no evidence against her could be unearthed.

Renard advised the Queen that the most satisfactory answer to the problem would be to have both the Lady Elizabeth and Edward Courtenay beheaded. "It seems to me," he told the Emperor, "that she ought not to spare [either of them], for while they are alive there will always be plots to raise them to the throne and it would be just to punish them, as it is publicly known that they are guilty and so deserve death." The Spanish ambassador agreed that the Lady Elizabeth would have to die, "since while she lives it will be very difficult to make the Prince's [Philip's] entry here safe." Gardiner also thought that the Lady Elizabeth should be executed for the security of the State. But other Councilors objected that her guilt was far from established and that it would be impossible to prove it were she to be tried. Admittedly a trial would not be necessary if Parliament were to pass an Act of Attainder, pronouncing her guilty of high treason; but Parliament could never be persuaded to adopt such a course. Lord Paget argued that it would be better to have her married to some harmless foreigner than to risk her execution, which might precipitate another uprising, while the Earl of Arundel expressed his conviction that "her Grace spoke the truth." For his part he "was sorry to see her troubled about such vain matters."

For two months she was kept where she was, tired and unwell, in constant fear of the scaffold which she could see on her walks, so desolate and despairing, she confessed years later, that she thought only of asking her sister for permission to be executed by a swordsman, as her mother had been, rather than by the axe. Her feelings at this time were imagined three centuries afterwards by Alfred, Lord Tennyson:

> I would I were a milkmaid,
> To sing, love, marry, churn, brew, bake, and die,
> Then have my simple headstone by the church,
> And all things lived and ended honestly.
> I could not if I would. I am Harry's daughter . . .
> I never lay my head upon the pillow
> But that I think, "Wilt thou lie there tomorrow?"
> How oft the falling axe, that never fell,
> Hath shock'd me back into the daylight truth
> That it may fall to-day! Those damp, black, dead
> Nights in the Tower; dead – with the fear of death –
> Too dead ev'n for a death-watch! Toll of a bell,
> Stroke of a clock, the scurrying of a rat
> Affrighted me, and then delighted me,
> For there was life – And there was life in death –
> The little murder'd princes, in a pale light,
> Rose hand in hand, and whisper'd, "Come away,

1. Princess Elizabeth, aged about thirteen; a painting on panel attributed to William Scrots.

2. A copy of a wall painting in the Privy Chamber of Whitehall Palace showing Henry VIII standing on the step below his father, Henry VII, and, to the right, Henry VIII's mother, Elizabeth of York, above his third wife, Jane Seymour.

3. Anne Boleyn, Elizabeth's mother, by an unknown artist.

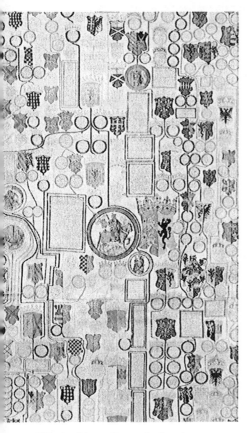

4. Elizabeth's pedigree depicted on a parchment roll that traces her ancestry back to Adam.

5. The Queen in her coronation robes, the frontispiece to Saxton's *Atlas of England and Wales*, 1579.

6. Painted panels from Nonsuch, now at Loseley Park, the center one with the initials of Elizabeth's kindly stepmother, Catherine Parr.

7. A detail from Joris Hoefnagel's *Panorama of English Society* (1570), usually known as *A Marriage Feast at Bermondsey*.

8. Sir William Cecil, later Lord Burghley, the Queen's faithful and industrious chief Secretary of State and, from 1572, Lord High Treasurer.

9. A miniature by Nicholas Hilliard of Robert Dudley, Earl of Leicester at the age of forty-four.

10. The Queen in 1585 from a portrait attributed to William Segar, known as the "Ermine" portrait after the little animal, a symbol of purity, on her left sleeve.

11. (*Opposite, top*) The Queen being borne along in procession by attendants and courtiers, including her Master of the Horse, the Earl of Worcester, whose bald head is immediately below the Queen. The Procession picture, attributed to Robert Peake, was painted not long before the Queen's death, but the artist has given her the face of her younger self.

12. (*Opposite, bottom*) Elizabethan London, an engraving by Cornelius de Visscher showing shipping on the Thames, St. Paul's Cathedral and, on the south bank, the bear garden and the Globe Theatre, which was built in 1598–9.

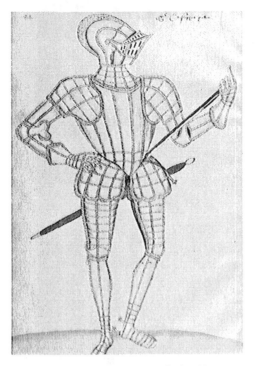

13. A suit of armor made for Sir Christopher Hatton in the 1580s, as illustrated in *An Elizabethan Armourer's Album*.

14. A miniature of Sir Christopher Hatton by Nicholas Hilliard.

15. A portrait by François Quesnel of King Henry III of France, who, as Duke of Anjou, had been considered as a husband for Queen Elizabeth.

16. A miniature of Sir Walter Ralegh by Nicholas Hilliard.

The civil wars are gone forevermore:
Thou last of all the Tudors, come away,
With us is peace!" The last? It was a dream;
I must not dream, not wink, but watch.

On April 11 Sir Thomas Wyatt – weakened by the tortures he had undergone in a vain effort to make him "confess concerning the Lady Elizabeth" – was beheaded on Tower Hill, having made a speech on the scaffold exculpating both her and Edward Courtenay. He was subsequently disemboweled and his body cut into quarters which were displayed on gibbets in various parts of the city. His head, similarly exhibited, was stolen. Some seventy other rebels were executed in different parts of the country. Edward Courtenay was sent into exile and died suddenly in Padua the following year. The Lady Elizabeth still expected to die also. When told that a large body of men in armor and blue liveries had arrived at the Tower on the morning of 19 May, she felt sure that they had come to witness her execution and she asked if the scaffold on which Lady Jane Grey had been beheaded were still standing. She was assured that the men had come there for a quite different purpose; they had come to escort her to a more comfortable place of confinement. She was to be taken to the royal manor at Woodstock near Oxford and there held in the care of Sir Henry Bedingfield, a trustworthy Norfolk landowner, whose father had been Catherine of Aragon's custodian at Kimbolton. One of the earliest of Queen Mary's supporters, he had been appointed a Privy Councilor soon after her accession and had lately been granted part of Sir Thomas Wyatt's forfeited estate. A conscientious man, ever mindful of the orders he had been given, he was profoundly to regret having accepted the responsibility of looking after so difficult a prisoner.

Removing the Lady Elizabeth from the Tower on 19 May, he and Lord Williams of Thame, Sheriff of Oxfordshire, took her by boat as far as Richmond, being much embarrassed on the way when the gunners on Steel Yard Wharf fired their cannon in riotous salute. Although Bedingfield had strict orders to protect his charge from attack by overzealous Catholics as well as from rescue by a Protestant mob, the prisoner herself still believed her life to be in danger. When she arrived at Richmond, she said to Lord Williams, "This night I think to die"; and the next day, as her escort rode on from Richmond to Windsor, she sent one of her guards to a group of her servants who had collected to see her pass by, asking him to deliver this message to them, "*Tanquam ovis*" – like a sheep to the slaughter.

Although orders had been given that her transfer from London to Oxfordshire should be as discreet as possible and that demonstrations must
be avoided at all costs, her journey was more like that of a triumphant
progress than the removal of a prisoner from one place of confinement to
another. At Windsor, where she stayed the night at the Dean's house, the
schoolboys of Eton came out to greet her; and in the Thames Valley
villages through which she rode on her way to Sir William Dormer's house
at High Wycombe the people welcomed her so enthusiastically, throwing
cakes and biscuits and showers of presents into her litter, that Bedingfield
felt obliged to write to Queen Mary, explaining rather lamely that the
people "betwixt London and this place be not good and whole in matters
of Religion." Nor were they apparently in Aston, where the church bells
rang out in greeting and where Bedingfield thought it as well to have the
ringers arrested and cast into the nearest jail. Nor were the servants at
Lord Williams's house at Thames where the next night was spent and
where Williams himself was such a hospitable and respectful host, going so
far as to ask several of his neighbors to a dinner in Lady Elizabeth's honor,
that Bedingfield felt obliged to remind his colleague that she was after all
their prisoner, not an honored guest.

At Woodstock, however, she was to be left in no doubt as to her status.
Bedingfield's orders were exact: the girl was to have no visitors other than
those of whom her custodian approved and these must not speak to her
except in his presence. Bedingfield must also accompany her when she
took walks in the gardens; her servants were to be watched as closely as
she was herself; she was to have no cloth of state above her place in the
dining hall; she was to receive no letters nor to write any; she was to be
treated with appropriate respect, but any additional favors for which she
might ask must be referred to the Privy Council. She was to be lodged not
in the palace itself but in the gatehouse. She was not to have Mrs. Ashley
back to live with her; nor was she to have Thomas Parry, who was to look
after her accounts from rooms in the Bull Inn in the village.

Bedingfield followed his instructions precisely. He was anxious not to
offend her. He seems, indeed, to have found her too intimidating to treat
otherwise than with cautious correctitude; but he was equally anxious not
to do anything that might earn the disapproval of the Queen or the Council. He found his charge extremely demanding: she wanted more books
and more maids; she wanted Cicero, and an English Bible as well as the
Psalms of David in Latin; she wanted to have a tutor sent to her so that she
could practice her foreign languages; she wanted permission to walk in the
park as well as in the garden; she wanted the return of one of her ladies

who had been sent away on the mistaken grounds that she was "a person of an evil opinion"; she wanted to have more paper and ink; she wanted to write to the Privy Council; she wanted to have the use of couriers to send messages to court. All requests – some granted, others not – were referred to court by Bedingfield who reported to the Privy Council that "her Grace saith she is sure your Lordships will smile in your sleeves when you know this my scrupulousness." But he was, as he confessed, "marvellously perplexed to grant her desire or to say nay." He annoyed her beyond endurance when, instead of granting her more simple requests, evasively replied that he would see what he could do.

She asked to write to the Queen, and this request was eventually granted her. Bedingfield brought her pen, ink and paper, scrupulously removing everything when she had finished. But the letter she wrote, which has not survived, was far from welcome. Renard reported it as being so disrespectful as to verge on the insolent. The Queen herself complained to Bedingfield of its contents, of its haughty tone and of the insincerity of her sister's nature which it disclosed. The Queen understood that she attended Mass and that, although this had at first been celebrated in English, it was now said in Latin; but was this a mere token observance? She would not receive any further "colourable" letters from her sister; if she had anything important to communicate she must do so through Sir Henry.

Frustrated and apprehensive, Elizabeth fell ill again. Her face swelled up; she was often in tears; she asked to be bled, for doctors to be sent to her, naming George Owen and Thomas Wendy, who had attended her before, and Robert Huicke who had treated both her father and her brother. She would, she said, submit the privacies of her body to these physicians but not to others unless the Queen commanded it. The doctors she had named came with a surgeon who, in Bedingfield's presence, bled her first from the arm, then from the foot. After that she was a little better, but her temper did not improve. Watching Bedingfield one day at his laborious task of unlocking six pairs of gates and then locking them all behind her, she lost her temper and upbraided him for being a common jailer. He knelt at her feet, asked her not to use such a word; he was merely doing his duty; he had been instructed to look after her.

She was a prisoner, though, all the same. With a diamond she is said to have scratched on a windowpane:

> Much suspected, by me
> Nothing proved can be,
>   Quoth Elizabeth, Prisoner.

While the days of early summer passed by slowly and tiresomely at Wood-stock, in London preparations were being made for the marriage of the Queen to King Philip of Spain who stepped ashore at Southampton in the pouring rain on 20 July 1554 and met his bride for the first time near Winchester three days later. He was twenty-seven, she was thirty-eight. Small and thin, with a strangely deep voice, she was by now extremely short-sighted and seemed much older than she was. One of King Philip's attendants noticed that she had no eyebrows, another that she had few remaining teeth, a third described her as "not beautiful, small, flabby rather than fat." King Philip himself, fair and distant, anxious, gloomy, restrained and mistrustful, regarded her without evident emotion, though he treated her with consideration and the utmost respect. He bent down to kiss her on the mouth in the "English fashion." They were married in Winchester Cathedral on 25 July by Stephen Gardiner who, as well as being Lord Chancellor, was bishop of the diocese. After the blessing and when the Mass was over, a herald proclaimed in Latin, "Philip and Mary, by the Grace of God, King and Queen of England, France, Naples, Jerusa-lem, Ireland, Defenders of the Faith, Princes of Spain and Sicily, Archdukes of Austria, Dukes of Milan, Burgundy, and Brabant, Counts of Habsburg, and Tyrol . . . "

For both of them the marriage had been conceived for reasons of state. But whereas Philip continued to regard Mary with polite indifference, she, starved of affection, fell in love with him and all that he promised and represented – her mother's dynasty, the prospect of a Roman Catholic heir, reunion with Rome – and she was as anxious to keep him by her side as he was to go home. He did his best to curb that religious fervor which had already brought Thomas Cranmer to trial for heresy, as well as Hugh Latimer, Nicholas Ridley and numerous others, many of them women and of humble birth, who were to perish in the fires of Oxford and Smithfield. Philip urged moderation on his wife and her ministers: if men and women were to be punished, he argued, let them suffer on political rather than religious grounds, let them die as traitors rather than as martyrs. The Spanish, who would be held largely responsible for their deaths, were disliked quite enough as it was. Mary closed her mind to all such argu-ments. She was not cruel. She knew her way to God and could not con-ceive that there was any other way. Men suffered for their refusal to accept it, not to be punished but to be saved. It was not that she had no sensibil-ity, but that she had no judgment. Courageous, unshakeably loyal to those she loved and to her religion, virtuous, conscientious and devout, she appeared more like a practical housewife or even a nun than a queen. "She is a perfect saint," one of Philip's attendants remarked, "and dresses badly." She was, as Philip himself observed, quite different from her sister.

Elizabeth was brought to court to see King Philip towards the end of April 1555. Bedingfield was as profoundly relieved at the prospect of being rid of his responsibility for her as she was to get away from him. Thereafter, however, she bore him no ill-will. When in later years he appeared in court she, "with a nipping word," remarked, "If we have any prisoner whom we would have sharply and straitly kept, we will send for you!" She continued to call him her 'gaoler'; but the nickname was bestowed with a kind of wry affection. It appears that she once even went to stay at his country house in Oxborough in Norfolk.

On her arrival at Hampton Court, the Lady Elizabeth was taken to apartments near those occupied by Reginald Pole, the Cardinal and recently appointed Papal Legate, who had returned home from exile on the Continent a few months previously and was soon to be appointed Archbishop of Canterbury. Here in private she welcomed her brother-in-law upon whom, she afterwards claimed, she made a most favorable impression. She was allowed to receive other visitors in her rooms, though few availed themselves of this privilege, but she was not invited to court functions or to dine in hall. Indeed, she was still treated as a prisoner and one to whom it might be dangerous to show undue sympathy. One day Gardiner came to see her accompanied by various Privy Councilors. "My Lords," she said to them, "I am glad to see you for methinks I have been kept a great while from you, desolately alone." Gardiner replied that if she wished to be restored to liberty she would have to throw herself upon the Queen's mercy and confess her guilt. How could she confess a guilt where no guilt existed, she responded angrily. She would rather stay in confinement for the rest of her life. Queen Mary was told of this outburst and expressed her deep displeasure.

Mary believed herself to be pregnant, and, although her ladies did not think her so, there seem to have been symptoms to account for her illusion, perhaps those of ovarian dropsy. She certainly ceased to menstruate and had an emission of milk from swollen breasts. Everything depended on an heir, Renard told the Emperor. "If God is pleased to grant her a safe delivery," he wrote, "things will take a turn for the better. If not, I forsee disturbance and a change for the worse on so great a scale that the pen can hardly set it down. It is certain that the order of succession to the Crown has been so badly arranged that the Lady Elizabeth comes next, and that means heresy again and religion overthrown." Yet even worse to contemplate was the possibility of Elizabeth's not being accepted as Mary's heir.

The legitimate heir would then be the granddaughter of her father's elder sister Margaret, wife of James IV of Scotland – the twelve-year-old Mary Stuart who was one day to become Queen of Scots and who was at that time betrothed to the heir to the King of France. The idea of the English Crown passing into French hands was, to a Spaniard, unthinkable. It was essential that this should never be allowed to happen, that Queen Mary should be dissuaded from depriving Elizabeth of the succession, that King Philip should do all he could to speak out on her behalf, to gain her friendship.

So convinced was Queen Mary by her symptoms that ambassadors were commanded to carry the news abroad as soon as the child was born and letters in French were prepared announcing the birth, the word *fil* written with a short space after it so that *fille* might if necessary be inserted instead. On 30 April it was announced that a baby had arrived. Bells were rung and bonfires lit. The next morning it was given out that the news was false and soon afterwards Mary was told by her doctors that there was no baby, nor ever likely to be one. As though she had already become aware of this herself she had spent hours that summer sitting in silence on cushions on the floor, staring at the wall, her knees drawn under her chin. Her husband told her that he could wait no longer: there were other countries besides England that needed his attention; he must leave before the end of August. The Queen was distraught. As much in love with him as ever, she discounted or was unaware of improbable stories of his "gross licentiousness," of such urges as that which induced him to peep into the dressing room of one of her more attractive young ladies, Lady Magdalene Dacre, who struck him a sharp blow with a stick. Ill as she was, she insisted on accompanying him to Dartford and was with difficulty dissuaded on going with him all the way to Dover.

Before he left, Queen Mary was induced to receive her sister for the first time for more than a year. Elizabeth was summoned at ten o'clock at night by the Mistress of the Robes, who instructed her to wear her best clothes. She was escorted across the garden by torchlight and admitted to the Queen's apartment by a side door. Inside the privy chamber she behaved with appropriate submission, kneeling before the Queen in her bedroom and tearfully declaring that she was now and always had been a devoted subject. Mary listened, then turned away and in her deep, masculine voice said, "God knoweth." She still did not trust her: not long before she had observed to Renard, "She is what I have always thought her."

Even so, the Queen was kind to Elizabeth after her husband's departure, as he had advised her to be. Now that his wife's health was so poor,

he was looking to the future, to the time when his sister-in-law would be
Queen of a country whose help he needed against the power of France. In
compliance with Philip's suggestions, the Queen relaxed the rules for Elizabeth's confinement and appointed as her custodian Sir Thomas Pope, once
a friend of Sir Thomas More, a Privy Councilor who had acquired extensive estates at the Dissolution of the Monasteries and had in March 1555
obtained a charter for the foundation of Trinity College, Oxford. A very
rich man, trained as a lawyer but of wide interests, contentedly married to
his third wife, Pope was a far more compatible person than Bedingfield,
and the Lady Elizabeth found him as congenial as she found Bedingfield
exasperating. They talked to each other at length about Pope's plans for
Trinity College, to which he was lavish in his benefactions, occasionally
being joined in their discussions by Roger Ascham who had by now returned to his pupil, though her mind was becoming so well stocked, he
told a friend, that he learned more from her than she did from him.

In October, Elizabeth asked for leave to go to her own house at Hatfield. Permission was granted her; the Queen wished her farewell and, as
usual, gave her parting presents. At Hatfield her life was less circumscribed
than it had been at court; but she was not happy, conscious always of
being watched. "No one," reported the Venetian ambassador, "comes or
goes and nothing is spoken or done without the Queen's knowledge." Kat
Ashley, who had been permitted to go back to Lady Elizabeth's household, was arrested together with the Italian tutor, Castiglioni. They were
soon released; but later Mrs. Ashley was arrested again and, although
released again, was dismissed from the household.

Constantly there came to Hatfield reports of the burning of Protestants,
both young and old, many of them poor and obscure. There were growing
protests at these executions, demonstrations in support of the condemned
to whose legs were sometimes tied bags of gunpowder to bring them a
quick death. There were murmurs that the Spaniards were to blame, that
better times would come under Elizabeth. Protestant refugees in France
plotted to precipitate these times: supporters of a young man resembling
Edward Courtenay proclaimed her Queen and her "beloved bedfellow,
Lord Courtenay, King." The impostor's few supporters were soon rounded
up, and plots to assassinate Mary all came to nothing. But Elizabeth was
frightened that she might be suspected of complicity as she had been in Sir
Thomas Wyatt's time, that the Queen's religious fervor might induce her to
order the burning of her own sister. Elizabeth professed her loyalty in long
letters to the Queen, full of flattering assurances and pious sentiments; she
attended Mass regularly and even went to confession. Her protestations that

she had nothing to do with these recent plots were accepted by the Council; yet her popularity with the people, distressing to the Queen, remained to herself a source of acute fear as well as of pleasure. When she went to London for a week that autumn, accompanied by two hundred horsemen in red and black liveries, the people cheered her as she passed through the city on her way to Somerset House and cheered her again when she departed.

There were no such cheers for the Queen, whose life was becoming ever more desolate and whose people were becoming ever more disillusioned by poor harvests, economic depression and religious persecution. Her husband came over to England again in March 1557; but it was only to talk to Elizabeth about her marrying his protege, Emmanuel Philibert of Savoy, or, failing him, Alexander Farnese, son of the Duke of Parma, and to try to persuade the Queen and her ministers to join him in war against France. England obediently declared war; and in this war Calais, which had been held by the English for over two centuries, was lost to the French, who triumphantly renamed it and the surrounding region the Pays Reconquis. The Queen was dismayed. She is said to have declared, in the one utterance of hers which is now remembered, that when she died and her body was opened up, the doctors would find the word Calais lying in her heart.

A few weeks after this blow she received the Lady Elizabeth again, and greeted her as though she knew she had not long to live. Elizabeth herself had been ill once more, suffering from the breathlessness that had concerned her physicians in the past; she had also had jaundice. In her weakened state she had been on the point of succumbing to the blandishments of the French who, through their ambassador, Antoine de Noailles, had long been pressing her to leave England for their country where she would find more sympathy and support than she had received at her sister's court. She had sent one of her ladies, Lady Sussex, to see the ambassador. De Noailles had by then been recalled and his place taken by his brother, who strongly advised Lady Sussex against her mistress going to France. Were she to do so, he said, she might indeed be more handsomely treated than she was in England, but she would forfeit all chance of becoming Queen. No further thought was given to this matter and Elizabeth took care not to take such a risk again. When the King of Sweden proposed to her that she should consider marriage to his son, Prince Eric, she immediately declared that she could never entertain any such offer that did not come to her by way of the Queen, and she did not fail to tell her sister of this reply. Besides, she told Sir Thomas Pope, she had no intention of marrying anyway. Pope hinted that she would make a different response were a more attractive offer made to her in the future. "What I shall do hereafter, I know not," she had replied firmly. "But I assure you . . . I am not at this time otherwise minded than I have declared to you." She wished, she added, expressing a preference that Pope ascribed to maidenly modesty, "to remain in that estate which of all others she best liked." There was no other "kind of life comparable unto it."

The Queen had obviously been gratified by her sister's candor in the matter of the Swedish offer. Their meetings thereafter, rare though they were, were marked by a more easy familiarity than those of the recent past. One day Elizabeth went to visit Mary at Richmond, being escorted there in one of the Queen's barges decorated for the occasion with freshly picked flowers. On a return visit to Hatfield, the Queen was entertained with an exhibition of bear-baiting, a play performed by the boys of St. Paul's School, which had been founded in their father's time, and an evening of music during which Elizabeth played for her sister on the virginals. Their last meeting in February 1558 also passed pleasantly enough; but by now, while Elizabeth was recovering from her recent illness, it was clear that the Queen was dying. Already she was suffering from cancer of the ovaries which was to kill her before the year was out at the age of forty-two. Unhappy and in pain, and so much in fear of assassination that she had taken to wearing armor, she became fractious and unpredictable. After his father's death her husband sent his confessor, Francisco Bernardo de Fresneda, to England with instructions to advise the Queen officially to proclaim her sister as heir to the throne. The Queen petulantly refused: Elizabeth was not her sister; she was the daughter of a notorious woman who had behaved inexcusably both to herself and to her mother, her father's rightful Queen. She would certainly not recognize Anne Boleyn's child as heir. Philip's confessor persevered: he had strict instructions from his master, the Queen's husband. Mary gave way; but within forty-eight hours she had changed her mind.

The Spanish ambassador, the Count of Feria, had an easier, more pleasant time with the Lady Elizabeth, even though she was surrounded by people whose religious opinions were far from sound, by "young folk, heretics and traitors," sworn enemies of the old religion. Feria had gone down to Brocket Hall in Hertfordshire where she was staying to give her assurances of his master's high regard for her. He had enjoyed a jolly meal with her, laughing "a great deal," so he reported; and afterwards, when she had sent her ladies from the dining hall apart from one or two who spoke only English, they had a serious discussion. She told him that she was grateful to Philip for the kindness he had always shown her and that she wanted to remain good friends with him. So long as Calais was in French hands, she would never come to terms with France. The conversation was perfectly amicable; but there was something in her manner that put Feria on his guard. He had the feeling that she was not being altogether sincere, that she would not come down on Spain's side against France when she was in a position to influence policy. Moreover, he concluded, she did not have the modesty becoming in a woman. She was undoubtedly clever but "very vain."

She was certainly a mistress of ambiguity; childhood experiences had taught her to be wary, tentative and guarded. One of the Queen's last acts was to send her a message urging her to do all she could to preserve the Roman Catholic religion for whose sake so many heretics had perished in the flames. Cardinal Pole, who was also dangerously ill, sent her a similar message. The Cardinal's secretary said that her response was satisfactory; but what she had actually said was never made clear. His master died at seven o'clock on the evening of 17 November 1558. Queen Mary had died at seven o'clock that morning.

The Lady Elizabeth had asked to be given news of her sister's death at Hatfield as soon as it occurred and to be brought, as proof of it, the betrothal ring from the Queen's finger. She had been waiting anxiously for a week, as horses and carriages streamed out of London carrying courtiers, suitors and place-seekers from one Queen eager to pay their respects to the next. She had discussed the transfer of power with Sir William Cecil, who, modifying his religious observances to suit the demands of the time, had faithfully served her father, her brother and her sister.

On the morning of 17 November, Sir Nicholas Throckmorton rode from St. James's to Hatfield with the dead Queen's ring. Already on the road were several Privy Councilors and it was they who arrived first. They found the new Queen in the grounds. It was reported afterwards that, disregarding the winter cold, she was sitting under an oak tree reading the Bible in Greek. It was also said that when told of her accession, she knelt down on the grass and quoted in Latin these words from the 118th psalm: "This is the Lord's doing; it is marvellous in our eyes."

4

"Oh, Lord! the Queen is a Woman!"

"It is no marvel to teach a woman to talk . . . far harder to teach her to hold her tongue."

In the great hall at Hatfield the new Queen, pale, composed and confident, announced the appointments she had decided to make. Sir William Cecil was to be Principal Secretary of State and the enormously fat and highly capable Nicholas Bacon, who was married to a sister of Cecil's wife, was appointed Lord Keeper of the Great Seal. These choices surprised no one and pleased most. Even the Spanish ambassador, while regretting that Cecil was a heretic, acknowledged him to be a "prudent and virtuous man."

Cecil was now thirty-eight years old, astute, industrious, trustworthy, a master of statecraft and a pragmatist who was to prove himself, when necessary, as ruthless as the welfare of his Queen and country might require. The son and grandson of courtiers, he had been born in Lincolnshire and, after attending the local grammar schools, had been entered at the age of fourteen at St. John's College, Cambridge, an institution to which he remained devoted for the rest of his life. At Cambridge he had fallen in love with Mary Cheke, sister of the Greek scholar John Cheke, whose widowed mother kept a small wine shop to help support her family; and, to the great distress of his father, who had hoped for some more profitable match, he married the girl, and by her had a son. Removed from Cambridge by his disgruntled father, he had been sent to Gray's Inn where he had shown himself to be as apt and conscientious a pupil as he had been at the university. Having secured a well-paid post in the Court of Common Pleas, he had married, soon after his first wife's death, Mildred Cooke, the eldest of the clever daughters of Edward VI's governor, by whom he was to have six more beloved children. Brought into contact with the court by his marriage, his rise was thereafter rapid. Appointed

Master of Requests, he had become Member of Parliament for Stamford, secretary to the Duke of Somerset and, surviving the Duke's fall, a Secretary of State and Privy Councilor. Knighted in 1551, he had succeeded to his father's extensive estates in Lincolnshire, Northamptonshire and Rutland the following year; and from then until Queen Elizabeth's succession he had made his cautious way in and out of office, as innately conservative as was the Queen herself, also like her a confirmed believer in the established social order and the means whereby it was maintained. Carefully avoiding identification with the excesses of his time while remaining a firm Protestant at heart, he had gradually increased his reputation as a man of sound common sense and integrity as well as of learning. "This judgment I have of you," the Queen said to him when selecting him as her principal adviser, "that you will not be corrupted with any manner of gifts, and that you will be faithful to the State; and that, without respect of my private will, you will give me that counsel which you think best." The trust was not misplaced. Cecil was able to make an enormous amount of money out of the office of Master of the Court of Wards which the Queen granted him in 1561; and out of that of Lord Treasurer to which he was appointed eleven years later. He received up to a hundred letters a day from people soliciting his patronage and favor and let few opportunities pass of increasing his wealth or influence by granting requests to suitable candidates. Nor did he shrink from spreading false rumors, lying and even blackmail when the pursuit of his policies seemed to require deceit. Yet he was almost universally regarded as a minister of exceptional worth and honor, intent upon the nation's well-being.

Some other of the Queen's appointments, not so generally welcomed, were seen as mistaken choices natural to a women, a creature who, by virtue of her very sex, was liable to make perverse decisions.

Katherine Ashley, not the most discreet of women, was made First Lady of the Bedchamber; her husband, John Ashley, became Keeper of the Queen's Jewels; Blanche Parry was to be Keeper of the Royal Books; Thomas Parry, who had not been too exact in his office as the Lady Elizabeth's cofferer in earlier days, was appointed Treasurer of the Household and granted the immensely lucrative office of Master of the Court of Wards. Catherine Parr's brother, Sir William Parr, who had been sentenced to death for his complicity in the Lady Jane Grey affair and was considered most fortunate to have escaped execution, was restored to the Marquessate of Northampton and made a Privy Councilor. An even more devoted Protestant, Sir Francis Knollys, the husband of the Queen's cousin, Katherine, was also made a Privy Councilor and appointed Vice-Chamberlain of the Household; and another outspoken Protestant, Sir Nicholas Throck-morton, who had been a frequent guest of Elizabeth at Hatfield where his more extreme views had earned him occasional rebukes, became Chief Butler and Chamberlain of the Exchequer and, later, British ambassador in Paris. Fierce Protestant as he was, however, Throckmorton advised a care-ful approach to reform. The Queen must strive "to succeed happily through a discreet beginning," to have "a good eye that there be no inno-vations, no tumults or breach of orders."

The Queen had scarcely need of such advice. It was generally conceded that, on the whole, in her more important appointments, she had chosen well to maintain stability, retaining the most capable members of the old nobility on her Privy Council while dropping several Catholic Councilors who were too closely connected with the policies of her predecessor. Francis Talbot, fifth Earl of Shrewsbury, who was Lord Lieutenant not only of Shropshire but also of Yorkshire, Nottinghamshire, Derbyshire, Staffordshire and Cheshire, was kept on the Council. So was William Her-bert, Earl of Pembroke, one of the four peers who had given Queen Mary away at her wedding in Winchester Cathedral. So, too, was Edward Stan-ley, third Earl of Derby, whose influence in the north could not be disre-garded, even though he was a strong opponent of religious change. The ninth Lord Clinton and Saye was retained as Lord High Admiral; and Henry Fitzalan, twelfth Earl of Arundel, was appointed Lord Steward of the Household. William Paulet, Marquess of Winchester, was confirmed in his office as Lord Treasurer; Thomas Radcliffe, third Earl of Sussex was reappointed Lord Deputy of Ireland; and Sir Henry Sidney, whose sister was married to Sussex, was made Lord President of the Marches of Wales.

The Marquess of Winchester was over seventy at the time of his ap-pointment, Lord Shrewsbury nearly sixty. Most of the other Councilors were in their fifties, Cecil being considerably the youngest. But the Queen had need of experienced men whose appointments would be seen as evi-dence of that consensus in government she hoped to achieve and whose acceptance of office would allay fears that the new government was intent upon precipitate change. While Protestant views might now predominate in her counsels, there were several staunch Roman Catholics among her advisers; and only in the case of her ladies and maids of honor did she make a complete break with Mary's court, dismissing most of those ladies who had served her sister and bringing in more lively and younger mem-bers of Protestant families in their place. She was always to like young people, and she liked them better if they were good-looking. Indeed, she took pains to ensure that ugly people were not employed in her household, once going so far as to refuse employment to a man who, otherwise wholly unexceptionable, had a front tooth missing, and always, so Nicholas Bacon said, taking into consideration the "mien and appearance" of candidates for preferment.

One appointment that did arouse both contention and jealousy was that of Robert Dudley, son of the executed Duke of Northumberland and grandson of Edmund Dudley who had also been executed, to be Master of the Horse.

No one could deny that Dudley, widely disliked and distrusted as he was, looked the part. Tall and extremely handsome with a skin so dark he was known as "the gypsy," and with exceptionally long, well-shaped legs, he was one of the most skilled horsemen in England. He had greatly distinguished himself in royal tournaments while still in his teens and had been appointed Master of the Buckhounds when he was twenty. Three years before this, at the royal palace of Sheen, he had been married to Amy Robsart, daughter of the Lord of the Manor of Siderstern, Norfolk. It seems to have been a contented marriage at first, though Amy was left at home when his father took Robert to Court. She went to visit her husband when he was imprisoned in the Tower with other members of his family after the arrest of his sister-in-law, Lady Jane Grey, and she welcomed him home when he was pardoned and released. But it was widely supposed that he now hoped to dispose of her in some way so that he could marry the Queen, who was undoubtedly much taken by his "very goodly person" and who indulged what the Spanish ambassador described as his "over-preposterous pretensions" by lavish preferments.

Dudley was created a Knight of the Garter; he was appointed a Privy Councilor; he was given lands at Kew, the sites of monasteries in Yorkshire and large sums of money to meet his expenses as Master of the Horse and to sustain his position as an influential figure at Court upon whose support and services the Queen would always be able to rely. He was granted a valuable license to export woolen cloth duty free as well as an annuity chargeable upon the London customs; he was made Constable of Windsor Castle. At Whitehall, when he complained of the dampness of his quarters, he was given others on a higher floor, closer to the Queen's own apartments.

The Queen, who had known him since they were children, who had been imprisoned in the Tower at the same time as he had been and who had been a guest at his wedding, made no secret of her extreme fondness for him. She spoke of him frequently, praising his talents, his marvelous expertise in the tournaments that she was determined should be held with the splendor of her father's time, his undoubted skills as an impresario of court displays and entertainments. She abruptly contradicted anyone who referred to him slightingly. He was, it had to be said, a man of many parts as well as of fine physique and seemingly tireless energy. He was interested in architecture and gardening as well as jousts and warfare; he was an entertaining conversationalist whose interests ranged far wider than those of most young men about court. He could talk in Italian to a Venetian envoy as easily as he could in his own language to the fawning followers who formed his entourage and to whom he referred patronizingly as his creatures. At one moment he could be seen earnestly discussing a new play with one of the dramatists he encouraged, or, with his steward, some improvements at Kenilworth, the sprawling, ramshackle royal palace that the Queen had given him, the next dancing the galliard, that quick and lively, complicated dance in triple time involving the five steps of the *cinque pace* and the leap of the *cabriole* that the Queen loved to perform with him, jumping into the air "after the Florentine style, with a high magnificence that astonished beholders."

One night, when riding back to Richmond from Dudley's house at Kew where she had spent the evening, she spoke to the torchbearers of their master's great qualities, of the further honors she intended to bestow upon him. Gossiping with a friend, one of the torchbearers repeated the Queen's words. Perhaps she was going to make him a duke? Or perhaps she was going to marry him when he had disposed of his wife? The conversation was reported to the Privy Council. Cecil was deeply concerned, and sought to bring pressure to bear upon her by intimating to the Spanish ambassador that he was thinking of resigning. "He perceives the most manifest ruin impending over the Queen through her intimacy with Lord Robert," the ambassador reported. "Lord Robert has made himself master of the business of the State and of the person of the Queen, to the extreme injury of the realm, with the purpose of marrying her." It was not only that there were other possible husbands to be considered who were far more suitable, but that a marriage to this admittedly gifted though unreliable and arrogant young Englishman would raise all kinds of unwelcome difficulties. Besides, on more than one occasion when Cecil needed to talk to the Queen about some important matter of state she was either out riding with Dudley, indulging with him in her well-developed taste for hunting, or occupied upon some peculiarly female pursuit.

Indeed, Cecil, who once admonished a diplomat for discussing with the Queen a matter of weight "too much for a woman's knowledge," felt driven to ask if a woman were fit to rule at all. It was a question often posed. Some time before Thomas Becon, a Norfolk clergyman and prolific author, had vehemently complained and was soon to complain again in a passionate prayer to God: "Thou has set to rule over us a woman, whom nature hath formed to be in subjection unto man, and whom thou by thine holy apostle commandest to keep silence and not to speak in the congregation. Ah, Lord! To take away the empire from a man, and give it to a woman, seemeth to be an evident token of thine anger towards us Englishmen."

A woman, it was generally agreed in this man's world, was naturally subject to her father or her husband. One man fined for mercilessly thrashing a servant expressed a common sentiment when he indignantly expostulated that he did not know what the world was coming to when a mere servant could not be corrected thus. Why the day would soon come when a man might not beat his own wife! If a woman's place was in the home, obedient, quiet and submissive, how could a woman, a creature of unpredictable moods, lacking a man's strength and intellect, possibly be an adequate ruler? Such questions had been asked by the Scottish reformer John Knox in his *First Blast of the Trumpet against the Monstrous Regiment of Women*. This had been directed principally against the rule of Mary Tudor, but its arguments were held to apply equally to any female monarch; and, although Knox himself later modified his propositions to suggest that God might make exceptions in favor of queens regnant in particular cases, it was generally accepted that it was perfectly proper to contend, as King Philip of Spain contended, that it would be far better for the Queen "and her Kingdom if she would take a consort who might relieve her of those labours which are only fit for men." There were those among her subjects, in fact, who found it difficult to believe that they were actually ruled by a woman. "Oh, Lord!" exclaimed an astonished housewife who saw her Majesty passing down a London street, "Oh, Lord! The Queen is a woman!"

The Queen herself was ready to admit that women were the weaker sex; and she often presented herself – with a mock modesty that men found appealing – as a person, who, because of her sex, was lacking in those physical and intellectual characteristics bestowed upon men. She would refer to herself as a "mere woman" and once, when congratulated upon her gifts as a linguist, she replied that it was "no marvel to teach a woman to talk"; it was "far harder to teach her to hold her tongue." At the same time she insisted that, although a woman, she was a very special woman. She was a queen because God had chosen her to be a queen. She was an instrument of God's will, she once told Parliament: the successes of her reign must be attributed to God who by his divine will had called her to the throne. This was not idle, sanctimonious talk. She did have a genuine sense of her own divine calling. In her prayers she thanked God for raising her through his "providence to the throne," for "pulling [her] from the prison to the palace, for placing [her], a sovereign princess, over the people of England." And, as her reign progressed, the English were encouraged to believe that their Queen not only ruled by divine will but was in some sense divine herself.

Her processions through the streets were stage-managed so that she appeared to be a goddess rather than an earthly monarch. In the painting known as *Queen Elizabeth going in procession to Blackfriars,* she was presented as an ageless, gorgeously clad figure being carried along in majesty, sitting enthroned upon a triumphal cart beneath an embroidered canopy, surrounded by bare-headed Knights of the Garter, guarded by Gentlemen Pensioners armed with halberds and followed by ladies more plainly dressed than the Queen but with starched lace ruffs like hers and with large pearls in their hair. On St. George's Day each year she would take part in a grand procession of her Knights of the Garter on foot, seeming to glide along behind the nobleman who bore the Sword of State, her heavy cloak trailing behind her as she passed by, walking with carefully measured step so that the crowds of spectators could see her clearly as they sank to their knees in homage at her approach.

Festivals such as St. George's Day and her birthday, her Accession Day and St. Elizabeth's Day – a saint's day formerly considered of little importance in the calendar of hagiolatry – began to assume a significance which rivaled the feast days of the Christian Church; and the worship of Queen Elizabeth, Gloriana, Belphoebe, Sweet Cynthia, Deborah, the "beauteous Queen of Second Troy," the Virgin Queen, Astraea, the goddess who dwelt on earth and was metamorphosed into the constellation Virgo, became a cult almost in contention with that of the Virgin Mary, a cult dedicated to "a Monarch maiden Queen, whose like on earth was never seen," the "second Maid," the "second sun."

On these feast days dedicated to the Queen as the virginal genius presiding over a new golden age, there were celebrations not only at court but all over the country. At the royal palaces there were splendid tournaments at which the Queen and her ladies looked down from their windows upon the "many thousand spectators," upon the combatants riding towards the barriers to the sound of trumpets, and upon the combatants' servants, "disguised like savages, or like Irishmen, with the hair hanging down to the girdle like women."

Others had horses equipped like elephants [wrote a German witness of an Accession Day tournament]. Some carriages were drawn by men, others appeared to move by themselves . . . When a gentleman and his horses approached the barrier, on horseback or in a carriage, he stopped at the foot of the staircase leading to the Queen's room, while one of his servants in pompous attire mounted the steps and addressed the Queen in well-composed verse or with a ludicrous speech, making her and her ladies laugh. When the speech was ended he offered the Queen a costly present in the name of his lord. [Then the contestants] rode against each other, breaking lances across the beam.

Elsewhere in towns and villages people were encouraged by the government to celebrate the reign of the Lord's Anointed, the Virgin Queen whose sanctified rule kept the nation's enemies and the forces of evil and Popery in check. There were fireworks and dancing, military parades and mock battles. Sermons were preached; anthems were sung; bells were rung; ballads recited and popular tracts passed from hand to hand:

> The noblest Queen
> That ever was seen
> In England doth reign this day . . .
> To the Glory of God
> He hath made a rod
> Her enemies to subdue;
> And banished away
> All papistical play
> And maintains the gospel true.

Alms were presented to the poor; doors of houses were thrown open; guests sat down to splendid feasts; and, as at Liverpool in 1576, a huge bonfire was lit in the market square and smaller fires in other parts of the town, while the Mayor and aldermen held a banquet, distributing sack, white wine and sugar to all comers, "standing all without the door, lauding and praising God for the most prosperous reign of our most gracious sovereign."

Those who worked closely with the Queen recognized that behind the propaganda designed to present her as an almost supernatural being, behind the mask thrown over her to disguise the frailty that common prejudice attributed to her as a woman, there was a monarch of stern practicality if not always of sound sense, a woman of majestic hauteur whom weak men were reluctant to oppose. She commanded obedience, giving her orders and having her own way, as one foreign envoy said, "as absolutely as her father." Despite her delight in Lord Robert Dudley's company, she was prepared to work hard. She regularly attended meetings of the Privy Council, being present at seventeen meetings in the first full month of her reign alone. Nor was her presence there merely ornamental. As Cecil had already realized, her understanding of political realities was peculiarly astute for a woman of twenty-five, while she was deeply interested in the machinery of government and the exercise of power. She had inherited an unhappy realm in which – as the government constantly insisted, exaggerating the problems they faced – prices had risen far faster than wages, the coinage had been debased and one bad harvest had followed another. Foreign entanglements had proved disastrously expensive and religious animosities had led to bitter social strife. The Queen recognized as clearly as Cecil did that they must do all they could to keep the country out of expensive wars in the future, to impose such economies as would restore the national credit and to bring about a religious settlement that would be acceptable to all reasonable people, Catholic and Protestant alike.

5

Subjects and Suitors

"I do not live in a corner."

Ten days after her accession, wearing a dress of deep purple velvet that emphasized the paleness of her skin and the fairness of her hair, the Queen had taken formal possession of the Tower of London and had ridden in an open carriage as far as Cripplegate, then, on horseback, surrounded by Sergeants-at-Arms, through streets specially graveled in her honor, to Tower Hill.

The Lord Mayor and Garter King of Arms led the procession, followed by the Earl of Pembroke carrying the Sword of State. Riding behind the Queen on a black horse was Lord Robert Dudley as Master of the Horse. The church bells rang; choirs sang hymns of praise; the Tower's guns were fired in welcome. All fell into silence as the Queen dismounted and walked into the fortress. Before entering the White Tower she climbed the stairs of the Bell Tower where she had been held as a suspected traitor. She was heard to say that there were those that had fallen from being princes to being prisoners there. She, though, had risen from being a prisoner to being a prince.

The pleasures of that day were enjoyed again early the next year at the time of the Queen's coronation. John Dee, a learned astronomer, mathematician and astrologer who had been presented to the Queen at Whitehall Palace by Lord Pembroke and Robert Dudley, could determine by astrological calculation, so Dudley suggested to the Queen, the most suitable day for her ceremony to take place. A Fellow of Trinity College, Cambridge, Dee had been offered one of the chairs in mathematics at the University of Paris. Although he had a notorious reputation as a necromancer, he was a scholar of undoubted learning and the possessor of one of the largest libraries in Europe. At Cambridge, so it was said, he "applied himself to his studies with such diligence that he allowed only four hours for sleep, and two for his meals and recreation." The Queen, who shared the widespread belief in astrology, was much impressed by him; and over the years this tall, thin man with a "long beard as white as milke," was often to be seen at court where he is supposed to have supervised the construction of the astrolabe by which she set such store. Having had her horoscope cast by him, she asked to see the magic looking-glass into which he called up images of his spirits, and she inquired as to its powers and properties. She consulted him about the likely effects of a comet that had suddenly appeared, about the elixir of life that he was attempting to discover and about the dangers to be apprehended from a waxen image of her with a pin struck through its breast, which had been found in Lincoln's Inn Fields. She instructed her doctors to confer with him over treatment for her toothache; she asked him to examine her title to countries which had been discovered in different parts of the world where he envisaged the creation of a "British Empire"; she consulted him about the Archbishop of Canterbury's comforting assurance that she had no need to fear assassination when her birth sign, Virgo, was in the ascendant. Even when shunned by others as an "invocator of devils," Dee continued to be held by the Queen in great esteem, and when he was sick she ordered her own physicians to attend him, sending him "divers rarities to eat," according to his own account, "and the honourable Lady Sidney to attend upon him and comfort him with divers speeches from her Majesty, pithy and gracious." She promised him rewards which were not always received and preferments which rarely came his way, including the Mastership of the hospital of St. Katherine-by-the-Tower, which had been under the patronage of the Queen of England since the beginning of the thirteenth century. When Dee proposed Sunday, 15 January 1559 as the appropriate day for the Queen's coronation, the date was accepted without question.

On the Saturday before, as cannon boomed "in a great shooting of guns [whose] like was never heard before," she set out from the Tower on another procession, this time to Whitehall, dressed in cloth of gold with an ermine cloak and seated in a cushioned litter beneath a velvet-draped canopy held aloft by four knights. Again the Lord Mayor was in attendance, together with the aldermen and the Masters of the City Livery Companies in their splendid robes of office. The Yeomen of the Guard had been provided with new uniforms of scarlet, silver and gold. The members of the Queen's household, even the jesters, had also been given new clothes; so had the Privy Councilors. The Queen's ladies had all been allowed long rolls of velvet and two yards each of cloth of gold.

The Queen's reception was as enthusiastic as any she had known and her response to it as skillfully performed as though she had been rehearsing the part all her life. At well chosen moments she brought her entourage to a halt to talk to a person in the crowd, to inspect one or other of the tableaux, to listen to a schoolboy's Latin speech, the recitation of a verse, the singing of a hymn. At Cornhill, according to the official account, the tableau represented "pure religion" treading upon "superstition and ignorance," "love of subjects" treading upon "rebellion and insolence," "wisdom" treading upon "folly and vainglory, justice upon adulation and bribery."

When someone shouted above the cheers, "Remember old King Harry the Eighth!" she smiled approvingly; when a boy from Christ's Hospital, founded by her brother ten days before his death, gave a long and tedious oration in which she was praised for saving the Reformation from its enemies, she listened intently, her eyes cast to heaven, her hands raised as though in ecstasy like Teresa de Cepeda y Ahumada, the mystic whose Carmelite convent was to be opened in Avila three years later. As she listened to a child introducing another tableau, it was noted "in the Queen's Majesty's countenance . . . besides a perpetual attentiveness in her face, a marvellous change in look, as the child's words touched either her person, or the people's tongues and hearts." Later, when a child presented her with an English Bible, which she declared she "oftentimes read," she took it eagerly with both hands and clasped it closely to her breast. When the Recorder presented her with a purse containing a thousand gold marks, she replied, "Be ye assured that I will be as good unto you as ever queen was to her people . . . Persuade yourselves that for the safety and quietness of you all, I will not spare, if need be, to spend my blood. God thank you all."

The whole day's celebrations were a brilliant exercise in propaganda, a successful attempt to ram home the government's thesis that Elizabeth's reign would inaugurate a new and palmy era in the history of the nation, that the follies of Queen Mary's time were not to be repeated, that past wrongs, real and invented, were to be redressed and past policies, which had brought the country close to ruin, to be rejected, that reconciliation and concord were to be the themes of the future.

The next day the Abbey at Westminster was crowded to the doors with peers and their ladies, with Privy Councilors and knights of the shires, with city dignitaries and representatives of provincial towns, with bishops and "with every notability of the realm whom her Majesty's grace desired to see her crowned as undisputed Queen."

She walked into the Abbey across a blue carpet which the crowd snatched up when she had passed to cut themselves pieces from it. Inside the church pipes were played and drums beaten above the notes of the organ and the voices of the choir. The Queen moved slowly forward to her anointment, her long red velvet train carried by the Duchess of Norfolk beneath hundreds of burning tapers and lamps.

The crowning was performed by Owen Oglethorpe, Bishop of Carlisle, since Parker had not yet been appointed Archbishop of Canterbury; the Archbishop of York had asked to be excused on grounds of conscience, and the senior bishop of the province of York, the Bishop of Durham, pleaded that he was too old. So, wearing robes that the Queen had required Bishop Bonner to lend to him, Dr. Oglethorpe placed on the Queen's head the heavy Crown of St. Edward. Wearing a lighter crown, she was then presented to the congregation, the bells ringing so loudly above her head, the organist playing his instrument with such force and the pipers and trumpeters blowing so hard and the drums being beaten with such energy that the Venetian envoy said it sounded like the end of the world. He also noted that the Mass was said in Latin but that the celebrant did not elevate the Host, that the epistle and gospel were read out in English as well as in Latin, and that the coronation oath was administered from an English Bible.

The coronation banquet was held in Westminster Hall, as it was to be until the coronation of George IV in 1821. The Queen, clothed once more in purple, sat at a table on the dais beneath the great window, the eight hundred guests at four tables stretching from one end of the hall to the other. She spoke little during the meal as Lord Howard of Effingham, the Lord Chamberlain, and the Earl of Sussex, Chief Steward by hereditary right, supervised the placing of the dishes before her. The Earl of Arundel, Lord Steward of the Household, and the Duke of Norfolk, Earl Marshal, rode up and down the hall between the tables, after Sir Edward Dymoke, whose family had held the office of Champions of England since the fourteenth century, had appeared in full armor to issue the traditional challenge by throwing down a gauntlet and daring anyone to impugn her Majesty's title.

The banquet which had begun at three o'clock on Sunday afternoon was not over until one o'clock on Monday morning; and the Queen was so tired that a tournament arranged for that day had to be canceled and, because she had caught a bad cold, the opening of Parliament arranged for 23 January had to be postponed for forty-eight hours.

When this ceremony took place her people were once again given an opportunity to see their Queen to whom, in the words of Sir Nicholas Bacon, there was nothing so dear, "no worldly thing," "as the hearty love and goodwill of her subjects." Certainly she congratulated herself constantly upon this love which was, indeed, genuine enough, especially in

London where, so the Venetian envoy was told, she received "such blessings from the people as though she had been another Messiah."

As she made her way to the Palace of Westminster on that January day in 1559, wearing a crimson dress, with a cap encrusted with pearls on her head, the crowd called out, "God save and maintain thee!" And she called back, "God a' mercy, good people!"

Not long before, she had said to a deputation of judges who had come to offer their respects, "Have a care over my people . . . They are my people. Every man oppresseth them and spoileth them without mercy. They cannot revenge their quarrel nor help themselves. See unto them, see unto them, for they are *my* charge."

They were also one of her principal safeguards. She had need of the love which she took so much trouble to generate between them and herself. Her throne was still far from secure, and her realm far from stable, "weaker in strength, men, money and riches" than Sir Thomas Smith, who sat for Liverpool in the House of Commons and had long experience as a statesman, had ever known it: he had much affection for his country and his countrymen but he had become ashamed of both. As for Elizabeth's title to be Queen of this disordered realm, there were many to dispute it, even though many claimants had been executed in the course of establishing and safeguarding the Tudor dynasty. Some malcontents pressed the claims of Lady Jane Grey's sisters or those of her cousin, Lady Margaret Strange; others urged those of the third Earl of Huntingdon, who was descended on his mother's side from Edward IV's brother, the Duke of Clarence. Some preferred the Earl of Derby or the Earl of Westmorland; a few Catholics looked to the descendants of John of Gaunt's daughter Philippa, who had married King John I of Portugal. Most were aware that Queen Mary had often asserted that Elizabeth was not her sister, that King Henry VIII was not the girl's father, that Elizabeth's real father was Anne Boleyn's lover, the lute-player Mark Smeaton, to whom, so Mary said, she bore a marked resemblance. Did not Elizabeth's frequent public references to the greatness of her father, King Henry VIII, betray a determination to fix this paternity, rather than the baser one, in people's minds?

Elizabeth's right to the throne therefore remained in dispute, and so long as she had neither husband nor successor, her life must always be considered in danger. Cecil, constantly concerned for her safety, drew up a memorandum which he headed "certain cautions for the Queen's apparel and diet." She was warned to be on her guard against presents to her by strangers, particularly against scented clothing and "all manner of things that might touch any part of [her] Majesty's body bare." She was told to be sure that she never risked infection by the plague, whenever threatened by which her father had become, so the French ambassador, Marillac, said, the "most timid person in the world." Once when the court was at Windsor and the plague raged elsewhere, a gallows was erected in the town for hanging anyone from the infected area who disobeyed the Council's order and came near the Queen's most precious person.

Councilors were also concerned by the constant threat of an assassin's knife, by frequent reports of foreign plots by agents of Philip II, the Duke of Guise and others of the Queen's enemies. There was danger also from enemies at home, as the Queen herself was only too well aware. She "had to deal with nobles of divers humours," she told the French ambassador, "and peoples who, although they made great demonstrations of love towards her, nevertheless were fickle and inconstant, and she had to fear everything." In London more than once she found herself eyed by vagabonds, or by gypsies who, when taken up, were tortured in attempts to extract information about their accomplices; and despite the great care taken by the officials and guards responsible for her safety, she was always liable to be surprised. One day a deranged sailor, who professed to be wildly in love with her, contrived to get into the Presence Chamber and there produced a dagger; another day, William Parry, the highly excitable Welsh Member of Parliament for Queenborough, who may well have been mad also, penetrated her Privy Garden with the intention of assassinating her while she was walking there, and was prevented, so he said, only by her striking resemblance to her grandfather, Henry VII. On yet another occasion a man from Warwickshire in a "frantic humour" announced his resolve to murder "the serpent" and to set her head upon a pole.

So alarmed did her Councilors become on occasions that they apparently invented and engineered plots to frighten her into being even more circumspect than she naturally was.

She was rarely alone, even in her Bedchamber where one of her ladies also slept and four chambermaids were always on call, day and night. Permanently on duty in daytime were fifty or more Gentlemen Pensioners, while the corridors and outer chambers of the court were constantly bustling with officials and servants, visitors, foreign envoys and their suites, and petitioners with favors to ask for themselves, their friends or families, watching for any opportunity to approach her Majesty and to take advantage of a cheerful mood to make their solicitations. Her Presence Chamber, so the Spanish ambassador discovered to his astonishment, was always "crammed with people" crowding round her, trying to catch her attention, to talk to her, to beg a favor, to offer a present. No one could doubt that an armed enemy might lurk anywhere undetected in that medley, waiting his chance to strike.

Councilors became even more worried about the Queen's safety when in 1570 Pius V issued a Bull of Excommunication, *Regnans in Excelsis,* against "Elizabeth, the Pretended Queen of England and those heretics adhering to her." "Peers, subjects and people of the said Kingdom and all others upon what terms so ever bound unto her," the Sentence Declaratory ran, "are freed from their oath and all manner of duty, fidelity and obedience . . . They shall not dare to obey her or any of her laws directions or commands." A curse was laid upon those who did "anything to the contrary"; while a subsequent directive from the papal Secretary of State decreed that the assassination of Queen Elizabeth would not be regarded as a sin:

> Since that guilty woman of England rules over two such noble kingdoms of Christendom and is the cause of so much injury to the Catholic faith and loss of so many million souls, there is no doubt that whosoever sends her out of the world with the pious intention of doing God service, not only does not sin but gains merit, especially having regard to the sentence pronounced against her by Pius V of holy memory. And so, if those English gentlemen decide actually to undertake so glorious a work, your Lordship can assure them that they do not commit any sin. We trust in God also that they will escape danger.

The Queen was acknowledged to be brave. One day on the Thames near Greenwich a man in a nearby boat suddenly discharged a gun in her direction, wounding one of the royal oarsmen. The Queen, disregarding the possibility of a second shot, jumped forward in the barge, tearing off her scarf to bind the man's bleeding arm and calling out to him not to be afraid for she would take care of him. But over the years the strain of her constant exposure to danger, and her efforts to appear indifferent to it, had their effect. On occasions when a procession had been arranged she would alter the route at the last minute. In 1575, the night before she was due to ride in state over London Bridge, she sent a message to the Lord Mayor, urging him not to allow a large crowd to gather there. Soon afterwards she sent another message: the citizens who did gather were not to be armed. A third message followed almost immediately: she would not go over London Bridge at all.

Once, so the Spanish ambassador was informed, when the Queen was on her way in procession to Chapel she was suddenly seized by a "shock of fear." She could not bring herself to go on; and, to the "wonder of those present," hurried back to her private apartments. On another occasion she rushed for safety to Lord Robert Dudley's house on finding a threatening anonymous letter thrown into a doorway on one of her morning walks. She dismissed all her Italian servants when she heard stories that a poisoner from Italy was lurking about the court and she had all the locks of doors leading to her Privy Chamber changed on learning of some other potential danger. In later life she slept with an old sword by her bed.

The ever-present threat to her safety made the matter of the Queen's marriage and the birth of an heir of urgent importance. Not only her own throne and life but the lives of the Councilors who had cast their lot with hers, and the whole religious settlement which was being evolved between them, were in peril. "Everything," as the Spanish ambassador said, "depends upon the husband this woman takes." He himself naturally hoped that she would take his own master, but when such a match was proposed to her she was so evasive and ambiguous in her response that Feria did not know what to make of her. She was equally ambivalent when a marriage to Philip's nephew, the Archduke Charles, was suggested; and she was no more forthcoming though considerably more histrionic when a parliamentary delegation waited upon her at Whitehall to beg her to consider marriage. She would do as God directed her, she told her visitors. It might perhaps be God's will that she should not marry, and if that were so, he would no doubt make other provisions. For her own part she would be perfectly content if one day a marble tombstone should declare "that a Queen, having reigned such a time, lived and died a virgin." She pulled the coronation ring from her finger, held it up to them and solemnly declared, not for the first or last time, "I am already bound unto a husband which is the Kingdom of England."

Her reluctance to commit herself was endlessly discussed by her Councilors, to few of whom did it ever occur that a woman of such independence of spirit might actually prefer to remain single than submit to the loss of freedom that a marriage would entail, that she might prefer to remain a virgin rather than enter that state which, in a society dominated by men, was considered one that all normal women by their very nature must desire. Some said the Queen would brook no master, relishing as she did the exercise of her sole authority; others that so long as she had no husband she could use the possibility of taking one in endless diplomatic maneuvers; yet others that it was useless to talk to her about a foreign match since she had made up her mind to marry Lord Robert Dudley anyway. A few contended that she used her single, vulnerable state to strengthen the loyal devotion of those to whom she turned for her protection. This, too, it was supposed, was why she steadfastly declined to name her successor, though she disingenuously maintained that she did not do so because she would not place anyone in the dangerous predicament she had known when she herself had been her sister's recognized heir.

It was also whispered that she would not marry because she knew she could not bear a child. This, however, was not Cecil's opinion. He had consulted physicians as well as women "most acquainted with her Majesty's body"; and they had assured him that she was "very apt for the procreation of children."

Considering the proportion of her body [Cecil wrote in a private memorandum], having no impediment of smallness in stature, of largeness in body, nor no sickness, nor lack of natural functions in those things that properly belong to the procreation of children, but contrariwise by judgement of physicians that know her estate in those things and by the opinion of women, being more acquainted with her Majesty's body in such things as properly appertain, to show probability of her aptness to have children.

Besides, Cecil added, it would be good for the Queen's health for her to have sexual relations and to bear a child, for "it were to be remembered the likelihood of Her Majesty's pains in her cheeks and face to come only of lack of the use of marriage, a thing meeter by physicians to be advocated to Her Majesty than to be set down."

Convinced as Cecil was, however, that the Queen could have children, the chatter and doubts persisted. Were not those rare, irregular menstruations significant? And why did she so often ask to be bled? Both the Count de Feria, who had a well-informed English wife, Jane Dormer, a former lady-in-waiting to Queen Mary, and Feria's successor, Alvaro de la Quadra, heard that she was supposed to be barren. "It is the common opinion," Quadra reported, "confirmed by certain physicians, that this woman is unhealthy and it is believed that she will not bear children." The Venetian ambassador told the Doge that he had heard similar reports and that many people said things that he did "not dare to write." Some believed that she fought shy of marriage because, through some physical deformity, she was incapable of the sexual act; while others maintained that she was far from being the virgin whom poets celebrated. Certainly she liked men and women about her who were sexually attractive; and this led to much gossip, particularly in foreign courts.

Those who knew her best set little store by such rumors. "I can say with truth," wrote Michel de Castelnau, the Sieur de Mauvissiere, who

was appointed ambassador by Henry III of France in 1575 and who saw
her regularly thereafter until her death, "that these [stories of her love
affairs] were sheer inventions of the malicious, and of the ambassadorial
staffs, to put off those who would have found an alliance with her useful."
Cecil, Nicholas Bacon and Lord Howard of Effingham all discounted the
stories; so did Francis Walsingham, who became her Secretary of State in
1573. "I do not live in a corner," she said herself. "A thousand eyes see all I
do, and calumny will not fasten on me for ever."

The names of possible husbands for this "best marriage in her parish,"
as one of her ministers described her, were repeatedly suggested. The
names of King Eric XIV of Sweden, the Dukes of Holstein and Saxony, the
Earl of Arran and the Earl of Arundel were all repeatedly canvassed. So
were those of that "brave, wise, comely English gentleman," Sir William
Pickering, a former ambassador in Paris, as well as the Archduke Charles
of Austria. It was said that even the Pope, Sixtus V, who had spent his
early years as a swineherd in the bleak mountains of the Marche, had his
eye on her, proponent of the Counter-Reformation though he was. "Just
see how well she governs!" he was said to have exclaimed. "She is only a
woman, only a mistress of half an island, and yet she makes herself feared
by Spain, by France, by the Empire, by all . . . Our children would have
ruled the whole world."

Cecil, who prayed that "God would send our mistress a husband, and by
time a son, that we may hope our posterity shall have a masculine succession," persisted in his gentle persuasion, telling her of his hope that God
"would direct your Highness to procure a father for your children." There
were persistent canards that the Queen was already pregnant and that the
father was Lord Robert Dudley. Her reputation, Cecil lamented, was sinking
dangerously. "The cry is that they do not want any more women rulers,"
the Spanish ambassador reported of the English people, "and this woman
may find herself and her favourite in prison any morning."

In August a Brentford woman, Anne Down, was sent to jail for publi-
cizing a story about the Queen's pregnancy, a story that was nevertheless
repeated by others, who suffered the same punishment. Thereafter, intermittently throughout her reign, rumors about the Queen's wantonness
spread from alehouse to alehouse and village to village: she was as sexually
voracious as her mother had been; she had had more than one child; she
forced courtiers to lie with her on pain of execution; she had, so the
Venetian ambassador in Spain was told, at least thirteen natural children;
in Norwich in 1570 certain persons, who persisted in spreading treasonable
slander against the Queen and her wanton court, were executed. Suspi-

cions about her and Dudley were much intensified in September 1560 when reports reached London of a tragic accident at Cumnor Place, Oxfordshire.

For the past few months Dudley's wife, Amy, who was probably suffering from cancer, had been living in seclusion in apartments reserved for her and her servants at the isolated Oxfordshire home of her husband's former steward, Anthony Forster, Member of Parliament for Abingdon. On Sunday, 8 September she gave her servants leave to go to Abingdon fair. When they returned to Cumnor Place they found her lying at the foot of the staircase in the hall with a broken neck. Apparently she had been playing backgammon with some other ladies who were staying in the house, had suddenly left the room and fallen downstairs to her death.

Dudley was brought the news while he was with the Queen at Windsor. He immediately ordered the most particular inquiries to be set in hand, maintaining that "the greatness and suddeness of this misfortune" much distressed him and that he could take no rest until it had been fully investigated, "considering what the malicious world will bruit." When a jury brought in a verdict of accidental death he suggested that a second jury be empaneled to continue the investigation. Yet stories that Amy Dudley had killed herself, or, more likely, that her husband had somehow been implicated in the affair, were soon rife and continued to be spread. The dead woman's maid declared that she had heard her mistress "pray to God to deliver her from desperation"; a local clergyman told the Privy Council of the "grevious and dangerous suspicion and muttering" about foul play in the surrounding villages; at court, where Dudley was said to have spoken not only of divorcing but of poisoning his wife, gossip grew more and more wildly speculative. The Spanish ambassador reported it was a matter of fact that the Queen and Dudley were "thinking of destroying Lord Robert's wife . . . They had given out that she was ill, but she was not ill at all. She was very well and taking care not to be poisoned . . . The Queen on her return from Hunting [four days before Amy Dudley's death] told me that Lord Robert's wife was dead or nearly so, and begged me to say nothing about it." In Paris, so the English ambassador, Sir Nicholas Throckmorton, reported, it was generally accepted that the woman had been murdered and that her husband was responsible.

In fact, the Queen – whom sensible men supposed would surely not have welcomed the death of a woman whose removal made possible a marriage she may well have liked to fancy but would never bring herself to undertake – told one of her secretaries that the verdict of the jury left no room for doubt that the death was accidental. This was also the expressed opinion of Sir Henry Sidney, Lord President of the Council in the Marches of Wales, who was married to Dudley's sister, and who was an eager proponent of a marriage between the Queen and his brother-in-law. This, too, was the conclusion reached by Sir William Cecil, distrustful of Dudley though he was and devious as he had been in his efforts to render their marriage impossible by encouraging rumors that Dudley and the Queen had been plotting to poison the dead woman.

Certainly the Queen's regard for Dudley was not impaired by the tragedy. She sent him from court until the funeral, which he did not attend and at which she herself was represented by her old friend Lady Norris after other ladies whom she had approached had evaded the duty, so great was the scandal. But Dudley was soon welcomed back at court and the Queen seemed to be even more fond of him than ever and he as self-confident and bold. One day, during a boating party on the Thames where Dudley was behaving in an exceptionally flirtatious manner – which the Queen found appealing, and her courtiers both irritating and offensive – he declared impudently that Alvaro de Quadra, who, as well as ambassador, was Bishop of Aquila, might just as well marry them there and then. The Queen expressed her doubts that the ambassador spoke English well enough to perform the ceremony adequately. This drew from the ambassador the sardonic observation that he would happily play the part of priest if the Queen would dismiss Sir William Cecil and all the other Protestant heretics in her service. Sometimes, however, Dudley went too far even for the Queen's indulgence. There were quarrels and reprimands. The Queen agreed to create him a peer, but when the time came to sign the patent she crossly cut it up with her paper knife.

The rumors of an imminent marriage to some other suitor persisted; and the Queen clearly took deep pleasure in the negotiations, the attendant compliments, the stories of urgent, longing suitors, of desirable admirers, of the value of her hand. Yet when details were discussed there were the familiar evasions and ambiguities; and talk once more returned to Lord Robert Dudley, even though Dudley himself maintained that "Her Majesty's heart is nothing inclined to marry at all, for the matter was ever brought to as many points as we could devise, and always she was bent to hold with the difficultest."

There were persistent reports that she was betrothed to Dudley, that she had married him in the house of Lord Pembroke, who was said to have once proposed to her himself, that she was "a mother already." Sir Nicholas Throckmorton, writing anxiously from France, dreaded the very thought that she would "so foully forget herself," and sent his secretary to keep her informed of French opinion. The secretary found her looking "not so hearty and well as she did by a great deal," and added in his report, "Surely the matter of my Lord Robert doth much perplex her." Eventually he came to the conclusion that the marriage was "never like to take place"; and this, despite all the rumors, was becoming a common enough opinion. When it was suggested that the King of Spain should lend his support to the marriage on condition that England became a Roman Catholic country once more and that, in talking to her about this plan, Quadra had gathered the impression that she approved of it, Philip had replied with his customary scepticism, "Get it in writing with her signature." Quadra himself could not make the woman out. One day she seemed inclined to marry, the next day not. "Your Lordship will see what a pretty business it is to deal with her," he wrote to his predecessor, Feria, who had left his post resigned to the fact that no good could be expected of "a country governed by a Queen." "I think she must have a thousand devils in her body, notwithstanding that she is for ever telling me that she longs to be a nun and to pass her time in a cell praying."

The Queen was now twenty-seven years old. The matter of her marriage would soon become more urgent than ever, so urgent, indeed, that the Earl of Sussex, who disliked Dudley intensely, was prepared to support a marriage between him and her Majesty if that was the only way to secure an heir to the throne. Her immediate successor, as matters stood at present under Henry VIII's will, was Lady Catherine Grey, the great-granddaughter of Henry VII and younger sister of Lady Jane Grey, a susceptible, attractive girl eight years younger than Elizabeth with a strong sense of *amour-propre* who had already aroused the animosity of the Queen, ever fearful of the consequences of having a recognized successor, by expressing dissatisfaction at not being formally accepted as heiress presumptive. She had been married as a child to Henry Herbert, afterwards second Earl of Pembroke, who had arranged for a divorce after the execution of her sister. Unknown to the Queen, she was now deeply attached to Edward Seymour, Earl of Hertford, son of the executed Duke of Somerset; and both his mother and hers encouraged her to hope that they might be married, though it seems that at first the young man was not much taken with the idea until stimulated by his persuasive sister, Lady Jane Seymour, one of the Queen's maids of honor and Lady Catherine's closest friend. If they were to marry, however, the Queen's consent had to be obtained, since by an act of 1536 it was treason for a person of royal blood to do so without the sovereign's permission. It was hoped that the Duchess of Suffolk might prevail upon the Queen to agree to the match; but the Duchess died before this projected interview had taken place and, since no other intermediary could be persuaded to tackle the Queen on a matter that was sure to enrage her, the marriage was conducted secretly and illicitly, in the bridegroom's house in Cannon Row, Westminster, towards the end of 1560 by a priest whose identity was never discovered.

Soon afterwards the bridegroom was sent to the Continent to accompany Sir William Cecil's young son, Thomas, on a prolonged tour; while his bride was left behind at court to hear stories at secondhand of the dissipations of the young Cecil, whose father expressed the fear that his son would return home "like a spending sot, meet only to keep a tennis court." Afraid that her husband might be indulging in these excesses himself, and that her pregnant state would soon come to the Queen's notice, Lady Catherine sought the advice of Lady St. Loe, the wife of the captain of the Queen's Guard, a formidable woman of "masculine understanding and conduct," who had been married twice before and was to die, widowed for the fourth time, as the immensely rich, insatiably ambitious Countess of Shrewsbury, known to history as Bess of Hardwick. She did not welcome Lady Catherine's confidences, upbraided her for having made her a party to them and gave her scant comfort. The distraught girl then turned to Lord Robert Dudley believing that, since his brother had been married to her sister, he might take pity on her plight. But Dudley was so alarmed by her creeping into his bedchamber, where her presence might be reported to the Queen, that he got rid of her as quickly as he could and the next morning told the Queen all that his sister-in-law had confessed to him.

Lady Catherine was immediately sent for questioning to the Tower where her husband on his return from France was also incarcerated. Intolerable as it was for the Queen to learn that the girl, claiming to be her successor, had married without her consent, it was even harder for her to bear the knowledge that she was to have a child. Fortunately, not only was the priest who had married her not to be found, but the only other witness to the ceremony, Lady Catherine's sister-in-law, Jane Seymour, had since died, while a deed of jointure made out in the husband's name, settling an annuity of £1,000 a year on the bride, had unaccountably been lost. The commission appointed to look into her "infamous conversation" and "pretended marriage" could, therefore, find that no marriage had, in fact, taken place. This the commission duly and obediently did find, and Lady Catherine's baby, a son, Edward, was declared illegitimate.

Taking pity on the mother, or accepting a bribe from the father, a jailer in charge of them disobeyed the orders he had received to keep them apart; and in course of time they had another baby, Thomas. The Queen was, of course, appalled. Summoned before the Star Chamber, Lord Hertford was fined £15,000; and, although most of this sum was subsequently remitted by the Queen, she required him to find £1,000 without delay. When the money had been paid, the Hertfords were separated. He was entrusted to the custody of his mother and of her second husband, Francis Newdigate, at Hanworth; she was sent to the house of her uncle, Lord John Grey, at Pirgo, Essex, and later to Sir William Petre's house at Ingatestone, Essex. And, for the rest of her life, transferred from Petre to Sir John Wentworth and from Wentworth to the custody of Sir Owen Hopton at Cockfield Hall, she remained in custody, her pleas to be allowed to see her husband being ignored. Her husband also remained in custody until she died; and thereafter, for the rest of his long life, he kept as much in the background as he could, spending most of his time in the country and accepting the appointment of English ambassador in Brussels only after the Queen was dead. When on her deathbed she was asked if she might consider his elder son, Edward, as her successor, she roused herself to reply firmly: "I will have no rascal's son in my seat."

The Queen had been close to death forty years earlier. She had been on one of her progresses through East Anglia where, distressed already by the Catherine Grey affair and the badgering by her Councilors about her marriage, she was so upset by the state of the cathedral and college at Norwich, cluttered up with the untidy belongings of the wives and children of the clergy and masters, that she there and then drafted an ordinance to be sent to the Archbishops of Canterbury and York forbidding the presence of women in cathedral lodgings. Looking tired and ill, she also berated the civic authorities at Ipswich because of the filthy condition of their streets.

When she returned to London the Queen was feeling rather better, but by October 1562 she was out of sorts again. She decided to have a bath. She did not often do so when she was well. Few ladies did, contenting themselves with washing at a basin, then sprinkling their bodies and clothes liberally with scent. Occasionally the Queen would lie in a bath for pleasure or for her health's sake, but although there were bathrooms in her palaces she did not indulge herself by using them regularly. This autumn, after her bath at Hampton Court, she went outside for a walk in the gardens in which her father had taken such interest and which she herself was improving, supervising the layout of the flower beds, planting trees and shrubs, and stocking the hothouses with rare plants brought back from distant lands. It was noticed that on these daily excursions round the grounds she walked "briskly when alone"; but, when she was conscious of being watched, "she, who was the very image of majesty and magnificence, went slowly and marched with leisure." On this occasion she felt tired rather than refreshed after her walk, and was soon running a temperature. Dr. Burcot, a skillful though extremely irascible German physician, was sent for, and immediately diagnosed smallpox.

The symptoms of this disease had recently been described by Thomas Phaer, a lawyer who combined a study of medicine with his legal practice in Wales and whose *Regiment of Life* was one of the most widely read medical treatises of his day. It was a "common and familiar" disease, Phaer wrote,

> called of us ye smal pocks . . . The signs are itch and fretting of the skin as if it had been rubbed with nettles, pain in the head and back etc: sometimes as it were a dry scab or lepry spreading over all the members, other whiles in pushes, pimples and whayls running with much corruption and matter, and with great pains of the face and throat, dryness of the tongue, hoarseness of the voice, and, in some, quiverings of the heart with sownings.

Since the Queen was suffering from so few of these symptoms, she refused to believe Dr. Burcot's diagnosis and demanded that "the knave" should be removed from her sight. Four days passed and still there were no marks on her pale skin, yet her temperature soared, her mind began to wander and for long periods she lapsed into unconsciousness. Her doctors, fearing for her life, sent for her Councilors. They gathered round her bed. Regaining consciousness and seeing them standing above her, she bemusedly asked them to appoint Lord Robert Dudley Protector of the Realm with the enormous salary of £20,000 a year. She also asked them to allow his confidential servant, Tamworth, who slept in his room, £500 a year. As though sensing their unease, she called upon God to witness that, although she loved Lord Robert and had always loved him, there was nothing untoward in their relationship. She asked the Councilors to care for her servants and mentioned as well her cousin, Henry Carey, Lord Hunsdon, a straightforward, honest and intelligent man, one of her favorite courtiers and a future Lord Chamberlain of her Household. She then fell into silence. "Death," she said afterwards, "possessed almost every part of me."

Messengers were sent galloping off to Dr. Burcot to beg him to come back to do what he could to save the Queen's life. "By God's pestilence!" the man cried out, refusing to overlook the insult that had been offered him. "Call me a knave for my good will! If she be sick let her die!"

Outraged by these words, a servant drew a dagger and threatened to drive it through Burcot's body if he did not immediately put on his cloak and boots and take horse for Hampton Court. The doctor then stormed out of the room, galloped off to the palace, came to the bedside of the Queen, and looking down upon the patient, delivered himself of the opinion that he had arrived "almost too late."

There was, however, a cure for smallpox which, adopting an old Arabic remedy, the physician, John of Gaddesden, author of the earliest English treatise on medicine, the *Rosa Anglica,* had described in the early fourteenth century. This was to "let a red cloth be taken, and the patient be wrapped in it completely, as I did with the son of the most noble King of England [Edward of Caernarvon, the first Prince of Wales, and later Edward II] when he suffered those diseases. I made everything about his bed red, and it is a good cure, and I cured him in the end without marks of smallpox."

Relying upon this remedy for the cure of the Queen, Burcot had her body, with the exception of her head and one hand, wrapped in a length of scarlet cloth and laid on a mattress in front of the fire in her room. He then put a bottle to her lips and told her to drink as much of its contents as she wanted. She swallowed the liquid which she said was "very comfortable." Before long, red spots began to appear on her hand. Noticing these, she apprehensively asked Burcot what they signified. " 'Tis the pox," he replied with complacence, adding irritably with a favorite oath when his patient began to moan, "God's pestilence! Which is better? To have the pox in the hand or in the face, or in the heart and kill the whole body?"

John of Gaddesden had advised the pricking of the eruptions with a golden needle, but this was not considered necessary in the Queen's case. Slowly she recovered; the red spots disappeared; her pale skin was left scarcely blemished. But Lord Robert Dudley's sister, Sir Henry Sidney's wife, Lady Mary Sidney, who had nursed her through the illness, was not so fortunate. She contracted the disease and was left with a skin as pitted as the Queen had feared her own might be. "I left her a full fair lady, in mine eyes at least the fairest," her husband said, "and when I returned I found her as foul a lady as the smallpox could make her, which she did take by continued attendance upon her Majesty's most precious person." Thereafter Lady Mary "chose rather to hide herself from the curious eyes of a delicate time than come upon the stage of the world with any manner of disparagement." Burcot also disappeared into obscurity, rewarded with a grant of land and a pair of golden spurs that had belonged to the Queen's grandfather, Henry VII. The Queen, as Edmund Bohun said, "wished never to be reminded of her illness."

6

Papists and Puritans

*"Leave that! It has nothing to do with
your subject and the matter is
threadbare."*

The conjectures of theologians, the Queen once said, were "ropes of sand or sea-slime leading to the moon." She was well enough versed in theology herself, but endless and fruitless disputes about doctrine exasperated her. Her own position in the matter of religion was clear enough. She warmly approved of a statute passed in her father's time, an Act Abolishing Diversity in Opinions; yet, provided people outwardly conformed to Christian belief and accepted practice, she did not much care what their inner beliefs might be. She had no wish, as Francis Bacon observed, to "make windows into men's hearts and secret thoughts." A Protestant at heart, she liked her services, which she attended regularly, to be conducted in English, but she also liked to have crucifixes and candles in her private chapels, a predilection that the Archbishop of Canterbury, Matthew Parker, felt called upon to censure. She liked clergymen to wear vestments, provided that they were not too elaborate, and for services to be accompanied by the lovely voices of her choirboys – "unfledged minions flaunting it in silks and satins," as a puritan pamphleteer described them – and by the music of her composers, among them Catholics whom she protected from persecution. Yet she did not approve of those ceremonial parts of the Mass that supported belief in the real presence of Christ in the elevated Host; and when Owen Oglethorpe, whom Queen Mary had nominated as Bishop of Carlisle, raised the Host during a celebration of Mass in the Chapel Royal at Whitehall Palace, she told him to lower it. He refused to do so; so she walked out, hurrying away with that characteristically brisk and hasty step of hers, so markedly in contrast to her slow and almost choreographic movements when on processions of state.

She was constantly at odds with her bishops. When Edmund Bonner, the fat and caustic Bishop of London who had burned Protestant heretics in his diocese with apparent enthusiasm, came to do homage to her with

various City dignitaries, she snatched her hand away from his and turned
her back on the man who, having been criticized for ordering an old man
to be scourged, responded with cheerful alliteration, that it was surely a
"good commutation of penance to have thy bum beaten to save thy body
from burning."

When John White, Bishop of Winchester, who was also famous in the
pursuit of Protestant heretics and who had conducted Queen Mary's
funeral service, tactlessly chose as his text for a sermon he preached in
Queen Elizabeth's presence the words from Ecclesiastes 4:2, "I praised
the dead more than the living," he was immediately commanded to
"keep his house." And when John Christopherson, Bishop of Chiches-
ter, in preaching at St. Paul's Cross, violently attacked the doctrines
recently set forth by William Bill, a future Dean of Westminster, who
had spoken of Protestantism as the "true religion," he was summoned
before the Queen who had him sent to prison. Yet the punishments of
these bishops were nothing like as severe as those which would have
been imposed for comparable misdemeanors by Protestants in Mary's
time. White was soon released from house arrest; and Christopherson
would also have been freed had he not died a few weeks after his imprisonment. Oglethorpe continued as Bishop of Carlisle, and Bonner as
Bishop of London. "Let it not be said," the Queen declared, "that our
reformation tendeth to cruelty."

The Queen strongly disliked most sermons and hated long ones, to
which she frequently did not trouble to listen, using the time to consider
personal problems or affairs of state, sometimes ostentatiously closing the
shutters of her closet window, at others revealing her inattention by
thanking the preacher for a sermon of which she could not conceivably
have approved. When she did listen, she did not hesitate to interrupt
tedious preachers and those who strayed from religious into political matters or who expressed views at variance with her own. "Do not talk about
that," she called out loudly when the Dean of St. Paul's, preaching before
her one Ash Wednesday, contentiously condemned the display of crucifixes and candles in private chapels. "Leave that!" she shouted when the
Dean, unabashed, elaborated upon his theme. "Leave that! It has nothing
to do with your subject and the matter is threadbare." The Dean then
brought his sermon to an abrupt close and the Queen strode from his
presence, looking very cross.

It was said that the Catholics were as elated by this display as they had
been downcast when she had walked out of the Chapel Royal upon the
elevation of the Host and when, at the time of her coronation, she had

called out in protest at priests holding candles by the door of Westminster Abbey, "Away with those torches! We see very well!"

The Queen also disliked the idea of married clergymen, particularly married bishops. This was reflected in her treatment of Richard Fletcher, Bishop of Worcester, who, not long after the death of his first wife, married a pretty, rich widow of somewhat dubious reputation. It was a sensible match, it was said, because he was Dr. F. and she was Mrs. Letcher. But for the Queen the marriage was no laughing matter. Dr. Fletcher was forbidden the court and suspended from his episcopal functions. Through Cecil's good offices he was soon restored as bishop, but he and the Queen were never fully reconciled and he died not long after his suspension while smoking a pipe of tobacco, a novel practice to which he had become addicted.

Even those clerical wives, demure and discreet, like Mrs. Parker, were not welcome in the eyes of the Queen who after a visit to Lambeth Palace was heard to take her leave of the Archbishop's wife with the words, "Madam I may not call you; mistress I am ashamed to call you; yet, as I know not what to call you, I thank you."

To Parker himself the Queen was much attached. A shy and quiet man, reluctant to make his opinions known at meetings of the Council, he came from a modest home, the son of a calenderer from Norwich. He had gone as Bible-clerk to Cambridge where he became associated with the group known as the Cambridge reformers, though he had strong reservations about the doctrines of Martin Luther by which most members of the group were so influenced. Elected Master of Corpus Christi College in 1544, he became Vice-Chancellor of the University the following year and Dean of Lincoln in 1552. Having lived in obscurity during the reign of Queen Mary, he was approached with the offer of the Archbishopric of Canterbury soon after Elizabeth's accession. He was most reluctant to accept the appointment, wishing to return to a quiet life at Cambridge; but the Queen, knowing how closely his views coincided with her own, and prepared to overlook the existence of the excrescent Mrs. Parker, pressed him to take up the office for which he was so well suited. He succumbed to her blandishments and for the next fifteen years was Archbishop of Canterbury, patiently submitting to the Queen's attacks on his indulgence in the "holy estate of matrimony" – of which she occasionally spoke with such "bitterness' that he was "in horror to hear her" – presiding over the direction of the Anglican Church on its course between the extremes of Romanism and Puritanism, obeying as best he could her Majesty's injunction to stamp out "diversity, variety, contention and vain love of singularity from the Church" and to bring to heel such troublesome nonconformists as Thomas Sampson, Dean of Christ Church, Oxford, who persistently declined to wear vestments, an offense for which the Queen decreed that he should be deprived of his deanery.

The middle course that the Queen and Parker contrived to steer required extremely skillful navigation. They were both well aware of the passions that the most finical points of doctrine could arouse, and proceeded towards settlement with caution, knowing that while the House of Commons might be in favor of far-reaching reform, the House of Lords and its sixteen bishops were certainly not. In the first Proclamation of her reign, any unauthorized alteration in the religion of the people, still largely Roman Catholic outside London and the southeast, was expressly forbidden. A subsequent Proclamation decreed that the Lord's Prayer, the Litany, the Ten Commandments and the lesson of the day should be read out in church services in English. This did not cause too much disquiet. But a Bill that proposed the abolition of papal supremacy and the appointment of the Queen as "Supreme Head of the Church of England" was altogether too much for most bishops and for many lay peers. Nicholas Heath, Archbishop of York, maintained that, while her Majesty was no doubt "as virtuous and as godly a mistress" as the English people had ever had to reign over them, biblical authority had it that a woman could no more be "Supreme Head" of the Church than she could be a preacher or a doctor. The title was consequently abandoned. "Supreme Governor" was inserted in its stead; and penalties for refusing to take an oath acknowledging the Queen's position were laid down. Refusal to take the Oath of Supremacy in Henry VIII's day had been punishable by death. This was now reserved for a third offense. The first offense was to be punished by a fine, the second by imprisonment.

The Bill was passed in the House of Commons without much dissent. In the House of Lords, however, the bishops voted against it *en bloc*. They also refused to accept the third Book of Common Prayer which, referring to "ministers rather than priests," restored the Protestant communion service in place of the Roman Catholic Mass, even though the Queen had ensured that this prayer book did not contain either the offensive references to "The Bishop of Rome and his detestable enormities" or the prayer for the conversion of Roman Catholics, as well as that of Jews and infidels, which had outraged Catholics in the first.

The recalcitrance of the bishops – their refusal to take the Oath of Supremacy as required by an Act passed in 1559 or to make use of the new prayer book in accordance with the 1559 Act of Uniformity – could scarcely be ignored. Examples, it was agreed by the Queen and Council, had to be made: the Bishop of London who perversely continued to celebrate Mass in the old Roman Catholic way was sent to the Marshalsea prison in Southwark where he died ten years later; the Bishops of Lincoln and Winchester were imprisoned in the Tower; all the others, with the exception of Anthony Kitchin of Llandaff, who was induced to sign a declaration of acceptance of the Queen's Supreme Governorship of the Church, were deprived of their bishoprics and replaced with more amenable men. These were mostly Cambridge men whose names were advanced by William Cecil and whose Protestantism was in several cases a good deal more advanced than that of the Queen herself, though none was prepared when it came to the point of standing firm against her moderate policy. Robert Horne, Dean of Durham, accused in the past of infecting his whole-diocese with Protestant error, was appointed Bishop of Winchester; Edmund Grindal, Master of Pembroke Hall, Cambridge, a friend of Nicholas Ridley and an exile in Queen Mary's reign, was chosen as Bishop of London. Thomas Young, also an exile in Mary's time and later Archbishop of York, became Bishop of St. David's. Yet the strength of opposition to the government's wishes, and to some of these diocesan appointments obliged the Queen to modify her plans. She had told Sir Francis Knollys to assure the House of Commons that, since she was "termed the Defender of the Faith," so would she be found the "protector of the Protestants." But she felt forced to take note of conservative opinion, and saw to it that the reformist movement was kept in check.

The lesser clergy proved more amenable than the bishops. About four hundred of them resigned or were deprived of their benefices over the next five years, but over half of them departed for offenses other than their determination to refuse to abandon their Roman Catholicism. Such offenses were unearthed by commissioners sent out into the parishes of England to enforce the new law, to instruct the clergy to preach against papal malpractices, against superstition and the veneration of relics, to make sure the Bible was placed in every church and that all churches also had pulpits. At the same time clergy were required to wear proper vestments, not to marry without the permission of their bishops and of two Justices of the Peace, and to ensure that their congregations attended to the service reverently and lowered their heads at the name of Jesus.

Most commissioners were of strongly Protestant inclination and their decrees were much disliked in those many parishes where the people clung affectionately to the traditions of the ancient past. They protested against the removal of altars and their replacement with communion tables, the whitewashing of wall paintings, the burning of images, rood lofts and ornaments, the installation of box pews so that the better-off parishioners could listen to boring sermons and long readings from the Bible protected from draughts and hidden from the eyes of their neighbors if they were to go to sleep.

The Queen sympathized with the people's resentment at the loss of their churches' traditional fittings, and she did what she could to stem the outburst of iconoclasm, protesting vainly against the wanton destruction of Cheapside Cross, that "ancient ensign of Christianity," and against the defacement of "monuments of antiquity set up in the churches for memory not superstition." She learned with dismay that James Pilkington, the recently married Bishop of Durham, eagerly supported by his Calvinist Dean, William Whittingham, who had been an elder of the church at Geneva, was zealously stripping the Cathedral of all its decorations, even going so far as to deface what they took to be idolatrous figures from the cathedral plate. She said that she was not surprised to learn that people were beginning to absent themselves from church on Sundays for the more lively pursuits of dancing, football, bowls, morris-dancing or bear-baiting to such an extent that Nicholas Bacon felt constrained to ask in Parliament in 1563, "How cometh it to pass that the common people in the country universally come so seldom to common prayer and divine service?"

Penalties were meant to be imposed upon absentees, but they rarely were; and so long as those who remained Catholic at heart were loyal to the Crown rather than to the Pope, as indeed most of them were, the Queen had no wish to be coercive, particularly so since the heads of many if not most leading Catholic families were prepared to make token appearances at their parish churches despite the Pope's ruling that they were under no obligation to do so. In the northern counties, indeed, where a large proportion of the people remained Catholic, little attempt was made to force observance of any of the provisions of the Acts of 1559.

Confident that they were loyal to her, the Queen not only overlooked the disobedience of the leading Catholic families to the letters of her laws, but was prepared to show them her favor by going to stay at Cowdray Park with the family of Anthony Browne, Lord Montague, who had outspokenly condemned the Acts of Supremacy and Uniformity in the House of Lords. She remained there for over a week and clearly approved of the lavish, not to say spectacular entertainments provided for her.

Both the Queen and Parker, "the Pope of Lambeth," were attacked by stricter Protestants for their leniency; and both were concerned by the puritan leanings of so many members of the Privy Council and other men about the court, among them Sir Francis Knollys, who commended puritan preachers as "diligent barkers against the popish wolf." Even Cecil was not as critical of the behavior of Puritans as the Queen would have liked. "The comfort that these Puritans have, and their countenance, is marvellous," Parker wrote in March 1573, "and but that we have our trust in God, in her Majesty, and in two or three of her Council, I see it will be no dwelling for us in England."

Two years after this letter was written several Dutch Anabaptists, whose extreme Protestant teachings were considered a threat to the social order, were discovered at a prayer meeting in London. Brought to trial on a charge of heresy, five of them recanted and the others were found guilty of a crime the punishment for which was burning at the stake. Since the extinguishing of the fires at Smithfield in 1558 there had been no burnings for heresy in Elizabeth's reign, and most members of the Privy Council were reluctant to resort to a punishment now associated with Queen Mary apd the Spanish Inquisition. The condemned were accordingly all reprieved except for two of the most unrepentant and recalcitrant. Strong pressure was put upon the Queen to reprieve these men too, both by representatives of the Dutch Protestant Church in London and by Englishmen who begged her not to resort to a punishment belonging "more to the example of Rome than to the spirit of the Gospel." The Queen replied that she had left the matter of punishment to those who had sentenced the offenders to death. When the death warrant was brought to her for signature, she put her name to it, displaying great anger, so it was afterwards said, when her maids of honor presented to her a petition for mercy. The two offenders were burned at Smithfield, perishing in the flames "in great horror, with roaring and crying."

After this unpleasant episode, the Queen remained as determined as ever to protect Anglicanism from Catholic and Protestant agitators alike. She would neither "animate Romanists," she said, nor "tolerate newfangledness." When Parker died in May that year and was succeeded, at the instigation of Cecil, by Bonner's successor as Bishop of London, Edmund Grindal, a wealthy farmer's son and convinced Protestant sympathetic towards the Puritans, there was further trouble.

Elizabeth had deeply disapproved of the caustic Bonner's violent Catholicism; but she was almost equally at odds with Grindal, who was with the utmost difficulty persuaded to order the clergy in his diocese to wear surplices and who, after succeeding Parker as Archbishop of Canterbury, declined to suppress "prophesyings," those meetings held by zealous cler-

gymen for the discussion of scripture to which the Queen, always distrustful of the religious enthusiasm of parsons, took strong exception. More
than once the Queen asked Grindal to suppress the meetings which were
bound to do harm, attended as they were by "the vulgar sort" who must
be prevented from listening to disputations "unmeet of unlearned people."
Grindal replied that his conscience would not allow him to do so; he must
"choose rather to offend your earthly Majesty than to offend the heavenly
Majesty of God." "Remember, Madam," he added rashly, "that you are a
mortal creature."

The Queen determined to suspend the impertinent man from his duties
as Archbishop; and this, after various Councilors had done their best to
save him, she contrived to do.

Grindal died soon after being suspended as Archbishop and was succeeded, as the Queen's required, by John Whitgift, a learned, brave and
stubborn man whose views were much closer to her own. Like his two
predecessors, Whitgift was a Cambridge man, a former Master of Trinity
College, Regius Professor of Divinity and Vice-Chancellor. He had been
enthroned as Bishop of Worcester in 1577, and was nominated Archbishop
of Canterbury in 1583. By then extremely rich, having inherited a fortune
from his father, a Lincolnshire merchant, he lived in the most splendid
style at Lambeth Palace where he was able to entertain the Queen (who
called him affectionately her "little black husband") with that sumptuous
ceremony which she always so much enjoyed.

As anxious as the Queen to bring that uniformity into the Church which
Grindal in his indulgence towards puritan doctrine had failed to do,
Whitgift required of all the clergy, on pain of suspension, that they accept
the Thirty-Nine Articles, the doctrinal statements of the Church of England
that had been enacted by Parliament in 1577. He also, again with the
Queen's approval, brought forward a decree that imposed a prison sentence
upon any printer who issued material of a religious nature which had not
been licensed by the Archbishop or by the Bishop of London. This severe
measure, and the subsequent execution of several Puritan pamphleteers,
aroused widespread opposition in Protestant circles; but Whitgift refused to
be deflected from his purpose and the Queen warmly supported him in his
stand, convinced that the Puritans, natural enemies of the established hierar-
chy, were far more of a threat to her authority than the Catholics – an
attitude that astonished Sir Francis Knollys who marveled that her Majesty
could be persuaded that she was "in such danger of such as are called
Puritans as she [was] of the Papists." Yet she persisted in this view, hearing
with relief of the death of the influential puritan leader John Feild, sanction-

ing the execution of three prominent sectarians, Henry Barrow, John Greenwood and John Penry, and exasperating the Puritans by her popular support of sports and pastimes which kept people away from their sermons. She particularly annoyed the Puritans by her support of the theatre, by having her own company of players known as "the Queen's Men," by vetoing a Bill that sought to ban all kinds of sports from bull-baiting to rowing on a Sunday, and by contemptuously dismissing a plan to make blasphemy and adultery capital offenses.

Gradually Puritanism as a movement within the Anglican Church was defeated. Anglicanism became identified with conservative patriotism, and with the Protestant victims of the previous reign who were celebrated in John Foxe's *Book of Martyrs*. This immensely long and influential book was deemed of such importance that copies were required to be placed in every cathedral and most parish churches beside the Bible. Tactfully overlooking Queen Elizabeth's attendance at Mass in earlier years, Foxe's *Book* welcomed her to the ranks of Protestant heroines and gave thanks to the Almighty for "the miraculous preservation of the Lady Elizabeth, now Queen of England, from extreme calamity and danger of life in the time of Queen Mary her sister."

Yet Queen Elizabeth, sincere Protestant though she undoubtedly was, remained antagonistic towards Puritanism to the end. Indeed, it was often complained that after the failure of the last of the dangerous conspiracies to place a Roman Catholic sovereign on her throne, she was more severe with Puritan dissidents than ever, treating them far more harshly than Catholics. In 1587, when certain Puritan Members of Parliament introduced a Bill to replace the Book of Common Prayer with a Book of Discipline, she ordered the Members responsible to be sent to the Tower for attempting to usurp the prerogative of the Crown by interfering with the affairs of the Church of England: she was perfectly well satisfied "by her own reading and princely judgement" with the reforms she had already made in the Anglican Church.

Towards the end of her life, however, political considerations, the Spanish menace and the fulminations of the Pope induced the Queen to give way to Protestant demands for more punitive measures against Catholics, particularly priests trained in the seminaries of the Continent who were coming over to England to preach sedition. Elizabeth ordered that the most intensive efforts should be made to keep them out of the country and those who slipped through the net should be banished rather than executed, since executions created martyrs and she thought it as well that John Foxe's martyrs should not have rivals. But executions could not always be avoided; nor, it was felt, could torture; and scores of priests were hanged – as traitors rather than as heretics – after suffering dreadful pain in attempts to extract from them the names of their confederates.

Torture was a method of persuasion that the Queen did not condemn. Indeed, on occasions, she ordered it, as she did in the case of William Holt, a Jesuit priest captured on the Scottish border, who was racked on instructions sent to his jailer: "Her Majesty doth earnestly desire that Holt might be substantially examined and forced by torture to deliver what he knoweth." Similar orders were given in the case of the Jesuit, Edmund Campion, whose graceful eloquence much impressed the Queen when she visited Oxford in 1566. She offered to spare Campion, but on terms which his conscience would not allow him to accept; and so he was mercilessly racked before being taken with two other prisoners to the scaffold at Tyburn. Here the crowds of spectators were assured by government officials that his punishment had nothing to do with religion: he was to be executed as a traitor to the Queen. He was praying for the Queen, for whom he wished a "long quiet reign with all prosperity," when the cart was drawn away to leave him hanging at the end of the rope. It was noticed that his fingernails had been torn off.

Robert Southwell, the poet and Jesuit chaplain to the Countess of Arundel, was also tortured before being hanged at Tyburn, having been arrested by Richard Topcliffe, a notorious persecutor of Catholics who wrote triumphantly to the Queen, "I never did take so weighty a man if he be rightly used." Topcliffe had been granted authority by the Council to examine suspects at his house in Westminster churchyard, where he subjected then to unspeakable tortures which Southwell at his trial described as being far worse than those of the rack. Topcliffe, Member of Parliament for Old Sarum and holder of some minor office at court, boasted not only of the instruments of torture he had assembled at his house but also of the liberties the Queen had permitted him to take. He had, he said, put his hand into her bosom and seen her naked thighs. He was himself arrested and imprisoned in the Marshalsea, but after a few months he was released and returned to his old vile practices. He excited the loathing of Protestants as well as Catholics. When the head of his victim, Southwell, was displayed to the crowd around the scaffold, there were none of the usual shouts of "Traitor!"

Soon after Southwell's death, the Queen expressed her dislike at such punishments. She told the Council that, if they were intent upon converting Catholics to Protestantism, it would best be done by the example of their lives. She herself, concerned by Cecil's warning that cruel persecution was arousing widespread sympathy for the Catholics, declared that she would persecute no more as she had done in the past. Her orders to have the Jesuit William Holt tortured were not, however, the last such orders she gave.

7

The Queen in her Privy Chamber

"I like silk stockings well."

The Queen was not, as she said herself, "a morning woman." Sometimes she rose so early that she was ready to grant an audience at eight o'clock; but usually she was in bed when the rest of her household were about their duties, and could often be seen, "unready in her night-stuff," looking out of her bedchamber window or walking in the garden long after the others had finished their breakfast. When she came in from the garden her ladies attended her to help her with her toilet, to brush her hair or perhaps to wash it with alkalized water, to place ready her favorite marjoram scent and the cosmetics of which she made increasing use as she grew older and which included a lotion of white of egg, alum, borax, poppy seeds and powdered eggshell to maintain the whiteness of her complexion. In a vain attempt to keep her teeth white and sound, she appears to have followed the advice of Sir Hugh Platt, author of a book of advice on such matters, not to resort to aqua fortis but to wash them in a mixture of white wine and vinegar boiled with honey. She no doubt also used the tooth-cloths that are to be found recorded in the lists of presents she received every year and one of the golden toothpicks that appear in almost every inventory.

Her ladies stood by to help her dress in her dark and over-scented tapestry-hung Privy Chamber, an operation that necessarily occupied a considerable time, especially on those days when her appearance had to be particularly impressive. Then – in studied contrast to her ladies and her maids of honor who were kept in black and white – she would wear the most striking colors, yellow or red with bright embroidery and shining jewels, and, increasingly in middle age, black "sumptuously embroidered with silver and pearls."

These were the kind of clothes we see in her portraits as, for instance, in the portrait known as the Rainbow Portrait, attributed to Marcus

Gheeraerts, in which she appears surrounded by cascades of pearls, embroidery and lace, and in the painting of her going in procession to Blackfriars in which she is shown resplendent in a white dress covered with jewels, her left hand resting on the gorgeous material to display her famously long fingers of which she continued to be manifestly proud: the Spanish ambassador, the Count of Feria, noticed how much a play she always made of taking off her gloves to reveal them to his gaze.

Vain as she was, the Queen was apparently reluctant to sit for painters, the only documented likeness from the life being that of Federico Zuccaro; but she well understood the usefulness of portraits in creating the image of her as a woman and as a queen which she wished to present both to her own people and to foreign courts. And she and the Council did all they could to prevent unseemly and pretended likenesses of her being hawked about the streets and sold at fairs. Attempts were made to have all portraits done by unskillful "common Painters" cast into the fire – particularly those that made her look old – and to oblige "all payntors and gravors" to follow the pattern of "a portraicture" by "some speciall person that shall be by hir alowed." Such injunctions seem to have been far from effective, however. So were subsequent orders that no more portraits of her should be produced "but such as the Serjeant Painter [at that time George Gower] should first have sight of." Numerous portraits were, in fact, produced to satisfy an ever-growing demand for them for the galleries of town and country houses in which a painting of the Queen would hang surrounded by family portraits as a demonstration of loyalty both by supporters of the Tudor regime and by those who might otherwise be suspected of opposing it. At the same time thousands of metal medallions, stamped with the Queen's features, were made for loyal subjects who could not afford the price of a picture.

Illicit portraits were rarely offensive in the manner of "a fowle picture" of which the ambassador in Paris had cause to complain: "This was of the Queen's majesty . . . on horseback her left hande holdinge the brydell of the horse, with her right hande pullynge upp her clothes shewing her hindparte." But from even the best of them, as indeed from her relatively few official portraits, it was difficult to gain an impression of what Queen Elizabeth looked like, or to speak confidently of the color of her eyes and hair. As one exasperated critic complained, "After what everyone tells me of her, and after the paintings I have seen, I must declare that she did not have good painters." But then foreign rulers often received equally unreliable reports about her from envoys who had actually seen her. When she was twenty-three, Giovanni Michiel informed the Doge in Venice: "She is comely rather than handsome . . . tall and well formed, with a good skin, although swarthy. She has fine eyes." A few years later Francesco Gradenigo reported that she was "short and ruddy in complexion; very strongly built."

For the depiction of her clothes as well as her features patterns were issued, and in the representation of these the portraits were more reliable. For some portraits, the clothes the Queen was wearing, and the symbols with which the artist surrounded her, were, in fact, considered almost as important as the representation of her appearance. When, for instance, she had her portrait painted for Catherine de Médicis during the protracted negotiations for a marriage of the Queen to a member of the Valois court, she had herself dressed "à la Françoise," a complimentary gesture which caused much pleasure in Paris.

When she did not have to sit for a portrait, and had no important guests to receive, the Queen dressed far more simply in more muted colors, often brown, orange or very pale yellow, with cloth-of-silver slippers, perhaps, and huge white pearls in her hair. And nearly always after 1560, when one of her servants gave her a pair, she wore knitted silk stockings, a new pair every week, giving the others to her ladies. "I like silk stockings well," she declared, ignoring staid critics who considered them indecent since they revealed so fully the shape of the leg when the skirt was raised. "They are pleasant, fine and delicate. Henceforth I will wear no more cloth stockings." She sometimes did so, however, in winter when, as the draughts blew through the long passages of her palaces, she wrapped up well, wearing a mantle over her knees when seated, pulling a cloak over her shoulders and a furred muff round her hands when out of doors, and sometimes holding a golden warmingball.

She had an immense wardrobe to choose from, since not only was her expenditure on clothes immense – in the one year, 1599, more than £700 was spent on "fine linen for her Majesty's person" alone – but so many of the presents which she received – and which, as the Count of Feria said, she was "very fond of getting" – were of wearing apparel. An inventory made towards the end of her life listed, among numerous other items, 102 "French gownes," 100 "loose gownes" and 67 "rounde gownes," 99 robes, 127 cloaks, 85 doublets, 125 petticoats, 56 "saufegardes [outer skirts] and juppes," 126 kirtles, 18 "lappe mantles" and 136 "forepartes" [stomachers].

Her collection of jewelry, also a large part being gifts, was one of the most valuable and varied in Europe: she possessed numerous jeweled watches as well as bracelets, necklaces, rings and brooches; and in one of her portraits there may be counted no fewer than 319 pearls and precious stones, not to mention a jeweled pomander and a jeweled ostrich feather fan.

Once she was fully dressed she set about her morning occupations with an energy that suggested she was anxious to make up for the time she had lost. She spent some time at prayer, then dealt with such business matters as required her attention, reading letters, approving answers or dictating or writing them herself, receiving reports of the Privy Council's deliberations, talking to foreign ambassadors, suddenly getting up to stride about the room as she elaborated some argument, swearing vehemently from time to time, laughing loudly, behaving in fact in a far more earthy and strident way than would have seemed possible in the pale princess whose demureness the Bishop of London had once found so appealing. She usually found time for some reading or scholarly work, taking pleasure in solving the problems of translating Latin or Greek into English, finding such work calmed her nerves when she was agitated or alarmed. "She was wont to sooth her ruffled temper with reading every morning," wrote Sir John Harington, one of her over a hundred godchildren. "She did much admire Seneca's wholesome advisings when the soul's quiet was flown away."

She also calmed herself with exercise. The Spanish ambassador once saw her flounce furiously out of her Audience Chamber and into the garden where she paced up and down plucking at her gloves. When she returned, so he said, she had control of herself once more. Usually she took her walks alone; but sometimes she would take one or more of her ladies with her, or some courtiers or visitors to the court. When necessary she was watched or followed by a guard; if out walking by a detachment of the Yeomen of the Guard, a body established by her grandfather, if riding by a detachment of Gentlemen Pensioners.

A skilled horsewoman, she went riding often and never lost her pleasure in hunting and hawking; and on days when it was warm enough, she "took great delight" in eating a meal al fresco.

Yet, however hungry her companions may have been after a day's hunting, the Queen herself was rarely seen to eat with much appetite. Most of her meals she had alone in her private apartments, served by her ladies. She ate little of the meats her father had so relished, preferring chicken and game. It was no great hardship to her to observe fast days; and on Wednesdays, as well as on Fridays, she nearly always had fish.

She was easy to entertain on her progresses since she made so few demands of her hosts' cooks. She did like her bread to be fine and white and she had a weakness for sweetmeats and sugary puddings. But otherwise her household could offer little guidance to those who asked for suggestions as to what her Majesty would like served at her table when she came to visit them. She was known not to drink much: she had a marked distaste for strong beer and had the small amount of wine in her glass diluted with three parts more of water. "She seldom drank above three times at a meal, and that was common beer," according to Edmund Bohun; "and she very rarely drank again till supper. She rarely drank any wine, for fear it should cloud her faculties. She loved Alicant wine above any other. She always religiously observed fasting-days; [but] when she made any public feast or dinners for her honour or her pleasure, she would then order her table to be served with all the magnificence that was possible, and many side-tables to be adorned with all sorts of plate. She had many of the nobility which waited upon her at the table at those times, and served her with great care and attention."

At these banquets it was noticed by foreign envoys that she toyed with her food, pushing it about her plate, reluctant to eat it yet unwilling to be seen to reject it, thankful when the meal was over and the evening's entertainment could begin. In her own court these entertainments were less robust, more decorous than they were in many others on the Continent. She did keep fools; she had an Italian jester as well as two dwarfs; and Will Sommers, her father's thin little hollow-eyed jester continued in royal service until his death; but none of these took much part in court festivities, which were likely to reflect the Queen's own interests and the pleasure she took in dancing, music and in the theater. One evening there might be a masque performed by some of her courtiers, such as the one presented one summer before Don Guzman de Silva in which the gentlemen were all dressed in black and white. Another evening there might be a play, a comedy perhaps, like Ben Jonson's *Cynthia's Revels* which was performed by the children of Queen Elizabeth's Chapel, or Shakespeare's *Twelfth Night,* which was acted for an audience that included the Count Palatine for whom the Queen and Lady Grey de Wilton took it in turns to act as interpreter. The musical interludes in these plays were always performed with high skill, since it was known how particular the Queen was in this regard and that, careful as she was over other expenditure, she did not stint herself when it came to the employment of singers and instrumentalists. She had nearly fifty singers in her choir and over forty instrumentalists; and after listening to them perform, the French ambassador said that he had never heard the like in all his travels in Spain and throughout his own country: "a concert of music so excellent and sweet as cannot be expressed." The Queen employed William Byrd as a Gentleman of the Chapel Royal; Thomas Tallis was organist there. John Bull was also a

Chapel Royal organist; and both Christopher Tye and Thomas Morley, who edited *The Triumphs of Oriana,* a collection of madrigals written in her honor, were Gentlemen of the Chapel. Dr. Tye, who seems to have taught Elizabeth for a time, was so sure of her favor that he did not hesitate to contradict her. Anthony Wood claimed that "the Queen would send the verger to tell him that he played out of tune, whereupon he sent word that it was her ears that were out of tune." It was Tye, perhaps, who was at fault for he had grown old in her service; and the Queen's ear was known to be reliable. She sang well; she played the lyre and lute, as well as the virginals, with an almost professional skill and composed both music and ballets. She played the virginals "excellently well" in the opinion of James Melville who once came into her presence unexpectedly, though perhaps not as unexpectedly as he thought. "She left off immediately as soon as she turned about and saw me," Melville recorded. "She appeared to be surprised to see me, and came forward, seeming to strike me with her hand; alleging she used not to play before men, but when she was solitary, to shun melancholy."

> She takes great pleasure in dancing and music [another diplomat, Hurault de Maisse informed King Henry IV in 1598]. In her youth she danced very well and composed measures and music and had played them herself and danced them. She takes such pleasure in it that when her maids dance she follows the cadence with her hand and foot. She rebukes them if they do not dance to her liking and without a doubt she is mistress of the art, having learnt in the Italian manner to dance high.

While the Queen did not resent the amount she spent upon her musicians and her chapel singers, she frequently expressed her exasperation at the huge cost of maintaining her household. She made do with a far smaller staff than her father had done. She had no more than three Gentlemen of the Privy Chamber, less than ten grooms, seven married ladies of high rank, four of lesser rank known as the Queen's Women and six Maids-in-Waiting, cheerful, often cheeky and rowdy girls whom the Queen swore at and often slapped in her nervous irritability but of most of whom she was clearly fond, treating them with exceptional indulgence except in the important matters of sex and marriage; and in these she could be most severe *in loco parentis,* peremptorily refusing permission to marry in some cases, soundly beating the applicant in others, and having those who got married secretly or became pregnant banished from court or imprisoned in the Tower. Lady Catherine Grey's sister Mary caused unforgivable offense by secretly marrying Thomas Keys, the Queen's huge sergeant porter, in his chamber by one of the watergates of Whitehall Palace. When she heard of this *mésalliance*, the Queen had Keys thrown into the Fleet prison for three years, while Lady Mary was handed over to the custody of William Hawtrey at Chequers in Buckinghamshire. She was never allowed to see her husband again, and her request to wear mourning when he died was peremptorily refused.

Provided she was approached with due modesty and respect and the proposed husband was unexceptionable, the Queen usually gave her maids permission to marry in the end. Several of them were, indeed, married without undue fuss; and, when she declined to give her assent to a marriage, she generally had good grounds for doing so. She used "many persuasions" against marriage, Frances Howard told her future husband, the Earl of Hertford. "She said how little you would care for me . . . how well I was here, and how much she cared for me. But in the end, she said she would not be against my desire. Trust me, sweet Lord, the worst is past, and I warrant she will not speak one angry word to you." In this case the Queen was quite right to have given the warning: Frances Howard's marriage was not successful, as the Queen had foretold.

Small as was her personal staff, and small as it continued to be throughout her reign, the general costs of her household increased year by year, going up to more than £1,000 a week by the time of her death, even though the lower servants were notoriously underpaid. She was constantly complaining to her ministers and to officials of the Board of Green Cloth, the ancient institution of the household, presided over by the Lord Steward, which was responsible for the administration of the court. But the complex organization and traditional corruption of the household seemed incapable of reform. From time to time investigations were carried out, and tables were drawn up showing the amount of food consumed at court, its estimated and actual costs and the amount that was lost in leakage, wastage, ullage, spillage or downright theft. Yet to keep an exact and reliable tally of the ingoings and outgoings of an establishment which annually consumed well over 20,000 sheep and lambs, 600,000 gallons of beer and more than four million eggs, which customarily supplied private meals to scores of courtiers, officials and distinguished visitors, as well as to tables in the great hall, and which had hundreds of cooks, turnspits and scullions, kitchen boys and dishwashers all keeping sharp eyes open for a chance to purloin a capon or a few pounds of butter, was a task quite beyond the wit of the most scrupulous investigator. The inefficiencies that occasionally came to light were scarcely to be credited: when the Queen complained at Windsor that her food was always cold, it transpired that it

was not cooked in one of the Castle's kitchens, numerous though these
were, but in the public oven in the town, a good ten minutes' walk from
her Privy Chamber.

Such incompetence exasperated the Queen, who was by nature a practical woman with a keen commercial sense considered unusual not to say
unnatural in a woman. She took a close and continuing interest in the
financial affairs of the nation and in the organization and economy of her
own estates, consulting such experts as the financier, Sir Walter Mildmay,
and Sir Thomas Gresham, founder of the Royal Exchange, who helped her
with her currency reforms, making sure that her lands yielded their proper
due without unnecessarily alienating any of her tenants, selling property
when she deemed it necessary and thus gaining the friendship of the pur-
chasers at a time when rich men were anxious to extend their existing
estates or set themselves up as country gentlemen, curbing extravagance
and waste wherever she came across them, accumulating what she called a
"war chest," dreading thoughts of weakness or poverty, insisting that the
Exchequer should never spend more money than it could afford and that
interest on borrowed money should never rise above ten per cent even in
times of emergency, saving, saving, saving. "The parsimony of her Majesty," Cecil said, "hath been a great cause of her majesty's riches, able to
perform these actions whereof heads are inquisitive."

When opportunities to make more money presented themselves, the
Queen was never overscrupulous in seizing them, whether it be in clandestine investments in piratical expeditions or in fleecing the Church. Not
only were bishoprics kept vacant for long periods so that she could lay her
hands on the re.enues – Bristol was without a bishop for fourteen years,
Ely for nineteen – but she also took advantage of a clause in an Act of
1559 to insist upon bishops granting long leases to the Crown either for
her own benefit or for that of some councilor or courtier whom it was in
her interests to reward. As her godson, John Harington, punned, her
courtiers were more often to be found preying on the Church than in the
church.

"As for her private expenses," the Chancellor of the Exchequer once
told the Commons, "they have been little in building. She hath consumed
little or nothing in her pleasures. As for her apparel, it is royal and princely,
beseeming her calling, but not sumptuous nor excessive."

Her wardrobe, in fact, remained enormous, as did the number of her
personal possessions, largely because of the presents that were continually
given to her and continually expected. Certain courtiers, like Lord Robert
Dudley whose fortunes depended upon her favor, loaded her with jewelry;

others with dresses and materials, ornaments and knick-knacks, writing tables, books, ebony cabinets, porcelain porringers and perfume pans, fans, crystal jugs, candlesticks, velvet girdles, silver forks and spoons with coral handles and, most often to be found in the long lists, gold – gold buttons, gold cups, gold bowls, gold bodkins, gold toothpicks, even a gold warming pan. Cecil presented her with gold plate as well as clothes, a rock-crystal ewer, a writing set of silver-gilt and mother of pearl with a penknife and sandboxes, among many other items. The Marquess of Northampton gave her white enameled bracelets; Lady Walsingham a cloth of silver muff with seed-pearl buttons; Lady Heneage "a pomander garnished with gold, enameled and garnished with sparcks of rubyes and a perle pendante"; the Countess of Huntingdon "one greene frogg, the back of emraldes, and a pendaunte emeralde with a chaine of gold to hang by." The lists were seemingly endless; the inventory books replete with entries. When the Queen went on progress it became customary to offer her presents. In this way she acquired a remarkable collection of silver spoons as well as gold cups, dishes and ornaments and of such items as the "mother of pearl tablet with an opal in it, garnished with golde and set with rock rubyes and emeraldes" which she was given at Warwick, and the "gyrdell of golde contayning XVI agathe Heddes and XV troches of perle, II perles in every troche," with which she was presented in Lincoln. Against unsuitable presents, disparaging comments were made in the inventory as, for instance, "very mean" set against a present of pearls from the Countess of Oxford; and such gifts as these were liable to be sold, or, in the case of precious metal, to be classed as "coarse rubbish" and sent to the Mint for melting down.

Having regard to the incompetence of the catering arrangements, it was surprising that court ceremonial was so well organized. Foreign envoys were almost unanimous in their praise of its well-regulated orderliness. A Venetian visitor had "never witnessed the like anywhere"; and for this the Queen herself and Lord Robert Dudley were largely responsible. Both were quick to fall upon the slightest breaches of the settled and well-practiced routine or of the proper etiquette. On feast days, when the Queen dined in public, visitors to court were permitted to see how well-rehearsed the ceremonial was. Escorted from Chapel by her guard in their black and red uniforms with her coat of arms embroidered in silver gilt on the back, she marched towards the Dining Hall behind Councilors bearing her scepters and her sword of state. Attended by her Lord Chamberlain, the Master of the House, the Lord Chancellor and the Lord High Admiral, she sat down alone at her table; and then her ladies took their seats at another table, ready to watch her closely throughout the meal so that, as soon as she showed herself ready to rise, which she was likely to do even before the second course was served, they might rise themselves and make two deep curtseys. Grace was said by two bishops; and after this an attendant brought in a gold basin and a towel. The Queen ceremoniously removed her rings, handed them to the Lord Chamberlain, washed her hands, dried them, then put the rings on again. After the meal there was dancing; and, while this was in lively progress, the Queen called up to her, one after the other, those to whom she wished to talk. Having spoken to the last of them she stood up, raised a long white hand in valediction and was escorted from the hall back to her Privy Chamber. And here, late though it might be, as often as not she settled down to work.

Before embarking upon an evening of festivities, she would often have a rest about six o'clock; for, although her energy seemed never to flag in the hunting field or in the Council chamber, or when appearing informally or in state before her people, she did weary of an evening at court when there was nothing of particular interest to engage her attention. In the privacy of her own chamber she amused herself with card games, chess or tables, a kind of backgammon, or by playing with her pets. She was said to have "loved little dogs, singing birds, parrots and apes."

The Queen was what nowadays would be called exceptionally highly strung. She often came close to hysteria, and more than once fainted when overpoweringly distressed. When she was first Queen it had been supposed that she was, in the words of the Spanish ambassador, "not likely to have a long life." Her constitution, he told his master, "cannot be very strong." There were reports of stomach pains, headaches and aching limbs; and once, when she had diarrhea, she was so ill she made Cecil and the other Councilors "sore afraid." In 1569 she developed a painful ulcer on her leg, which troubled her intermittently for years and gave rise to further reports that her life was in danger; and, when the discharge dried up, that also was considered dangerous since it was supposed to have compensated for her irregular menstruation. She suffered from eyestrain, insomnia and breathlessness, from occasional indigestion and fainting fits, sometimes also from gout in her thumb, and repeatedly from toothache and swellings in her cheeks; and she was not an easy patient for she hated to be ill or to be thought to be ill. When she first complained of the "desperate ache" in her right thumb and it was suggested that she might be suffering from gout, she would not have it. It certainly was not gout. "The gout it *cannot* be," one of her ministers commented, "nor dare not be." In fact, she concluded, there was no ache; but she would not sign her letters.

She was equally obstinate when her teeth ached. Once, when a tooth was giving her intense pain, it was decided that it must be extracted; but her physicians dared not tell her so, because she herself "doth not or will not think so." Eventually the Council decided that the tooth must come out, having listened to the opinion of a tooth-drawer who said that the only other possibility was to dress it with fenugreek which might make the neighboring teeth fall out as well. A body of Councilors went to try to persuade the Queen to agree to the extraction. She refused to do so, however, until the Bishop of London allowed the surgeon to pull out one of his teeth to demonstrate the ease with which the operation could be performed.

Yet for all her occasional illnesses, so quickly seized upon by foreign envoys who reported her as being "thin as a stick" or "pale as a ghost," the Queen's health seems to have improved as she grew older. She needed little sleep; she spent hours standing up; she continued to walk with energy and to ride with astonishing vigor.

8

The Queen in her Council Chamber

"I perceive they deal with me like physicians who, administering a drug, make it more acceptable by giving it a good aromatical savour."

"When her Highness is angry or not well disposed, trouble her not with any matter which you desire to have done," warned the experienced Clerk of the Council, Robert Beale, in a memorandum for the guidance of those who had matters to discuss with the Queen. It was well-considered advice. According to her godson, John Harington, a courtier came out of her presence one day "with an ill countenance" and pulled Harington "aside by the girdle and said in a secret way, 'If you have any suit today, I pray you put it aside. The sun doth not shine.'" Harington prudently decided "not to adventure her Highness's choler." His own method he described as follows:

> I must go in an early hour, before her highness hath special matters brought to counsel on. I must go before the breakfasting covers are placed, and stand uncovered as her highness cometh forth her chamber; then kneel, and say, "God save your majesty! I crave your ear at what hour may suit for your servant to meet your blessed countenance?" Thus will I gain her favour to the auditory.

Robert Beale also advised Councilors and petitioners to find out from "some of the Privy Chamber" what sort of mood the Queen was in before approaching her and then to make a "note of such things as you are to propound to her" so that her patience was not tried by a muddled presentation. It was, moreover, in Beale's experience, essential to keep on good terms with those closest to the Queen in the Privy Chamber, and often wise to divert her attention by talking lightly of other matters when there were important documents to sign, since she was all too prone to alter their wording or not to approve them at all at the last minute. "Avoid opinion of being new-fangled," Beale added, "and a bringer-in of new customs."

Instinctively conservative as she was, the Queen made no immediate changes in the constitution of the Council. At the beginning of her reign about half its members were peers, but these were often absent on other business in their counties and were gradually replaced by men whose offices kept them about the court, men more closely connected to the Queen and, for the most part, related to each other either by blood or marriage. This certainly made the Council more easily controllable, but it also made its membership conspicuously narrow. Assiduous as she was in the early months of her reign in attending meetings of the Council, which took place twice a week at one or other of her London palaces, the Queen soon took to relying upon individual members to report to her on the Council's deliberations, attending them herself infrequently, except in times of crisis or when she felt her presence necessary to promote policies she favored or block those she did not. She would also consult courtiers whom she liked and trusted but whom for one reason or another she excluded from the Council as she excluded the Earl of Sussex, whose appointment would have angered Lord Robert Dudley; and this exasperated her official Councilors, one of whom protested that it was "but a folly for them to debate things if she followed other's Counsel."

With few exceptions, her Councilors agreed with Beale that she was a "princess of great wisdom, learning and experience." Sir John Harington "never did find greater show of understanding and learning than she was blessed with." She was also extremely well-informed and had an astonishingly retentive memory. "She was so expert in the knowledge of her realm and estate," said Cecil "as no counsellor she had could tell her what she knew not before." In fact, so John Oglander concluded, there was nothing lacking in her "that could be desired in a prince, but that she was a woman." She read the reports that came to her from England and abroad and all Orders in Council with the most careful attention, or had them read to her, listening intently, occasionally making or dictating notes. She would then summon Councilors to discuss various points with her, either alone or in small groups, again making notes and sometimes later holding the opinions then expressed against those who had put them forward or catching them out in misstatements or contradictions. The papal Nuncio in Flanders once commented, "The Queen of England, I know not how, penetrates everything." It seemed perfectly appropriate that in the portrait of her at Hatfield her dress is embroidered all over with eyes and ears.

When the Baron de Rosny was sent over to England as his envoy by the

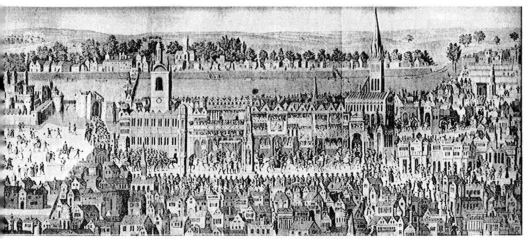

1. An engraving from a contemporary painting showing King Edward VI proceeding from the Tower of London to Westminster on 19 February 1547, the day before his coronation. The King can be seen riding beneath a canopy held by four outriders, approaching the cross in Cheapside.

2. Lady Jane Grey aged about sixteen, three years before her execution, from a painting attributed to Master John.

3. Queen Mary and King Philip of Spain, whose unpopular marriage took place in 1554, from a painting by Hans Eworth.

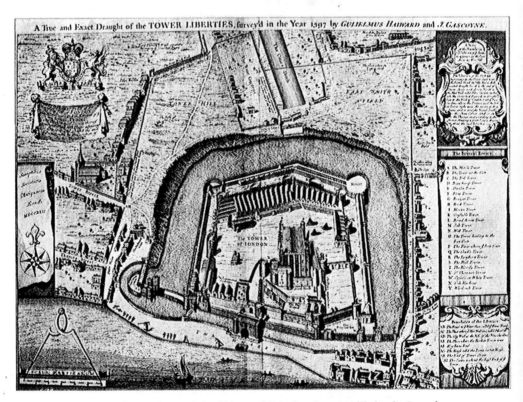

4. A bird's-eye view of the Tower of London in 1597. Traitor's Gate, by which Princess Elizabeth entered as a prisoner during her half-sister's reign, can be seen beneath St. Thomas's tower in the center foreground.

5, 6. Sketches for full-length portraits of Queen Elizabeth and the Earl of Leicester by the Italian Mannerist artist, Federico Zuccari, who visited England in the summer of 1575.

7. A miniature by Nicholas Hilliard of Henry Wriothesley, third Earl of Southampton, Shakespeare's patron and the Earl of Essex's friend.

8. Matthew Parker, who was consecrated Archbishop of Canterbury in 1559.

9. Sir Francis Walsingham, the Queen's outspoken Secretary of State, from a portrait attributed to John de Critz the Elder.

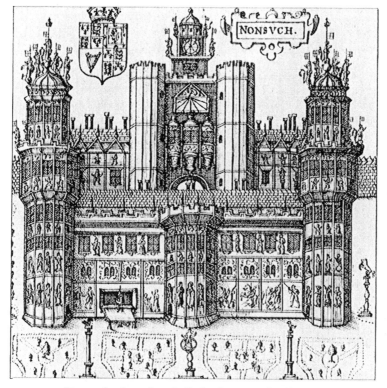

10. Nonsuch, the palace built in the 1530s for Henry VIII, where Elizabeth stayed on many occasions, enjoying the hunting.

11. Richmond Palace in 1562, the Queen's "warm box" and favorite of all her palaces.

12. The Queen being served a meal al fresco, from George
Turberville's *The Booke of Hunting*, 1572.

13. Anthonis van den Wyngaerde's view of Oatlands, one
of the Queen's manors, prized for the hunting to be
enjoyed there.

that the Prince oz chiefe (if so please them) doe alight into take
assaye of the Deare with a sharpe knyfe, the whiche is done

14. The Queen is invited to "take
assaye of the Deare with a sharpe
knyfe"; an illustration from
Turberville's *The Booke of Hunting.*

15. Ruins at Holdenby, Northamptonshire, the palatial house built by Sir
Christopher Hatton, who waited vainly for ten years for the Queen to come
to stay.

16. A portrait of the Queen in middle age by an unknown artist, who used one of the face-patterns issued from time to time under royal license to help painters produce acceptable likenesses.

King of France, the Queen undertook to give him her view of how matters stood in Europe. She did so with such fluency and knowledge that Rosny looked at her in silent amazement. She thought that he must have failed to follow her arguments; but he assured her that he understood her very well; he was just astonished by how much she knew. So she continued and when she had finished Rosny was fully persuaded that "this great Queen merited the whole of that great reputation she had throughout Europe."

This reputation, it had to be said, was combined with one of bossiness. She was as bossy as a "peasant upon whom a barony has been conferred," wrote one disapproving foreign envoy. "Since she came to the throne she is puffed up with pride and imagines she is without peer." She was also instinctively deceitful, and so reluctant to reveal her hand that even her closest advisers were often at a loss to gather what her true opinions were, so adept did she become at obfuscation, masquerade and camouflage.

All her ministers had constant cause to complain also of her vacillations and tergiversations, her reluctance to make up her mind and then, having made it up, her readiness to change it. Her equivocations and *voltes-face* over the proposed grant of the royal property of Newhall to the Earl of Sussex were a case in point. She said at first she would give it to him, but then, reflecting that if she did so, it would be gone forever, she thought perhaps she had better not part with it. Then "she thought it best you should have it," Cecil reported to Sussex, "but therewith she mixed speeches also after her accustomed manner, what a noble house it was and with what charges her father had built it." Even so, Cecil was bold enough to interject, her father had not much liked it when it was finished and had soon abandoned it as not a proper royal residence. "Then she wore a new doubt, considering the value of the property that was to leave her hands." Did not Cecil think she ought to charge a rent for the park? Cecil did not believe she could. Well, then, she did not know what to say and "would give no resolved answer yea or nay."

She was as reluctant to make up her mind, and as ready to change it, in small matters as in important ones. She would, for instance, repeatedly alter the date appointed for her departure from one house to the next; and once at Windsor, when she had changed her mind three times, she overheard a carter, who had been summoned to transport her wardrobe, cry out in anguish, "Now, I see the Queen is a woman, as well as my wife!" She thought it as well to throw the man some money out of the window. She also constantly changed her mind about the route to be taken on her progresses: once, so it was exasperatedly reported, the proposed itinerary "hath changed every five hours."

So irresolute and inconsistent was the Queen on occasions, and so distressed by the prospect of having to come to an irrevocable decision, that she seemed close to nervous breakdown. Sir Francis Knollys, the Vice-Chamberlain of her Household, once told Cecil that he sometimes doubted that she was really fit to govern, so difficult was it to pin her down; and, taking it upon himself as an old friend and cousin to be quite frank with her, Knollys warned her bluntly that it was impossible for her faithful Councilors to govern her estate unless she resolutely followed "their opinion in weighty affairs." It was a common sentiment. If only, her principal secretary once complained exasperatedly, she would, as other princes did, leave important affairs to "those best capable of understanding them," instead of wearing them all out by her tiresome "prolonging and mincing." "The lack of resolute answer from her Majesty," once drove Cecil "to the wall." Rather than come to a decision she would spend weeks and months in argument and in protracted, useless diplomacy, hoping that difficult problems would resolve themselves – as often, indeed, they did – if left to do so. "It maketh me weary of life," Sir Thomas Smith complained. "I neither can get the other letters signed, nor the letter already signed permitted to be sent away, but day by day, and hour by hour, deferred until anon, none, and tomorrow."

"This irresolution doth weary and kill her ministers, destroy her actions, and overcome all good designs and councils," Smith protested on a later occasion. "I wait whilst I have neither eyes nor legs to stand on. And these delays grieve me more and will not let me sleep in the night." Her ministers learned to rush away with papers she had signed in order to put authorization into effect before a message arrived "to stay those things that her Majesty had signed." Robert Beale advised all ministers to obtain written instructions from the Queen confirming their most important orders so she could not afterwards deny – as she was otherwise wont to do – that she had given them.

Of course, the main trouble, so it was generally agreed, was that her ministers had to deal with a woman. "They labour under two things at this Court," one of them once complained, "delay and inconstancy, which proceeded from the sex of the Queen." "This fiddling woman troubles me out of measure," another expostulated. "God's wounds! This it is to serve a base, bastard, pissing kitchen woman! If I had served any prince in Christendom, I had not been so dealt withal."

Nor was the Queen's indecision all that her ministers had to complain of. When she was in the mood to do so, she would talk incessantly, reminiscing discursively as though thinking aloud with no regard for the minister anxious to get back to his work. "It is her wont," complained one diplomat subjected to this cascade of words, "to make long digressions and after much circumlocution to come to the matter of which she wishes to speak." This habit was all the more exasperating because the amount of work her ministers were expected to get through was phenomenal; yet requests that they might have more clerical assistance were met with evasions, suggestions that the time had come for them to retire with assurances of their indispensability, hints that they might take a holiday, with either sympathy or scorn but rarely with permission to do so. They also had to grow accustomed to taking the blame for all her policies that turned out badly, just as they had to learn to concede to her the credit for all that went well. "All irresolutions and lacks are thrown upon us too in all her speeches to everybody," Cecil had occasion to deplore to one of his colleagues. "The wrong is intolerable." Moreover, the Queen was often highly impatient and sometimes in an extremely bad temper, and then she would swear and blaspheme "greviously by God and by Christ," so a contemporary author complained, "and by many parts of his glorified body, and by saints, faith, troth and other things." She would threaten to set her Councilors in the stocks or see to it that they were soon "shorter by the head." Several of them, from Burghley and Dudley to those less favored, found it expedient to stay away from court at times. But then she would suddenly forgive them, and welcome them back as though there had been no quarrel, teasing them slyly for what she might well pretend was a fit of sulks on their part, making some such remark as she was said to have addressed to a courtier who, "making his low obeisance" to her, "happened to let a Fart at which he was so abashed he went to travel seven years. After his returne the Queen welcomed him home and sayd, 'My Lord, I had forgot the Fart.' "

"When she smiles, it was a pure sunshine that everyone did choose to bask in if they could," wrote Sir John Harington; "but anon came a storm from a sudden gathering of clouds, and the thunder fell in wondrous manner on all alike." Councilors were then liable to be slapped on the face or to have a slipper thrown at their heads, an indignity once suffered by Sir Francis Walsingham.

Walsingham, the son of a lawyer from an old Norfolk family, who was one of London's leading citizens, had been trained as a lawyer himself after coming down from Cambridge without a degree. An ardent Protestant, he had spent the whole of Queen Mary's reign on the Continent where he gained the knowledge of European affairs and languages that was to prove

of such benefit to Elizabeth's government. On returning to England upon
her accession, he had entered Parliament for Lyme Regis; and, having been
recommended to the notice of Sir William Cecil, had been asked to obtain
information about the activities and probable intentions of foreign governments. Soon afterwards he was placed, unofficially, in charge of England's
secret service, which he brought to a pitch of remarkable efficiency, supervising the operations of over seventy agents and spies in Continental
courts, maintaining that "intelligence is never too dear."

In 1573, after serving for a time as ambassador in Paris, he was appointed a Secretary of State with special responsibility for foreign affairs.
Intelligent, wily, authoritative and astute, entertaining ambitious policies
which the more pragmatic Cecil, like the Queen, usually considered impracticable, he was an acknowledged master of his subject. He was always
asked for his opinion at every new turn of events, but his relations with the
Queen were never easy. He was a far more zealous Protestant than Cecil;
and whereas the Queen often differed with Cecil, who favored a more
forceful religious policy than she felt inclined to pursue, there were never
serious ruptures. With the less tactful and less patient Walsingham, however, the case was different; and so it was with those others of the Queen's
advisers, nearly all staunch Protestants, who came into prominence with
Cecil's elevation to the Barony of Burghley and his appointment as Lord
Treasurer in 1572. One of these was Sir Thomas Smith, another former
ambassador in Paris, who was appointed a Secretary of State at about the
same time as Walsingham. A Cambridge scholar, once Regius Professor of
Civil Law and Vice-Chancellor of the University, Smith's zealous Protestantism was never in doubt. Nor was that of Thomas Wilson, another
former Cambridge scholar who had been tortured as a suspected heretic
by the Inquisition in Rome and who succeeded Smith as Secretary of State
in 1577. William Davison, Walsingham's assistant, was also a staunch Protestant. So was Robert Beale, the Clerk of the Council, who had once been
Walsingham's private secretary. With all these men the Queen came into
conflict from time to time over the recurring problems of her marriage and
the succession, over the proper attitude to adopt towards Puritans in England and Protestant rebels in France and the Netherlands. But it was for
Walsingham as the most capable and influential of her advisers that she
reserved her particular resentment, knowing that it was he who was largely
responsible for the fact, always distressing to her, that she could not govern in the way her father had done, that while her ministers acknowledged
that they were in duty bound to obey her, they made it difficult if not
impossible for her to carry through policies which she favored and they

did not, finding occasion to delay in fulfilling her orders or contriving to evade them altogether, not always telling her the truth, concealing facts from her, communicating with each other in code, assuring themselves that as a woman she could not fully understand the complicated business of government, writing to ambassadors at foreign courts, as Walsingham often did, asking them to give her Majesty the gist of a problem but to reserve the details for his eyes only or telling them, as Walsingham once told the Earl of Huntingdon, to write a basically false report to persuade her to adopt a policy that she otherwise would have rejected. The Queen's Councilors, in fact, came to the view that the methods of deceit so often adopted in their dealings with the Queen were the only means whereby the state's affairs could be conducted. Her Majesty being a queen and having a special regard for the problems of rights of other sovereigns, could not, for example, regard the struggle of the Dutch Protestants against their royal masters in the same clear light as her Protestant Councilors did. Why then, ways must be found to implement a policy of which she disapproved, and efforts must be made to persuade her to change her mind. "We all must dutifully bear with her Majesty's offence for the time," Cecil wrote to Walsingham regarding the Dutch problem in 1578, "not despairing but, howsoever she misliketh matters at one time, yet at another time she will alter her sharpness, especially when she is persuaded that we all mean truly for her and her surety, though she sometimes will not so understand." If all efforts at persuasion failed there was always the threat of resignation, a threat that Cecil made more than once in order to get his way.

The Queen was, of course, far too astute not to realize that her ministers practiced certain subterfuges to gain their points. "I perceive," she said, "they deal with me like physicians who, administering a drug, make it more acceptable by giving it a good aromatical savour, or when they give pills do gild them all over." But she seems not to have been aware of the full extent of the measures they, and in particular Walsingham, took to modify her policies or actually to pursue their own in defiance of her wishes.

Declining to indulge the Queen's delight in compliments, however outlandishly extravagant, by praising her beauty or genius in that elaborately stylized way that had become a convention with her courtiers, Walsingham spoke to her bluntly in a manner that other ministers dared not do, going so far as to deride her ideas about marriage, to condemn her parsimony or to remind her of the limits of her power. When she endeavored to prevent the marriage of his daughter, Frances, to Sir Philip Sidney, one of those handsome young men about court, whose flattery and friendship she was always so anxious not to lose, Walsingham wrote firmly to the Lord Chancellor, "I pray you, sir, therefore, if she enter into any further speech on the matter, let her understand that you learn generally that the match is held for concluded, and withal to let her know how just cause I shall have to find myself aggrieved if her Majesty still show her mislike thereof."

The Queen respected Walsingham. She sometimes seemed even to be rather intimidated by him, as when, driven beyond endurance by her procrastination, he once burst out, "For the love of God, madam, let not the cure of your diseased estate hang any longer in deliberation." Yet she took pleasure in teasing him if he appeared to be on less than sure ground. When a possible marriage of Elizabeth to the Duke of Anjou was being discussed and Walsingham, who had previously been against it, came round to advocate it, she greeted him on his return from France with the words, "Well, you knave, why have you so often spoke ill of him? You veer round like a weathercock."

Yet, although she bestowed upon him one of those nicknames she gave to all her closest advisers and friends, she never really warmed to the dark-skinned "Moor," and favored him with a grudging hand. She knighted him; she appointed him Chancellor of the Order of the Garter and subsequently Chancellor of the Duchy of Lancaster; but, when he found himself in financial difficulties through his having paid for many of his secret service activities from the income he drew from his various offices, she refused to help him. In July 1581 he asked a courtier more intimate with her than he was himself to "put her Majesty in mind that in eight years' time wherein I have served her, I never yet troubled her for the benefitting of any that belonged unto me, either by kindred or otherwise; which I think never any other could say that served in the like place." But no recompense was forthcoming. Burghley, who was fully conscious of the invaluable services that Walsingham had performed for her, asked the Queen to help him out of his difficulties – which were increased by his taking over the debts of his son-in-law – by allowing him some of the forfeited estates of traitors whose convictions his vigilant eye had helped to secure. But she dismissed Walsingham's claims, keeping several of the estates herself and bestowing others on courtiers whom she found more accommodating and agreeable. These, Walsingham had cause to complain, were "unkind dealings."

It was a complaint that others had cause to make. It was true that some of her ministers and favorite courtiers made immense fortunes from the offices, the licenses and monopolies, the rights to levy fines or collect taxes, which she bestowed upon them, and from the taxes they contrived, with her connivance, to avoid. But others were not so fortunate, and promotion in rank and office was frequently very slow to come and financial rewards for many were not high. Most of the senior servants she employed received no more than £50 a year, while some of her most trusted ministers waited in vain for the honors which never came their way, as Walsingham did, or waited for year after year, like William Cecil who was not created Baron Burghley until 1571, the thirteenth year of his office. The following year Burghley was belatedly created a Knight of the Garter, but the Queen let it be known that this was an exceptional distinction for a man from his social background: it was an honor she otherwise reserved almost without exception for those of noble birth.

She did once ask Burghley to prepare for her a list of suitable candidates for the House of Lords, which was gradually diminishing in size; but when she had been given the names she pursued the matter no further. Concerned to maintain the riches and special status of the Crown, and to preserve the dignity and exclusiveness of the peerage, she continued throughout her reign to resist pressure to increase its numbers and refused to recognize honors received abroad, such as Countships of the Holy Roman Empire. She tartly informed Sir Nicholas Clifford when he came home with a decoration bestowed upon him in France, "My dogs wear my collars."

While declining in wealth, the great noble families still wielded much power; and it was essential for the Queen to have them on her side, to involve them so far as she could in any controversial decisions her government had to make. Frequently they dominated parliamentary elections; and, through their hold over the lord lieutenancies of their respective counties, they also dominated the local militia. Few had authority over so wide an area as did the Duke of Norfolk, whose power in East Anglia was formidable; but around their country houses, at Wilton and Arundel, for square mile upon square mile, the Earls of Pembroke and Arundel enjoyed undisputed authority in Wiltshire and Sussex, as the Earl of Bedford did in Cornwall, the Earl of Derby in Lancashire and Cheshire and the Earl of Shrewsbury in Shropshire, while in the north the Earls of Northumberland, Westmorland and Cumberland were almost a law unto themselves.

In order to placate, flatter and cultivate the support and friendship of such men – many of whom were, indeed, as anxious to please her as she was to please them – she gave them time to pay their debts; she allowed them to remain – as they long had been – undertaxed; she even granted some of them allowances when they were in need. She made over royal properties to them for use as London houses; she exchanged new years' gifts with them – more often than not, admittedly, to her own profit. She went out of her way to show interest in their family affairs, offering herself as godmother to their children; she paid visits to them when on her progresses; she found places for them when important embassies were to be sent to fellow-sovereigns; she was indulgent to the peccadillos and even the crimes of their wayward scions, and she treated them with honor when they came to court, encouraging them to shine brightly in that intriguing world within a world.

9

The Queen at Court

"When will you cease to be a beggar?"

"Let nothing draw thee from the Court. Sit in every Council." This was the advice given to one ambitious young man eager to make his name and fortune. The court was the key to success, at once the center of power and the fount of patronage. Here a man must seek a place if he were to be favored by the Queen and gain the profits and the influence that only positions at court could bestow. Men spent immense sums in endeavoring to become established at court and made immense sums once established there. There were enormously profitable offices to be had apart from licenses and monopolies: there were constableships of castles, keeperships of prisons; there were bribes to be collected, honors and rewards to be sought, favors to be granted in return for favors received. Banishment from court was a disgrace as well as a deprivation that men were constantly contriving to bring upon their rivals. Acceptance into the Queen's close circle was a prize of inestimable worth.

"The Queen did fish for men's souls," her Lord Chancellor said, "and she had so sweet a bait that no one could escape her network." She turned her courtiers into officials, and her officials into courtiers. In the later years of her reign it became fashionable for gentlemen at court to wear a portrait of her Majesty, a miniature or a cameo in a jeweled frame, as a token of their devotion to her and an acknowledgment of her authority over them: even Burghley, black-robed and somber, wore such a medallion in his hat. She liked it to be seen that courtiers and ministers alike were her admiring creatures, just as she liked to hear their declarations of love, their fulsome compliments, their praise of her intelligence as well as of her beauty. It was necessary to recognize her skill in small matters as well as in large: it was understood, for instance, that she was never to lose when playing cards.

Her ladies understood this as well as anyone. They were expected to show her a devotion quite equal to that of the men, and required to be even more tolerant of her tantrums. They were not to complain when she lost her temper, when she swore at a lady for her inefficiency in serving at table or jabbed at a clumsy hand with a knife. They were instructed not to dabble in politics, yet were required to be knowledgeable about the gossip of the court, while remaining innocent themselves of any hint of scandal.

It was safest for ladies not to get married. It was safest for men, too, though of all her favorite courtiers only one, Christopher Hatton, contrived to remain single.

Hatton, the son of a gentleman from Holdenby in Northamptonshire who claimed descent from one of William the Conqueror's knights, was a tall and agreeable young man, as graceful a dancer as he was skilled as a horseman. He had left Oxford without taking a degree and the Inner Temple without being called to the bar; but the favors that the Queen bestowed upon him and the presents she gave him were not lavished upon him merely because she found him so appealing. He·was a gifted man and, when it was required of him, capable of application. Industrious and loyal, he had an acknowledged ability for organization. His rise at court, however, was slow. He had been there for over ten years, accumulating debts of £10,000, before the Queen granted him the annuity she had vaguely promised him but hinted that he would not get if he asked for it. Once she had relented, however, his progress was smooth. From being a Gentleman of the Privy Chamber he rose to be Captain of her Bodyguard, then Vice-Chamberlain of her Household and one of her recognized spokesmen in the House of Commons, where he sat for Northamptonshire and where he was known to reflect her Majesty's views, particularly in matters of religion. When his appointment as Lord Chancellor was announced in 1587, the promotion occasioned a good deal of sardonic comment, since his knowledge of the law was slender and there were several other men whose claims to the office were suggested as being far more worthy of consideration than those of "the dancer" Hatton, who did not want the post anyway. But the Queen swept all such objections aside.

She gave him lands and profitable offices; she overlooked his involvement in rather suspect financial dealings and his manipulation of monopolies in the wine trade; she indulged him in his shady acquisitions of ecclesiastical lands. She obliged the Bishop of Ely to part with the freehold of Ely House and its surrounding estate in what is now Hatton Garden – which Hatton had rented for £10 a year, ten loads of hay and a rose picked at midsummer – and had not shrunk from implying that the Bishop, whom she heartily disliked, would be deprived of his see if he did not agree to the conveyance. She allowed Hatton almost twice as much as the other courtiers received on New Year's Day when it was customary to make presents to the Queen in exchange for various weights of silver plate.

He addressed her in letters of intemperate devotion, protesting that to serve her was heaven, to be parted from her worse than hell's torment. "Would God I were with you but for one hour," he once wrote. "My wits are overwrought with thoughts. I find myself amazed. Bear with me, my most dear sweet Lady. Passion overcometh me. I can write no more. Love me, for I love you." When an epidemic of smallpox broke out, he sent her a ring which, he said, contained a prophylactic and which he suggested she should wear round her neck, "betwixt the sweet dugs, the chaste nest of most pure constancy." "Your words are sweet," he wrote to her a few days later. "Your heart is full of rare and royal faith; the writings of your fair hand do raise me joy unspeakable."

She returned his devotion, sitting by his bedside when he was ill and then sending one of her own doctors to Spa whence he had gone to convalesce, bestowing upon him a fond nickname, always a sign of her particular favor. She called him her "mutton," her "belwether," and her "Lids," Lord Robert Dudley being her "Eyes." She was ever ready with her praise of him, once delivering a sharp retort to someone who commented that a certain *maestro di ballo* danced even better than Hatton, "Pish! I will not see your man – it is his trade."

The Queen knighted him; she invested him with the Order of the Garter; she had him appointed Chancellor of Oxford University. He repaid her with his flattery, his entertaining conversation, his good nature and constant attendance upon her, his easy ability to charm her with the notion of his being desperately in love. She dreaded losing him, and made it clear that she could not abide the thought that he might marry, which he never did, contenting himself with mistresses whom he was careful to keep out of her sight. It was natural that rumor-mongers whispered that the Queen and Hatton were lovers, that such rumors so distressed Archbishop Parker that he wrote to Burghley of his misgivings after a man had been taken up in Kent for "uttering most shameful words against her." The matter was "so horrible" that the Mayor of Dover who had examined the slanderer had felt unable to write down the words the man had used.

In fact when Hatton hinted to the Queen that they should become lovers, she replied with characteristic ambiguity, telling him that she had once been asked in a game of Question and Answer if anything should be denied to a friend, and that it was necessary to determine what true friendship meant.

Good tempered though he was, Hatton was quick to display his jealousy when he sensed he was being replaced in the Queen's affections by some rival. He did not, for instance, disguise his pique when the Queen's eye fell admiringly upon the Earl of Oxford, as dextrous and graceful a dancer as himself, as skilled and daring a horseman, a man in whom, so it was said, "the Queen's Majesty delighteth more in his personage and his dancing and valiantness than any other . . . If it were not for his fickle head he would pass any of them shortly."

Edward de Vere, seventeenth Earl of Oxford, was certainly a personable and gallant young man; but he was also selfish, arrogant and persistently quarrelsome. Whenever there was a fracas at court he was often to be found involved in it. He quarreled violently with Sir Philip Sidney who – though Oxford was as usual in the wrong – was reprimanded by the Queen for refusing to apologize for calling him "a puppy," for forgetting "the difference in degree between earls and gentlemen." "She laid before Sidney," Sir Fulke Greville wrote, "the respect inferiors owed to their superiors; and the necessity in princes to maintain their own creations, as degrees descending between the people's licentiousness and the anointed sovereignty of crowns; and how the gentleman's neglect of the nobility taught the peasant to insult both."

Oxford quarreled violently with Thomas Knyvett, a respected gentleman of the Privy Chamber; and the feud between the two men, after they had both been wounded in a duel, resulted in the death of at least five of their respective supporters and the wounding of several others. Again Oxford was protected, though when Knyvett killed one of Oxford's men, the Queen urged Hatton to arrange for a plea of self-defense to be accepted and to have the affair dealt with quietly during the legal vacation with the least possible fuss.

Oxford invited trouble, one of his rivals once said. He had inherited his father's title at the age of twelve, when Burghley became his guardian. He went to live at Cecil House, where he was soon at odds with almost the entire household and where, during one argument typical of many, he inflicted a fatal wound on an assistant cook. A jury was induced to bring in a verdict of suicide, death being conveniently attributed to the servant's having run "upon a poynt of a fence sword of the said erle." When Burghley's eldest and favorite daughter, Anne, fell in love with him, her father comforted himself in his snobbish way with the thought that the young man was, after all, the seventeenth Earl of Oxford, that he might improve with age, that he found in him even now "more understanding than any stranger to him would think."

He did not prove a fond husband, leaving his wife at home when he went to court. His mother-in-law looked askance at the Queen's excessive fondness for him. But her husband thought it better not to interfere: it was better to wink "at these love matters."

No one supposed that Oxford had ever been much in love with the Lord Treasurer's daughter, a kindly, retiring, rather plain girl of literary tastes. He himself told his cousin, Lord Henry Howard, that if she were ever to become pregnant he would not be the father. When it became known that she was pregnant, Howard – who thoroughly disliked Burghley and was resentful of the influence of a man whose descent was far more humble than he liked it to be supposed – spread abroad what his cousin had told him: Oxford was not only known to be a disloyal husband but was evidently a cuckold to boot. He was in Italy when the news of his wife's pregnancy reached him; and, on his return home with a present of perfumed gloves for the Queen, he told his father-in-law that he did not intend to go to see his wife until he was "satisfied on some points." Indeed, according to an entry in Burghley's diary, he was "enticed by certain lewd persons to be a stranger to his wife." Yet when Burghley asked him politely enough why he was behaving towards her in this way, he exploded in fury. "I will not blazen or publish it until it please me . . . I mean not to weary my life any more with such troubles and molestations as I have endured, nor will I, to please your Lordship only, discontent myself . . . Always I have, and I will still, prefer mine own content before others."

Burghley now thought it as well to write to the Queen in defense of his ill-used daughter who had always regarded the Queen with "fervent admiration." He could not explain his son-in-law's extraordinary conduct unless it arose from his having refused to give him any more money after having already been over-liberal in that respect.

The Queen was not disposed to blame Oxford for his treatment of his wife. Taking a proprietary interest in him, she did her best to protect him from harm and even from criticism. When she was told that his wife was pregnant, she jumped to her feet and exclaimed, "Indeed, it is a matter that concerns my Lord's joy chiefly, yet I protest to God that, next to them that have interest in it, there is nobody that can be more joyous of it than I am."

She welcomed Oxford back to court after his return from Italy, overlooked the extravagant dress he had now adopted, and the affectation of his speech and gestures. She encouraged him in his patronage of men of letters and musicians, praised his own lyrical poems, which were, indeed, of exceptional and surprising beauty, continued to reward his prowess on the tilting ground, forgave him his offenses in his protracted quarrel with

Thomas Knyvett and rewarded him with official employment. He remained apparently indifferent to his wife and although he had three daughters by her, as well as a son who died in infancy, he left the upbringing of these children to their grandparents. His wife died soon after the birth of the last of these children, and Oxford remarried without delay one of the Queen's maids of honor whose rich father enabled him to regain the fortune which his extravagance had dissipated.

Piqued as Sir Christopher Hatton was by the favors that the Queen bestowed upon the insufferable Earl of Oxford, he was even more jealous of another courtier also much younger than himself, Walter Ralegh.

Ralegh came from a family of squires in the West Country, where he had been to school and where, so it has afterwards been said, he spent hours talking to the sailors and fishermen on the beach at Budleigh Salterton. Certainly his Devonshire accent, even broader than that in which most of the gentry of that county were wont to speak, was scarcely less pronounced than that of the crew of his ship, the *Falcon*, of which he had been given command when he was still in his middle twenties. He had been a soldier, too, had served in France as a volunteer in the Huguenot army, and had commanded a company in Ireland where he had not scrupled to obey the Lord Deputy's orders and put to death some six hundred prisoners – an action considered unworthy of notice by the poet, Edmund Spenser, who was then the Lord Deputy's secretary, and approved of by the Queen, whose only objection to the slaughter was that the prisoners' senior officers had been spared.

Returning to England with dispatches at the age of about twenty-nine in 1581, Ralegh had immediately caught the attention of the Queen. Tall and strong, lively and outspoken, intelligent and forthright, with a full beard and thick black hair, extremely self-confident, dashing and flamboyant, he was just the kind of man who might well have thrown his new cloak across a muddy road for the Queen to step on. He was a poet, with an insatiably curious mind, as well as a man of action; and, although "damnably proud" in John Aubrey's words, and in Sir Anthony Bagot's "the best-hated man in the world: in court, city and country," such was his closeness to the Queen that men thought it as well to seek his friendship. He was soon on intimate terms with Sir Philip Sidney and with Lord Robert Dudley, who had him to stay at Kenilworth and Wanstead. He had recommended himself to Walsingham, and for a time also been close to Oxford, though with Oxford predictably the intimacy soon cooled, then turned to hatred. Like Oxford, Ralegh had a hasty and aggressive temper:

he was twice committed to terms of imprisonment, once in the Fleet, then in the Marshalsea, for causing an affray.

To Hatton it seemed that in the Queen's eyes this young interloper, whom as Sir Robert Naunton said, "she took for a kind of oracle," could do no wrong. She bestowed upon him one of her pet nicknames, a not very inspired epithet, "Water." She knighted him; she made him Captain of her Bodyguard in succession to Hatton; granted him estates in England and over forty thousand acres in Ireland, and she allowed him to occupy the "stately high" Durham House in the Strand, which she had required the Bishop of Durham, Cuthbert Tunstall, to surrender for refusing to accept her as Supreme Governor of the Church of England. She agreed, at his request, to give his impoverished friend, Edmund Spenser, a pension. "When will you cease to be a beggar?" she asked him, tapping him on the cheek with her hand. "When your Majesty ceases to be a benefactor," Ralegh replied with cheerful impudence. According to Edmund Bohun, during some performance at court the comic actor, Richard Tarleton, went so far as to point at Ralegh and, alluding to Ralegh's monopoly of playing cards, cry out, "See the Knave commands the Queen!" For this Tarleton was merely "corrected by a frown from the Queen."

She granted Ralegh patents and monopolies by which he could become, and did become, extremely rich. She appointed him Vice-Admiral of the counties of Devon and Cornwall; and, by investing in privateering expeditions against Spain, he became richer still, as did the Queen who gambled her own money on his none too scrupulous enterprises, later involving herself financially in the expeditions of another buccaneer, Sir Francis Drake, and doing her best not to let Burghley know what she was up to.

Ralegh had shares in voyages to Newfoundland and to the coast of America where, to a large area taken on her behalf, the Queen chose to give the name Virginia. Later, she allowed him to mount another expedition to found a colony in the New World, provided he did not go himself. Within a few years potatoes and tobacco were growing in the gardens of Cecil House; and Ralegh had taken to sucking a pipe, an activity at which the Queen was amused to watch him, taking the occasional puff herself. For all her indulgence, though, she was well aware of Ralegh's faults, his tactlessness, his unconcealed covetousness and his blurting out in public unpalatable truths that were best left unsaid: she never made him a Privy Councilor.

Exasperated by the Queen's fascinated attention to his entertaining talk, Hatton pettishly sent her a little bucket and a note in which he complained of being "destroyed by Water." She sent him in return a dove with an olive branch and a promise of no more "destruction by Water." But the intimacy between the Queen and Ralegh continued; and Hatton felt constrained to send her a jeweled bodkin in threat of suicide for love, as well as long letters protesting his devotion and chagrin. The Queen, evidently relishing his jealousy, attempted to reassure him with the present of a jeweled rainbow.

She knew of no reason to doubt Sir Christopher's own constancy. But with Sir Walter the case was different. "He loved a wench well," John Aubrey wrote of him; "and one time getting up one of the maids of honour against a tree in a wood ('twas his first lady) who seemed at first boarding to be something fearful of her honour, and modest, she cried, 'Sweet Sir Walter, what do you ask me? Will you undo me? Nay sweet Sir Walter! Sweet Sir Walter! Sir Walter!' At last as the danger and the pleasure at the same time grew higher, she cried in the ecstasy, 'Suisser Swalter Shwisser Swalter.' She proved with child . . . "

The Queen apparently heard nothing of this; but when she did hear that Sir Walter was making secret love to another of her maids of honor, Elizabeth Throckmorton, the tall, fair-haired orphaned daughter of Sir Nicholas Throckmorton, her anger knew no bounds. It was bad enough when she was told that the woman was pregnant; it was far worse when she learned that she and Sir Walter intended to marry. She had Ralegh sent to the Tower and had no compunction in sending Elizabeth Throckmorton there too. She could never bring herself fully to forgive Sir Walter, who had made her feel so old by abandoning her for a younger woman; and she could not forgive his wife who had so shamefully deceived her.

Ralegh's many enemies were delighted by his fall from grace. "The Tower will be his dwelling, where he may spend his endless days in doubt," one of these enemies wrote. "The Queen is most fiercely incensed, and threateneth the most bitter punishment to both the offenders. Sir W. R. will lose all his places and preferments at court, with the Queen's favour. Such will be the end of his speedy rising, and now he must fall as low as he was high; at which many will rejoice."

Ralegh was determined not to submit, to regain the Captaincy of the Queen's Bodyguard now held by a deputy. He had never much cared what other men thought of him, regarding their jealousy or dislike of him as a token of his success; but he cared much what the Queen thought, for his fortunes depended upon her good opinion. He had won her favor once; he would regain it now by writing letters full of the extravagant flattery which was so dear to her heart. He compared her to Alexander, to Orpheus, to Diana, to Venus; he wrote of the "gentle wind blowing her fair hair," her "pure cheeks like a nymph." Without her, he was lost: his "heart was never broken till now."

It was all to no avail. But then in the middle of September 1591 a Spanish carrack, the Madre di Dios, was brought into Dartmouth harbor. The treasure-laden ship had been captured, homeward bound from the East Indies, by a British privateering expedition which Ralegh had helped finance to the tune of £34,000. Fearful that the valuable cargo of diamonds and pearls, ebony and spices, pepper, drugs, carpets, scent and porcelain might all be lost to plunderers who had already looted a large part of it, the Queen was persuaded to authorize the release of Ralegh so that he could ride down to Dartmouth to use his influence there to prevent its further pillage. Greeted warmly at Dartmouth and congratulated upon his release by his West Country friends and the sailors of the port, he sadly replied, "No, I am still the Queen of England's poor captive." He did not, however, long remain so. But, although released from the Tower in unspoken recognition of his services in saving the treasure from plunderers, he was allowed no more than £36,000 as his share, a mere £2,000 more than he had ventured.

The Queen's own investment had entitled her to no more than a tenth of the profits, but she nevertheless took the lion's share, appropriating all the pepper, which was sold on her behalf for an enormous sum in yearly installments.

Years later she received Ralegh back at court, greeted him without rancor, reinstated him as Captain of her Bodyguard and entrusted him with various diplomatic missions since he was not only a man of much distinction but also a gifted linguist – "except in English," as his detractors said, deriding that still broad Devon accent. But his days as a particularly favored flatterer and courtier were over. Lady Ralegh, whom her husband truly loved, was required to remain in seclusion at their country home at Sherborne in Dorset.

10

The Queen on Progress

*"We come for the hearts and
allegiance of our subjects."*

In most summers the Queen left London for a progress through some part
of her realm to show herself to her people whose loyalty she considered to
be one of the great mainstays and safeguards of her rule. Their love for her
was boundless, she frequently assured foreign envoys, Parliament and the
people themselves, as though the constant reiteration of their devotion
would persuade them that they did, indeed, worship her as she told them
they did, that their love, in the words she once used to the students of
Oxford, was "of such a kind as has never been known or heard of in the
memory of man . . . It is such a love as neither persuasion, nor threats, nor
curses can destroy. Time has no power over it. Time, which eats away iron
and wears away the rocks, cannot sever this love of yours."

As well as nurturing this love, the Queen's progresses were intended to
lend encouragement to the trade of some deserving town and, in the pursuit of a shrewd economic policy, to oblige the richer of her subjects to
share the expenses of maintaining her court.

Once on the road, the household had to move often, for the smells of a
house occupied for several days by many people, and of stables and courtyards crowded with horses, could not be tolerated for long. It was peculiarly
offensive to Elizabeth, who had so extremely sensitive a nose that she could
not even bear the smell of book bindings treated with oil of lavender, who
was once dissuaded from reading some letters that a Secretary of State did
not want her to see by the warning that they had arrived in a filthily noisome
bag, who made clear her displeasure when men came to be presented to her
wearing new boots or afflicted with bad breath, and who, during the solemnity of her coronation in Westminster Abbey, complained that some ill-
smelling grease had been used instead of oil in the Abbey's lamps.

There were baths and jakes in most large houses and some had bathrooms as fine as those at Windsor Castle, which a German visitor described as having ceilings and wainscots of looking glass. But there were

no water closets in any of the royal palaces until 1597, when one was installed at Richmond Palace to the design of the Queen's godson, John Harington; and throughout her lifetime they were rare in the houses of even the grandest of her hosts. Instead, bedrooms had cupboards containing chamber pots, often of pewter and usually known as "jordans." "Jordans" were also kept concealed in close-stools. But even in the best regulated houses they were all too often ignored: according to the physician Andrew Boorde, whose *Brevyary of Health* was published in 1547, there was much "pissing in chimnies."

So, for personal reasons, for reasons both hygienic and political, through fear of the plague and lesser epidemics and because it was a not inconvenient and not unpopular way of saving money, the court in summer was more than usually peripatetic. And the people of southern England became accustomed to the sight of long lines of hundreds of carts and pack-animals trailing from house to house carrying piles of clothes and linen, table-ware, documents and furnishings, coverings for the Queen's bed, which always traveled with her, and all the valuables and clutter of an enormous household. When the court was on a major progress it was calculated that no fewer than four hundred wagons would be required and as many as 2,400 pack horses, traveling at the rate of about twelve miles a day. There were two principal departments in this caravan, the one controlled by the Lord Chamberlain, and the other and larger by the Lord Steward. The Lord Chamberlain had charge of the arrangements of the Queen's Privy Chamber, of the gentlemen grooms and yeomen, and of the ladies and maids of honor who were attendant upon her there. He had to ensure that all ceremonies were conducted in an appropriate style of grandeur, that visitors were received in a manner suitable to their rank, and – in consultation with the Captain of the Guard and the Master of the Horse – that the Queen's safety was never in jeopardy. The Lord Steward was in charge of all the more domestic departments as well as those of the Keeper of the Queen's Jewels and the clerks, cashiers and accountants of the Board of Green Cloth. Responsible for all the servants from grooms and stable boys to cooks, butlers and scullions, from seamstresses and laundresses to the woman whose sole task it was to sew seed pearls onto dresses, from the staffs of the Boiling House and the Bakehouse to those of the Pastry, the Confectionery and the Laundry, there were, on occasions, under the Lord Steward's control well over a thousand persons.

The Queen's choice of places in which to stay was very wide and varied. She had inherited numerous castles all over the country. Some of these had been demolished; many others allowed to fall into ruin; a few were leased or lent to men who could afford to maintain them. But there were several still available for her to use, notably Windsor Castle, where she built a fine stone terrace beneath the windows of her apartments on the northern side of the Upper Ward. Here in the evenings she liked to walk, moving very fast, as though she were hurrying away from a ghost or trying to keep warm in the cold air. She also built a gallery at Windsor, next to the tower that her grandfather had built for his Queen; and here, too, she walked when the weather was too bleak to take exercise on the terrace or in the garden she had created below it, "full of meanders and labyrinths."

As well as her castles, she had inherited several splendid palaces. But none of these did she alter or extend, refusing to spend money on building new works as her father had done, limiting her expenditure to the most essential repairs and looking very carefully into the estimates prepared by her surveyors. Indeed, Windsor was the only one of her residences where she authorized a work of construction rather than of maintenance. For after all, as she once remarked to Burghley, what need had she of new palaces? Her father had left her more than enough. There were the palaces around Westminster, the huge rambling Whitehall Palace, sprawling across more than twenty acres with its gardens and orchards, its tennis courts and cockpit, its tiltyard where tournaments were held and bears baited. There was St. James's Palace which her father had built on the site of a leper hospital for young women and made into "a goodly manor" of red brick with blue diapering; and there were the royal apartments in the Tower, though these the Queen avoided as often as she could, disliking the memories their surroundings evoked and the smell of the animals in the royal menagerie, their screeching and howling and roaring at night.

There were also the riverside palaces which she could reach so comfortably in one or other of the royal barges. There was Hampton Court, where she sometimes spent Christmas, since it was suitable for large-scale festivities, though as with the Tower, she did not like the place very much. There was Greenwich Palace where she had been born and where, from the gatehouse on the river front, she liked to watch the numerous craft splashing through the water below her; and there was Richmond. This was her favorite palace, as it had been that of her grandfather who had completely rebuilt it after the destruction by fire of the old medieval palace of Sheen and had renamed it after his earldom of Richmond in Yorkshire. It was a magnificent place, as comfortable to live in as it was splendid to look at, renowned alike for its eighteen kitchens, its lovely gardens and well-stocked orchards, the delicate gold and silver weather vanes that whirled about in the wind above the pinnacled towers and the painted domes that looked like the domes of Muscovy.

Not far away was Nonsuch, an extravaganza lavishly decorated in the Renaissance style, built by the Queen's father as a hunting palace and guest house for foreign visitors on the site of the church and village of Cuddington which were pulled down to make way for it. Here the Queen loved to hunt, wearing clothes and jewels more suitable for the audience chamber than the hunting field, and riding her horse so fast she often tired out her frightened companions. As a girl of fifteen she had cut the throat of a fallen buck; and throughout her life she continued, without apparent squeamishness, to kill "the great and fat stagge with her owen Hand." Once at Kenilworth the hart that she was chasing took to a pool in the park where it was caught alive. "Her Majesty granted him his life on condition that he lost his ears as a ransom." Even in old age she was not content to watch the greyhounds drive the deer along the coursing paddock and to shoot at the quarry from the stands as her ladies preferred to do. She liked to hunt and kill with the men.

As well as her palaces in and around London, there were royal manors further afield: Woodstock, near Oxford, where she had been held in custody by the tiresome Sir Henry Bedingfield; Hatfield in Hertfordshire where she had held her first Council meeting; Newhall in Essex; Enfield in Middlesex; Easthampstead in Berkshire; and Oatlands in Surrey where the hunting was as good as it was at Nonsuch, though the building was not large enough to house the whole court, the less fortunate of its denizens having to make do with tents in the courtyards and grounds.

The Queen never went too far from London, never north of Stafford or west of Bristol. Indeed, she had little interest in travel as such: not only did she never go abroad, she never evinced any desire to do so. She did, however, set great store by her visits to towns in her own country within not more than a few days' distance of London. The record offices of many English county towns, of Norwich and Southampton, of Worcester and Warwick, of Bristol, Canterbury, and Gloucester are replete with references to her visits to these cities and the gracious words exchanged between the mayor and corporation and her Majesty upon her entrance into a town and her departure from it. She seems to have behaved on these occasions with a nicely calculated mixture of regal condescension, good humor and dignified approachability, listening patiently to tedious orations, intently watching the most laboriously presented pageants, paying well-chosen compliments to the town's principal monuments, taking a mayor or alderman aside to flatter him by a private word, going out of her way to talk to people in the crowd, sometimes entering a house to accept a drink or a piece of cake, making sure that if any accident occurred the sufferers were compensated and her generosity made known. "Come hither, little Recorder," she said in Warwick after that dignitary had completed his lengthy oration. "It was told me you were afraid to look upon me, or to speak boldly; but you were not so afraid of me as I was of you; and I now thank you . . . "

Numerous stories were told – and assiduously disseminated by the Council – of her good nature during these visits, of her generosity in distributing alms to the poor, of the cheerful way in which she would kneel down to wash the feet of the poor on Maundy Thursday, then wipe them with a towel and, "making a cross a little above the toes, kiss them" – or the manner in which she would touch with her long fingers the sores of those suffering from the King's Evil, a scrofulous disease which it was believed could be cured by contact with the monarch's hands. Sometimes she felt unequal to the task. At Gloucester she protested to the victims of the disease who crowded around her, "Would that I could give you help!" But she could not, on that occasion, bring herself to do so. God, she told them, was the best physician of all. They must pray to him. Usually, however, she performed the ministration expected of her without qualms. "How often have I seen her with her exquisite hands, whiter than whitest snow, boldly and without disgust, pressing their sores and ulcers," wrote her chaplain, William Tooker, who pleased the Queen by publishing an account of "the power inherent in the rightful English sovereign of curing the King's Evil," thus proving the validity of her succession. "How often have I seen her, worn with fatigue, as when, in one single day, she healed eight and thirty persons of the struma."

On a progress through Huntingdonshire her carriage was hailed by a countryman who shouted to her coachman, "Stay thy cart, good fellow, that I may speak to the Queen." The carriage stopped; the man came up to it to speak to her; the Queen, who had laughed "as she had been tickled" at the man's impertinence, graciously replied and stretched out her hand for him to kiss. In Oxfordshire, where she took shelter from a storm in a barn, an old woman told her that her copyhold on her family's farm was soon to expire: she instructed the Council to see that it was extended. When she left Norwich, she said, "I shall never forget Norwich," and, proceeding onward, "did shake hir riding-rod, and said, 'Farewel Norwich!' with the water standing in her eyes." She brought herself to cry again when she left Worcester where a jar and a cup she had used were preserved as precious relics; the room she had occupied shown to subsequent visitors as a shrine; and a pear tree she had commented upon incorporated into the town's coat of arms. At Coventry she accepted a present of a purse containing £100 in gold. "It is a good gift," she said, gratified, "One hundred pounds in gold! I have few such gifts."

> "If it please your Grace," said the Mayor, "there is a great deal more in it."
> "What is that?"
> "It is the hearts of all your loving subjects."
> "We thank you, Mr Mayor. It is a great deal more, indeed."

Norwich's Mayor also offered her £100 in gold in a silver-gilt cup. Indeed, since gold was known to be her favorite present, it became customary to offer it in addition to other less valuable presents like sweetmeats and scented gloves. At one town she demurred. "Princes have no need of money," she piously assured its Mayor. "We come for the hearts and allegiance of our subjects." This worthy sentiment did not, however, prevent her from taking the proffered cup and handing it to a nearby attendant.

Preparations for the Queen's progresses were made with the greatest care, estimates of their cost to the Exchequer calculated with exactitude and precise lists made of the baggage and stores that would have to be packed, including the Queen's special beer, a lighter brew than the strong ale which she much disliked and might well be offered on her journey. If the beer she liked were not available when she wanted it, she might well become extremely grumpy, as she did one hot summer's day in 1575 when, so Lord Robert Dudley said, the undrinkable stuff offered her "did put her far out of temper." The household was thrown into uproar as empty bottles were carried post haste to nearby houses, and servants even sent to London for a more acceptable supply.

Once the route had been decided upon, the timetable worked out and the Queen's changes of mind, and insistence upon what were politely known as "by-progresses" allowed for, the towns and villages through which she would pass would be told of her coming, and the owners of houses in which she intended to stay warned of the duration of her visit and the numbers of people in her household for whom bed and board would have to be provided. Officials were then sent out to follow the course of the itinerary to ensure that all the necessary arrangements had been made, that the Queen's safety would never be threatened, that the sheriffs and leading gentlemen of the counties through which she would pass would be ready to greet her at the boundaries, that the roads were in a reasonable state of repair, and mended if they were not, that there were no reports of plague in the area. Officials were also sent to the places where she was to spend the night to inspect the rooms and stabling, the water supply and kitchens, to talk to the senior servants, to provide for tents if these were needed. She herself would be given some information about all the people she would be meeting for the first time, and briefed about the places she was to visit with the help of some such book as William Lambarde's *Perambulation of Kent*.

She generally traveled on horseback, occasionally by litter, sometimes in a coach as open as possible so that the people could get a good view of her; and she was quick to complain if the surface were too bumpy, as, for all the care taken, it only too often was: she once told the French ambassador that, after one particularly uncomfortable journey, she could not sit down for several days.

As soon as news was received of the Queen's intended arrival in a town, the mayor, his corporation and responsible officials set to work removing dunghills, pillories and stocks, covering the streets over which she was to pass with gravel and strewing the floors of the houses that she was to enter with rushes and herbs. There were fireworks to buy; Latin orations to rehearse; choirs and musicians and country dancers to be given repeated practices; gowns and dresses to be washed and pressed; mayoral regalia to be polished; stages to be erected; canvas forts and wooden castles to be built for the mock battles and military pageants "whereat the Queen's Majesty took great pleasure." City gates and market crosses were painted; royal arms set up; the fronts of houses whitewashed; beggars and pickpockets locked up; gallows removed from sight; the simple-minded kept indoors. Sometimes walls had to be pulled down to make streets wide enough for the grand processions that were to grace them. Special orders had to be issued prohibiting the driving of cattle through the town while her Majesty was there and instructing tavern keepers to have post-horses ready should they be needed. There were those who grumbled about the expense of it all, and those who had cause to complain that the royal purveyors were unconscionably slow in paying for the goods they ordered, that they not infrequently requisitioned them without payment at all. The story was told of one Kentish man who was evidently bold and angry enough to approach a group of royal attendants to demand, "Which is the Queen?"

"I am your Queen," said Elizabeth who was standing nearby. "What would thou have with me?"

"You are one of the rarest women I ever saw, and can eat no more than my daughter Madge, who is thought the properest lass in our parish, though short of you. But the Queen Elizabeth took for devours so many of my hens, ducks and capons as I am not able to live."

The man's case was examined and the grasping purveyor, so it was widely reported, was hanged.

In few cities, apart from London, did the Queen devote more care to the impression she created than she did in the university towns of Oxford and Cambridge.

She paid her first formal visit to Cambridge in August 1564, making of it a demonstration of royal favor and interest in the condition of the university. Lord Burghley, who had been appointed Chancellor five years before, took it upon himself to make all the arrangements, proposing what entertainments, disputations and plays were to be provided for the Queen's enjoyment, giving instructions about the behavior of the scholars who were to greet her with shouts of "*Vivat Regina!*" while on their knees, detailing the precautions to be adopted against the plague and the manner in which streets were to be boarded up to control the crowds, sprinkled with sand and laid with rushes, requiring that "uniformity should be shown in apparel and religion, and especially at the communion table," even suggesting where all the visitors were to sleep: the Earl of Leicester in Trinity, himself at St. John's, the Queen and her ladies at King's.

There were to be processions and banquets, speeches, lectures and sermons, plays in English and Latin and visits to the several colleges. A play by Plautus was to be performed in King's College Chapel where a stage had been erected over the nave and the Queen provided with a seat which made her as much a spectacle as the actors themselves.

She played her part, it was universally agreed, to perfection. She came into the town in a dramatic black velvet dress with pink slashes, her hair drawn up into a gold net sewn with pearls and set off by a black, gold-spangled hat adorned with feathers at the side. In this spectacular costume she rode into the front quadrangle of Queen's College where all her attendants dismounted, leaving her to be admired as she sat upright in her saddle while the speeches of welcome were delivered. Throughout her stay she let it be known whenever something displeased her; but everyone knew that she would do so and they were expecting it. In St. Mary's she expressed her disapproval of some of the Fellows' gowns; and during a disputation there she told the speakers several times to raise their voices and, when she still could not hear, moved so far forward that she was almost on top of them. In King's College Chapel she interrupted a Latin sermon to tell the preacher to put on his hat; though afterwards she did tell him how much she had liked his sermon, that it was the first she had heard delivered in Latin, and that she did not expect to hear a better. When it was suggested by Burghley that she herself might care to say a word or two in Latin – three words, he said, would suffice – she delivered herself of six hundred.

She clearly wanted to please as well as to impress. She said she thought the Chapel more beautiful than "all the others within her realm." She gave another speech in Latin in which she promised to found a college herself, and, with arch false modesty apologized for her own lack of learning, her incompetent command of the tongue in which she so fluently spoke: "It is time then that your ears, which have been so long detained by this barbarous sort of an oration, should now be released from the pain of it." She raised a laugh when, in handing back the staves of office which the Vice-Chancellor had ceremonially handed to her, she said she hoped he would minister justice uprightly in the university, otherwise she would take them back into her own hands "and see to it" herself. She put off her departure for a day, announcing that she would stay even longer if she could; and, although she begged to be excused from attending a Sophocles tragedy because she was so tired, having already sat through performances of *Dido, Aularia* and *Ezechias*, she did so with such grace that no one could be offended.

Her visit to Oxford in 1566 was equally successful, though less well organized since the Chancellor here was Robert Dudley who, while a masterly impresario, had not taken the trouble with the arrangements which Burghley had done at Cambridge. During a performance of Richard Edward's *Palamon and Arcyte* in Christ Church hall, which had been specially painted and gilded for the occasion, so many scholars were permitted to crowd in to see the Queen – who was given as prominent a seat as she had been in King's College Chapel – that a stairway and part of a wall collapsed and three young men were killed. When the play was resumed the next night there was another uproar when Theseus's hounds began barking in the quadrangle outside and the scholars rushed to the windows and began hallooing, thinking a real hunt was in progress. But the Queen delighted them all by seeming to enjoy the commotion as much as she had enjoyed the play, just as she had pleased them all the night before by showing herself much concerned by the collapse of the wall and sending her own doctor to see what he could do to help the injured. As at Cambridge she did not trouble to disguise her occasional displeasure: she curtly told the university Orator that he would have done well in making his speech had he had "good matter"; later in St. Mary's she twice told Herbert Westfaling, the Bishop of Hereford, a man of "great gravity of demeanour," to cut short his tedious oration, so muddling him that he lost the drift of his Latin text, and embarrassing him still further by interrupting a subsequent speech of her own in Latin to request, in English, a chair for Burghley before continuing confidently where she had left off. And, though smilingly on this occasion, she told the Vice-Chancellor – the leader of the "Puritan party who had opposed the ecclesiastical habits with great warmth of zeal" – "That loose gown becomes you mighty well. I wonder your notions should be so narrow. But I come not now to chide." She gave far more pleasure than offense. Her earlier undertaking to found a college at Cambridge was never fulfilled; but when Hugh Price, Treasurer of St. David's Cathedral, approached her for her support in founding Jesus College, Oxford, she readily consented to grant it, though characteristically claiming for herself the title of "foundress" while obliging Price to be content with that of "first benefactor."

The houses in which the Queen stayed were less often her own than those of a rich courtier or Councilor or local magnate. Some contemplated her arrival with alarm, perturbed by the expense or by apprehension that their houses were, for one reason or another, unsuitable to receive her. Sir John Thynne, for example, who had built Longleat to please himself rather than with any wish to gratify her Majesty, had to be reminded of the hospitality expected of a man who had made a vast fortune as steward to the Duke of Somerset and had married the daughter and heiress of the rich merchant, Sir Thomas Gresham. "I thought it good to let you know," a member of the Queen's Household reprimanded him, "how of late Her Majesty had speech concerning you, that you seem unwilling to receive her this yeare at your house, making excuses of sicknese and other letts thereby to divert her from the country."

But for most owners of large country houses the honor of entertaining the Queen, and the possibility of advancement if all went well, outweighed the worry, inconvenience and cost. It was, in any event, rare that the choice fell upon a house whose owner could not afford to pay for the hospitality required, since the costs of entertaining the Queen and her large retinue were inevitably very heavy, sometimes running as high as £1,000 a day at a time when some farm laborers contrived to live on 7d. a day. The cost of food alone was enormous, even though six pullets could then be purchased for 1s., sixteen white bread loaves for 4d., sixteen oranges for 2d., two gallons of white wine for 2s. and eggs were six a penny. When the Queen stayed for five days at Gorhambury in Hertfordshire in 1577, her host, Sir Nicholas Bacon, the Lord Keeper – who had to employ several London cooks for the occasion – was obliged to purchase 60 sheep as well as 34 lambs, 26 pigs, 18 calves, 8 oxen, 10 kids and dozen upon dozen of birds: over 350 chickens, more than 200 pigeons, twelve dozen ducklings and herons, ten dozen geese, sixteen dozen quails, as well as quantities of capons, pullets, bitterns, partridges, larks, curlews, shovelers, pheasants and mallards.

Food and drink were far from being the only exceptional expense. There were additional musicians to employ, deer to round up for hunting and for savaging by greyhounds. There were likely to be tents and marquees to hire, as well as hangings and Turkey carpets, perhaps temporary structures to erect such as the buildings, including a Great Hall and Room of State, put up in the park at Elvetham by the Earl of Hertford for the Queen's visit in 1591. Sometimes owners felt obliged to enlarge their houses, as Sir Nicholas Bacon did when the Queen went to stay with him at Gorhambury and declared, "You have made your house too little." At Osterley, where she stayed with Sir Thomas Gresham, she found fault with the courtyard "as too great, affirming that it would appear more handsome if divided with a wall in the middle. What doth Sir Thomas but in the nighttime sends for workmen to London (money commands all things) who do speedily and silently apply their business, that the next morning discovered the court double, which the night had left single before."

There was also work to do in the gardens, the construction of bowers or fountains, grottoes or even lakes for water pageants. Sir Francis Carew erected a tent over a cherry tree in his grounds at Bedington so that the fruit would not ripen until the Queen came to stay with him in August. There were also losses by pilfering to consider – in 1577 Sir Nicholas Bacon lost £6,15s.6d. worth of pewter and 50s.6d. worth of napery during the Queen's visit – as well as the restoration of lawns and gardens through which thoughtless courtiers rode their horses, trampling down flower beds and kicking out lumps of turf.

Then there was the cost of the gifts traditionally presented as tokens of esteem and gratitude to the Queen, who did not trouble to disguise her displeasure if they did not come up to scratch. Lord North for instance – who entertained the Queen at Kirtling in Cambridgeshire at a cost of £762 5s.2d. for two nights – spent £120 on a jewel for her.

As well as large amounts spent on presents, on house extensions, improvements and conversions, and on food, money had to be found for extra silver and plate, new hangings, paper, ink and waxlights, the provision of presence, privy and audience chambers, or, as in the case of Sir William Petre of Ingatestone Hall, Essex, for the work of bricklayers, carpenters and laborers in "making ranges, sheds and other necessaries against the queen's Majesty's coming." Lord Burghley, specifically for entertaining the Queen, was obliged greatly to enlarge his house, Theobalds near Waltham Cross, which was much nearer to London than Burghley, his house in Lincolnshire. "My house at Theobalds," he told a friend, "was begun by me with a mean measure but increased by occasion of Her Majesty's often coming, whom to please I never would omit to strain myself to more charges than building it. And yet not without some special direction of Her Majesty. Upon fault found with the small measure of her chamber (which was in good measure for me) I was enforced to enlarge a room for a large chamber, which need not be envied of any for riches in it."

Year by year improvements were made at Theobalds. A new courtyard was built, doubling the size of the house and making it the biggest in England after Hampton Court. No fewer than five galleries were constructed so that the Queen could take her exercise when it was cold or raining; the roof was flattened so she could walk there in fine weather when she chose not to walk in one of the house's four gardens. To keep these gardens well-stocked and in good trim, Burghley, who was advised by John Gerard, author of the classic *Herball*, had to employ about forty men in addition to his regular gardeners. He spent, in all, some £25,000 on Theobalds where the Queen stayed at least twelve times on visits which caused the utmost disruption in his household: his own servants had to move out of the house to sleep in a storehouse and to eat in the joiners' workshop; his steward had to vacate his lodgings to provide space in which to keep the royal plate.

Sir Christopher Hatton spent another fortune at the behest of the Queen on Holdenby House, a huge place in Northamptonshire paid for largely by money that Hatton managed to acquire through the offices to which she appointed him and the licenses she granted him. Modeled on Theobalds – "in direct observance of your house and plot at Tyball's," as Hatton himself put it in a letter to Burghley – it stood ready for ten years waiting for the Queen to come to stay. During the whole of that time she never did come. Hatton died a bachelor at the age of fifty-one, leaving his debts and Holdenby to a nephew who could not afford to live in it. The house was sold a few years later and within fifty years had been demolished.

Kenilworth, Lord Robert Dudley's castle in Warwickshire, had a longer life. The royal manor and lordship of Kenilworth had been given to Dudley in 1563. It was then in an almost derelict condition. But over the years he spent enormous sums upon it; and when the Queen stayed here during a progress in 1575 it had become both grandly imposing and sumptuous, filled with treasures, with tapestries and Turkey carpets, with huge four-poster beds hung with rich materials in the brightest colors, with elaborate looking-glasses and chairs "exquisitely carved," with an aviary crowded with birds of brilliant plumage. Dudley rode out to greet the Queen, meeting her at Long Ichington where a splendid banquet awaited them in an immense marquee. During the afternoon they went hunting; then rode back together through the park gates as the summer sun was beginning to set. Guns saluted them as they entered the courtyard; trumpets blared and figures in fantastic costumes came forth to welcome her, one of them, "The Lady of the Lake," "arrayed all in sylkes" and gliding forward upon a "moovable Iland from the midst of the Pool" to make a speech in "well-penned meter." She told the Queen "hoow she had kept this Lake sins King Arthurz Dayz" and was now offering it to her Majesty, an overture to which Elizabeth tartly responded that she had always supposed it was hers already.

During the following days the entertainments provided for the Queen set a standard to which few others of her hosts were able to aspire. There was hunting and there was dancing; there were plays, musical and acrobatic performances, banquets, water-pageants, morris-dancing, bride-ales and masques. There were displays of fireworks "with blazes of burning darts flying to and fro, beams of stars coruscant, streams and hails of fiery sparks, lightnings on water and on land, flight and shot of thunderbolts, all with such continuance, tempest and vehemence that the heavens thundered, the waters surged, the castle shook." There were savage bear-baitings "causing such expens of blood az a months licking [would] not recover."

Although she did not attend cockfights – which were considered a diversion for gentlemen rather than ladies – the Queen was known to take great pleasure in bear-baiting. She had her own bearpit in London and her own team of prize bears under the care of her Master of the Bears. She owned several mastiffs, immense and fearsome animals which were set upon the bears three at a time. She also enjoyed the spectacle of a monkey being set to fight a horse.

According to Robert Laneham, Clerk of the Council Chamber Door, the bear-baiting at Kenilworth was a sport very pleazaunt of theez beastz. The Bear with his pink eyes leering after his enmiez approch and the nimbleness of the Dog to take hiz avauntage, and the fors and experiens of the Bear to avoyd the assauts. If he wear bitten in one place, hoow he wood pynch in an oother to get free, and if he were onez taken then what shyft with byting, clawying and roring, tossing and tumbling he would woork to wynd himself awaie, And when he was loose, to shake his ears wyth the blud and slaver about his phiznomie was a pittance of a goodly releef . . .

Noow within also, in the mean time, waz thear sheawed by an *Italian* such feats of agilitie in goinges, turninges, tumblinges, hops, jumps, leaps, skips, springs, gambaud, somersauts, caprettiez and flights, backward, foward, sydewize, a doonward, upward and with sundry windings, gyrings & circumflexions, allso lightly and with such easiness as by mee in feaw words it iz not expressibl by pen or speech, I tell you plain . . . Toward night it liked her Majesty too walk afoot into the chase over the bridge where it pleased her to stand while upon the pool out of a barge fine appoynted for the purpoze too heer sundry kinds of delectabl muzik. Thus recreated and after sum walk, her Highness retired.

Part Two

II

Daughter of Discord

"Though I be a woman, yet I have as
good a courage, answerable to my
place, as ever my father had."

Mary Stuart, Queen of Scots, the third child and only daughter of King James V, had been born at Linlithgow Palace in December 1541, nine years after Elizabeth, whom she was always to consider a bastard and a usurper. Her mother was a daughter of the Duke of Guise, and Mary herself had spent much of her life in France after her betrothal to the Dauphin, the son of King Henry II. She had grown to become a very tall, graceful, extremely good-looking woman of many and varied accomplishments and of strong sexual magnetism. On the death of her father-in-law, her husband had been crowned King Francis II.

Before his death, Henry II had quartered the arms of England on his daughter-in-law's bearings as well as upon those of his son; and, on the grounds of Queen Elizabeth's alleged illegitimacy, he had laid claim on her behalf, as great-granddaughter of Henry VII, to the thrones of England and Ireland as well as of Scotland.

Ever since Queen Elizabeth's accession there had been fears that a French army would land in Scotland and from there march south, gaining support in the northern counties of England where the great landowners, with a power over their tenants unknown in the south, were still largely Roman Catholic. Then Spain, unwilling to tolerate French power so much augmented, would land troops from the Netherlands on the English coast and turn England into a European battleground.

French troops were indeed landed in Scotland, and in response to appeals for help from the Lords of the Congregation – signatories of a covenant to support the Protestant "Congregation of God" – Elizabeth had, at the end of 1559, sent troops to Scotland herself. Dreading involvement in a dangerous military adventure which would be costly in both lives and money, she had been most reluctant to take the step. The expense, she thought, would be ruinous: money would drain away and she would be

unable to check the waste. The difficulties of raising enough soldiers and
sailors would be formidable; the officers appointed to lead them might
turn out to be Roman Catholic in their sympathies; the King of Spain
might well have strong objections. A war with France could prove to be
catastrophic. Several of her Councilors agreed with her that an expedition
to Scotland was altogether too risky and expensive an undertaking, and
they approved of her initial decision not to accede to the request of the
Lords of the Congregation. Burghley, however, did not agree and he went
so far as to request a different appointment in her service if she did not
take action. Sir Nicholas Throckmorton returned from France to support
Burghley. Under their combined pressure, during the first week of December 1559, the Queen changed her mind: she would send troops after all.

Yet when the Spanish ambassador expressed strong disapproval of her
decision, and the British ambassador in Brussels warned Burghley that the
Spanish authorities in the Netherlands were convinced that England was
heading for a defeat from which King Philip would not save her, she began
to hesitate once more. The Councilors met and argued, some supporting
intervention, others opposing it. On 16 December the Queen reluctantly
sent orders to the naval commander, William Wynter, Surveyor of the
Navy, to sail for Scotland with supplies for the Congregation and the
promise of an army to follow. But by 28 December she had changed her
mind yet again. It was too late, though. Wynter had sailed the day before.

The operations did not go well: an attack on Leith was repulsed by the
French garrison who were assisted, so John Knox said, by their "harlots of
whom the most part were Scottish whores." These women loaded the
French soldiers' "pieces and ministered to them other weapons. Some
continually cast stones, some carried chimneys of burning fire, some
brought timber and impediments and weight which, with great violence,
they threw over the wall." Although orders were eventually given to send
reinforcements to the English army – whose scaling-ladders had proved
too short to reach the top of the walls and whose casualties numbered
over five hundred – Burghley feared for a time that the Queen would
choose to withdraw from the enterprise altogether. "God trieth us with
many difficulties," he wrote to Throckmorton. "The Queen's Majesty
never liketh this matter of Scotland." "I have," he added later, after he had
had the utmost difficulty in persuading her to send the reinforcements to
Leith, "had such a torment herein as an ague hath not in five fits so much
abated."

The French, however, were also in difficulties in Scotland; and when
Burghley arrived in Edinburgh to conduct negotiations, after a prolonged

journey of sixteen days from London, he was able to conclude a satisfactory treaty by which the French agreed to withdraw their troops and to leave the Scottish people free to choose their own religion, on condition that the English withdrew from their alliance with the Lords of the Congregation and did not press for the return of Calais. The French also agreed to renounce their claim to the English throne and not to press for the Queen of Scots's right to quarter the arms of England on her own bearings.

Favorable as these terms were from the English point of view, and widely as they were considered a triumph for Protestantism and for England, Queen Elizabeth expressed her disapproval of some of the concessions made. She told her delegates to break off negotiations, but by the time her letter arrived the terms of the treaty had been settled and the matter closed.

When she was given details of the treaty, the Treaty of Edinburgh, Mary Stuart expressed herself as dissatisfied with the settlement as Elizabeth had done. She was particularly annoyed that there had been any question as to her right to the English royal arms. As the Cardinal of Lorraine, Henry II's former foreign minister pointed out, the Queen of England still quartered the French fleur-de-lis on *her* coat of arms. English monarchs had provocatively done so for two centuries. Mary and her husband, Francis II, refused to ratify the treaty.

Soon afterwards, just before his wife's eighteenth birthday, Francis died; and his mother, Catherine de Médicis, became Regent for her younger son, the ten-year-old King Charles IX. Excluded from power by her mother-in-law, Mary was advised by her Guise relations to leave France for Scotland. She asked for a safe-conduct and permission to land at an English port should bad weather interrupt her voyage. This Queen Elizabeth refused her so long as she declined to ratify the Treaty of Edinburgh. Mary decided to sail anyway. "And if she be so hardhearted as to desire my end," she said, her cousin could "do her pleasure and make sacrifice" of her. Elizabeth's disposition to sacrifice her was not put to the test. Queen Mary arrived safely at Leith on 19 August 1561.

On several occasions during the next few years, Mary expressed a wish for a friendly relationship with Elizabeth. At the same time, however, she warned that if this friendship were denied her she had other wellwishers to whom she could turn, both in France and elsewhere. "I have friends and allies and such as would be glad and willing to employ their forces and aid to stand me in stead," she had told Throckmorton shortly before leaving

France, not troubling to veil her threats. "Your mistress doth give me cause to seek friendship where I did not mind to ask it . . . I do not trouble her state, nor practise with her subjects. And yet, I know there be in her realm some that be inclined enough to hear offers. I also know that they be not of the same mind that she is, neither in religion nor in other things."

For her part Elizabeth, though she had good cause to distrust her, said that she wanted nothing more dearly than to live in peace with Mary. She declined, however, to recognize her as her heir, believing, as she put it, that to do so would be to place a winding-sheet before her eyes, knowing "the inconstancy of the people of England, how they ever mislike the present government and have their eyes fixed upon that person who is next to succeed." At various times meetings were proposed. But the first of a long succession of civil wars of religion had broken out in France and it was decided that it would be better if a meeting did not take place; for Elizabeth was deeply involved in that war, having, on the advice of Burghley, Throckmorton and Dudley, declared her support for Protestantism throughout Europe and sent an English army to France to fight on the Protestant side under the command of Lord Robert Dudley's brother, Ambrose, Earl of Warwick.

Unlike her intervention in Scotland, her expedition to France proved a disaster. Her troops were obliged to evacuate Le Havre which had been seized in the vain hope that it might be used as a bargaining counter in the recovery of Calais; and, upon their return to England – hungry, bedraggled and unpaid, as Queen Elizabeth's soldiers so often were – an epidemic of the plague which they had brought with them spread throughout southern England, killing over 17,000 people in London alone, where a beggar in Bullein's *Dialogue* describes meeting "wagones, cartes and horses full loden with young barnes, for fear of the blacke Pestilence, and with them boxes of medicens and sweete perfumes. O God! How fast did they run by hundredes, and were afraied of eche other for feare of smityng!"

So long as the Queen of Scots's uncles were leading Catholic forces against the Protestants in France, it would obviously be embarrassing for the Queen of England to meet her in the formal ceremony that was being discussed. Even so, Elizabeth decided that such a meeting should be held and, against the advice of her Council, announced that she would travel to either York or Nottingham in the summer of 1562. A previous meeting at Nottingham had already been suggested, and arrangements had been made for the Queen of Scots's journey through northern England and for an overnight stay at Norham Castle in Northumberland. This meeting having been put off because of the troubles in France, Elizabeth professed herself determined that the meeting planned for the August or September of 1562 should take place. Under pressure from her Councilors, she eventually submitted, however, and sent Sir Henry Sidney to Scotland to convey her regrets about the "impeaching of the great desire" which she had to see her cousin "this present summer." He was to convey also her consternation about horrifying reports from Paris where the "common people" had been given authority "to kill and cut in pieces all such as had broken any church . . . an order never heard before, to give to the common people the sword, by means whereof many horrible murders were daily and yet to be committed by the rash vulgar sort and headless people, without regard to estate or degree."

She added that she hoped the postponed meeting might be held in quieter times the following year at Nottingham or, failing that, in York or Pontefract. In the meantime she put her mind to the problem of how she might retain her cousin's friendship by arranging for her a marriage that might bind them closer together. And for this purpose she decided that there could be no more suitable a husband than Lord Robert Dudley. By his marriage to Mary she would at once secure a close friend at the Scottish court, confer great honor upon a man of whom she was deeply fond, and scotch the tiresome stories that she intended to marry her supposed lover herself.

At first it seemed so outlandish an idea that when it was broached to the Scottish ambassador in London he did not take it seriously. The more Burghley considered it, however, the more he approved of the proposal, though there was no telling how sincere Elizabeth was in her advocacy of the match. "Of my knowledge of these fickle matters," he wrote, "I can affirm nothing that I can assure will continue." There were rumors that plans were afoot to marry Mary to either the Archduke Charles or to King Philip's son, the Infante Don Carlos, or perhaps to her cousin, Henry, Duke of Guise, or even to her brother-in-law, the boy King Charles IX. None of these matches would be in England's interest. So determined efforts must be made to present another suitor as being more attractive than any of them. Burghley and the Queen accordingly drafted their instructions to Thomas Randolph, their confidential agent in Scotland, with the utmost care, both of them rewriting parts of it before the letter was dispatched. Randolph was to assure Queen Mary that, while any marriage she might contract must naturally be a matter for her own choice, it might not be considered improper for the Queen of England to express an opinion about it from the English point of view. A marriage to "any mighty" foreign prince, for example, might be considered harmful to English interests and might make it difficult for Mary to be recognized as Elizabeth's heir. It would, however, be quite a different matter if Queen Mary were to marry "some person of noble birth within the realm of England, yea, perchance [such a person] as she should hardly think we could agree to," the clear inference of these words, which Elizabeth herself underlined, being that the person suggested was Lord Robert Dudley.

Dudley's name was not, however, initially mentioned by Randolph who, in obedience to his instructions, was noncommittal when questioned by Mary's advisers, as though embarrassed to put forward the name of a suitor who was widely supposed in Scotland not only to be his monarch's lover but the murderer of his wife. Persistently questioned, Randolph let the name drop at last, and waited for the expected objections. These were not such as he had foreseen. Mary's counselors merely protested that, while of noble birth, Lord Robert Dudley was not himself a nobleman and was the son of a man who had been executed for high treason. There was nothing to be done about the second of these objections but, as to the first, there were no problems about that: on 29 September 1564 Dudley was created Earl of Leicester by the Queen who, so Sir James Melville noticed, could not refrain from putting her hand down his neck and tickling him as she fastened the mantle around his shoulders.

Yet even if Queen Mary had been willing to marry the Earl of Leicester, whom she had not met, the Earl of Leicester was not prepared to marry Queen Mary. It was true that his position at the English court was not now as unassailable as once it had seemed. He had failed to fulfill his plans for replacing Burghley in Elizabeth's confidence; and she had more than once rebuffed him rudely. When the possibility of Elizabeth marrying the King of Sweden was being discussed and Lord Robert had ridiculed the notion, she had told him in her Presence Chamber that whether or not she married the King of Sweden, she would certainly never marry Robert, "nor none so mean as he." And when she heard that he had threatened to dismiss her Gentleman of the Black Rod for denying one of his protégés entrance to her Privy Chamber, she had flared up in a rage, exclaiming, "God's death, my Lord! I have wished you well, but my favour is not so locked up in you that others shall not participate thereof, for I have many servants to whom I have, and will at my pleasure, bequeath my favour. . . . If you think to rule here, I will take a course to see you forthcoming. I will have here but one mistress, and no master." She had allowed him much latitude in his behavior at court and in his collection of "creatures"; but he must never forget that he was always *her* "creature" and must do her bidding. He had long had his eyes on the vastly profitable Mastership of the Court of Wards, which became vacant on the death of old Sir Thomas Parry, but she declined to make it available to him, presenting it instead to Burghley.

Despite the Queen's occasional flashes of temper, however, and her angry reminders that it was she who ruled in England and could debase a favorite as quickly as she could honor one, the Earl of Leicester was still unrivaled in the Queen's affections. He also delighted in the pleasures of the English court of which he knew himself to be so brilliant an adornment. He had no wish to exchange his glittering life there for the grey gloom of Holyroodhouse and the company of dour lairds and glum provosts, however attractive the Queen of Scots was reported to be. Sir Thomas Randolph could not imagine how any man could not yearn to hold her "in his naked arms," and wrote glowingly of her ever-brightening beauty, the glory of which had never been surpassed, adding hastily "(our own most worthy Queen alone excepted)." Nor, as it happened, had the Queen of Scots any great desire to have the Earl of Leicester at the Scottish court as her husband. She now had another in mind, handsome, too, and twelve years younger than Leicester, and, what was more, a Roman Catholic as well as a great-grandson of Henry VII.

Henry Stewart, Lord Darnley, then nineteen years old, had carried the Sword of State before Queen Elizabeth when Lord Robert Dudley was created Earl of Leicester. The son of Matthew Stewart, Earl of Lennox, and of Lady Margaret Douglas, niece of Henry VIII, Darnley was undeniably handsome and physically alluring, graceful, tall and slender. He was also as lacking in modesty as he was in intelligence, an obstinate, arrogant man whose pride was described as "intolerable." Yet his claim to the English throne was a strong one; and, since he had been born in England at Temple Newsam, Yorkshire, there were those who agreed with his scheming and ambitious mother that it was quite as strong as the Queen of Scots's, if not stronger, and certainly to be preferred to that of Elizabeth Tudor.

Elizabeth knew well that Lady Lennox was busily suggesting that Darnley would be a better choice as husband for Mary than the Earl of Leicester. After the ceremony at which his earldom was bestowed upon Dudley, Elizabeth had asked the Scottish ambassador, Sir James Melville, what he thought of Leicester. Melville made some diplomatic answer to which Elizabeth responded, nodding towards Darnley, "And yet you like better of yonder lad."

She was naturally intrigued by Darnley, being intensely curious about everything that concerned her cousin in Scotland; and she questioned Melville closely about them both, anxious to persuade him, and to make him admit, that her skin was whiter than Mary's, her dresses finer, her skills as a musician and linguist more accomplished. Having artfully arranged for Melville to overhear her playing the virginals, she paraded herself before him in various styles; she delayed his departure from court so that he could see her dancing; she asked him who was the taller, Mary or herself. Mary he replied without hesitation. Then she is too tall, the Queen told him, for she herself was just the right height, neither too short nor too long.

Light-hearted as she appeared, the Queen, as Melville knew, was deeply concerned about the Queen of Scots and about a marriage that might induce Mary to make a joint claim with her husband to the crown of England. One day the French ambassador, Paul de Foix, arriving at court for an audience, was shown into her presence as she was playing chess. "This game," he observed, "is an image of the works and deeds of men. If we lose a pawn it seems a small matter; but the loss often brings with it that of the whole game."

"I understand you," the Queen replied. "Darnley is only a pawn but he may checkmate me if he is promoted."

For the moment his promotion seemed unlikely. The negotiations for the marriage of the Earl of Leicester to the Queen of Scots were still in progress. Sir Thomas Randolph was assured that Queen Mary would be pleased to agree to the match if she were officially to be recognized as Queen Elizabeth's heir. And Sir James Melville was persuaded that Elizabeth herself was also in favor of the match. Admittedly it did sometimes appear, as they went out riding and danced together, that Queen Elizabeth was too devoted to Leicester to allow him to leave her. One evening she took Melville into her bedchamber to show him some miniatures which she kept in a cabinet there. Each little picture was wrapped in paper on which she had written a name. One of them was marked "My Lord's picture." She took that out, and Melville asked to see it. It was a portrait of the Earl of Leicester. Melville asked if he might be allowed to take it to show the Queen of Scots but Elizabeth demurred: it was the only picture of Leicester she had.

It was still reported from time to time that the Queen and the Earl were already married: talk of another match for either of them was consequently pointless. It was said that after a game of tennis, Leicester had gone so far as to take a napkin out of the Queen's hand, as a husband might thoughtlessly have done, and wiped his face with it. But the Queen continued to deny that she would ever consider Leicester in the light of a husband. "The world thinks a woman cannot live unmarried," she confided to Don Guzman de Silva, the Spanish ambassador, "and if she refrains from men that she does so for some bad reason, as they used to say of me that I avoided doing so because I was fond of the Earl of Leicester whom I could not marry because he had a wife living. His wife is now dead and yet I do not marry him, although I have been pressed to do so, even by your King."

In fact, King Philip had now lent his support to a marriage between Queen Mary and Lord Darnley and had instructed his ambassador to tell them that if they did not rush into marriage but awaited a favorable moment when any attempt to frustrate their plans would be fruitless, he would "assist and aid them with the end they [had] in view." Learning of King Philip's attitude, and fearing that he might even attempt an invasion of England to place his Roman Catholic protégée on the throne, the Privy Council, now deeply alarmed, sent an envoy to Scotland to make counterproposals. The Earl of Leicester, whose talents and virtues had already been lauded by Burghley in letters to Edinburgh, was again recommended as a husband for the Queen of Scots. Failing him, it was suggested that she might consider the merits of other great Englishmen, the Duke of Norfolk, for example, or the Earl of Arundel. Marriage to any of these would ensure Parliament's recognition of her as presumptive heiress to the crown of England.

But now that she had set eyes upon Darnley, who had arrived in Scotland, the "lustiest and best proportioned long man" that she had ever seen, Queen Mary was as determined to marry him as the Earl of Leicester was reluctant to marry her. Defying her Protestant Lords, she had Darnley created Earl of Ross and Duke of Albany, then proclaimed him King of Scotland; and on 29 July – ignoring the protests of the English Queen and her Council who warned her that a match between her and Darnley would be "unmeet, unprofitable and perilous to the sincere amity between the Queens and their realms" – she married him in the chapel of Holyroodhouse.

Queen Elizabeth heard the news with exasperation. She blamed Leicester for not having pressed his suit with more enthusiasm; and she grew increasingly angry with him when, so it appears, she discovered that he had taken it upon himself to write a private letter to Scotland requesting that he should not be considered a suitor for Queen Mary's hand. In her anger she galloped through Windsor Park, hot as it was that August, leaving her ladies far behind, showing her irritation when they caught up with her. "The Queen's Majesty is fallen into some disliking with my Lord of Leicester," Burghley reported to Sir Thomas Smith who had been sent to France to join Throckmorton as ambassador; and in his diary Burghley added, "The Queen seemed to be much offended with the Earl of Leicester." From time to time she flared at him in a rage, using a favorite oath, "God's death!" And, as though to make him jealous, she began to flirt with Sir Thomas Heneage, one of the most attractive of her Gentlemen of the Privy Chamber. In retaliation, Leicester took ostentatious notice of one of the Queen's ladies, her cousin, Lettice Knollys, the daughter of Sir Francis Knollys, Vice-Chamberlain of her Household, an amusing, high-spirited, sensual young woman, the wife of Walter Devereux, Viscount Hereford. Thus provoked, the Queen displayed her jealousy: there were more cross words and quarrels; but the fire had gone out of the Queen's anger, and by the end of 1565 the Earl of Leicester was seen to be fully restored to her favor and as sure of himself as ever. He hinted to Burghley that his marriage to the Queen would not now be long delayed, patronizingly assuring the Secretary of State that he could rely upon his support and encouragement in the future. In the meantime, Leicester added, it would be as well if all negotiations for other matches were broken off. So close, indeed, were the Queen and Leicester once more that rumor had it at court that they had spent new year's night together in each other's arms.

Certainly the next year they were seen kissing on an open highway in London and driving in the Queen's coach to Greenwich Palace where Leicester was reported to have been seen in the Queen's bedchamber handing her the shift she was to wear when she got up. Again it was whispered that they were already married, but Burghley assured English envoys in foreign capitals that the rumors were false, that the Queen, though much attached to the Earl of Leicester, had never succumbed to his blandishments. "I affirm that the Queen's Majesty may be by malicious tongues not well reported," he wrote to Sir Thomas Smith in France. "But in truth she herself is blameless and hath no spot of evil intent." Leicester himself, while never disguising his hopes, sometimes revealed his resigned acceptance that they would never be fulfilled. One day he remarked to de la Forêt, Paul de Foix's successor as French ambassador, that the Queen had confided in him that if she were ever to marry an Englishman, he would be her choice; but she had "invariably declared that she would remain unmarried." "I have known her since she was eight years old, better than any man in the world," Leicester emphasized, and she had always insisted upon this. The Queen herself told de Foix that whenever the subject of her marriage was mentioned she felt as though her heart was being torn out of her breast.

Even so, while the rumors about the Queen and Leicester remained in circulation, the difficulties of arranging a foreign marriage were tiresomely aggravated. No one felt this more acutely than the Earl of Sussex who had been entrusted with the difficult negotiations over the proposed marriage of the Queen to the Archduke Charles and who believed that her involvement with the Earl of Leicester, whom he intensely disliked, was as much responsible as religious difficulties for the Queen's vacillation and his own consequent inability to bring matters to a head. Whenever they met the two Earls glared at each other and went so far as to quarrel fiercely and even to threaten violence in her Majesty's presence.

Exasperating Sussex with her hesitations over the Archduke Charles, the Queen's attitude was equally annoying to Sir Thomas Smith, who had to contend with Catherine de Médicis's plans to have Elizabeth married to her son, King Charles IX, an impressionable boy of seventeen who professed himself in love with Elizabeth, though she was a woman whom he had never seen and who was almost twice as old as himself. Elizabeth confessed to the Spanish ambassador that she found the idea of marriage to this mentally unstable French boy rather absurd, that people would laugh at the sight of "an old woman and a child" standing together at the church door. Yet, when the French ambassador approached her on the subject she took the proposal seriously enough for him to make the usual discreet inquiries as to whether or not the Queen could bear a child. "Your King is seventeen and the Queen is no more than thirty-two," one of her doctors was reported as having replied to this vital question. "Take no notice of what she says on the subject. If the King marries her, I will undertake that she could have ten children, and no one knows her constitution better than I do." This was, however, not Robert Huicke's opinion. Dr. Huicke, who had been elected President of the College of Physicians two years before, told the Queen that he did not think she ought to contemplate bearing a child, a piece of advice that brought him much abuse from both Councilors and Parliament.

Parliament had been reassembled in October 1566 in the expectation that the Queen would be granted the money of which she was constantly in need. But the Members were not so cooperative as she had hoped. "The Queen is not popular or beloved, either by Catholics or heretics," the Spanish ambassador explained. "The former do not like her because she is not a Catholic, and the others because she is not so furious and violent a heretic as they wish." All of them, he might have added, were dissatisfied by her apparent refusal to settle upon a husband, whether they were supporters of the suits of the Archduke Charles, King Eric XIV of Sweden or Charles IX of France. And, to her intense annoyance, the Commons began to debate – and to debate in increasing uproar – the question not only of her marriage but also that of her successor should she die without children. She demanded that they be prevented from committing so flagrant a breach of the royal prerogative and that those bishops and peers in the Lords who supported them must be sternly reprimanded. Her Councilors demurred. She shouted at them in rage. In calmer mood she discussed her problems with Guzman de Silva, complaining of the Commons' impertinence in making her marriage a condition of the vote of £250,000 that she and the realm so sorely needed. Guzman told her that this was all one could expect from heretics; she should "bear in mind the obedience and quietude of the Catholics, compared with the turbulence of the Protestants." "She answered me that she did not know what these devils wanted," Guzman reported to King Philip II. "I said what they wanted was simple liberty, and if Kings did not look out for themselves, and combine together to check them, it was easy to see how the licence that they had taken would end."

She had hoped that the Lords at least would support her, but the upper house was proving quite as difficult as the lower, and she berated its Members whenever she came across them at court. She attacked the Duke of Norfolk; she assailed the Earl of Pembroke; she angrily told the Earl of Leicester that he was utterly unworthy of the trust she had placed in him; she castigated the Marquess of Northampton, who had married his second wife before the divorce proceedings against his first wife were completed, telling him he was in no position to give anyone advice on matrimonial matters. The Marquess of Winchester had admittedly spoken up for her; but he was a useless old wreck, well over eighty, who was going deaf as well as losing his memory.

The Queen considered proroguing Parliament as soon as her subsidy had been granted; but this, she was warned, would lose her much popularity. How could Members return to their counties and satisfactorily explain what had happened? People would ask what had been decided about the succession, and they would have to reply, "We have done nothing but give away your money. The Queen hath what she looked for, but hath no care for us." The idea of dispersing Parliament was quickly abandoned, and on 3 November the Queen received a delegation of thirty Members from each

House at Whitehall Palace where she made a speech which she had taken much trouble to prepare.

They had been on the verge of committing treason, she told the delegates, and they would be well advised to desist from their folly. In a monarchy the feet should not try to tell the head how to proceed; it was the duty of the head to dictate to the feet to prevent them from running to disaster. She hoped to marry, and she hoped to have children by her husband. And it would one day be appropriate to consider these matters and that of her succession; but they were very delicate matters and must be considered with the utmost prudence and care. As she had told the Privy Council, there were grave difficulties in naming a successor to whom men might turn in times of crisis to her own dishonor and danger. Members were behaving as though the problems of her marriage and succession could be decided as easily as any other parliamentary business, and as though they had the welfare of the country more at heart than she.

"Was I not born in this realm?" she demanded of them. "Were my parents born in any foreign country? – Is not my kingdom here? Whom have I oppressed? Whom have I enriched to other's harm? What turmoil have I made in this Commonwealth that I should be suspected to have no regard to the same? . . . As for my own part, I care not for death; for all men are mortal. And though I be a woman, yet I have as good a courage, answerable to my place, as ever my father had. I am your anointed Queen. I thank God that if I were turned out of the realm in my petticoat, I were able to live in any place in Christendom."

It was a remarkable speech, strongly worded and delivered with vehement emphasis; and, for the time being, it achieved its purpose. The personality of the woman had awed the sixty men. Various Members of the Lords, so she told Guzman, came to her to ask pardon. The subsidy was granted her, and she graciously declined to take one third of it. The Commons conceded that it might be as well, after all, to leave the matter of the Queen's marriage to the Council; and, although they maintained their right to discuss the succession as a matter of public concern, the point was not pressed after the Queen summoned the Speaker to her presence, instructed him that Parliament did *not* have an automatic right to discuss the matter and added, "If any person thought himself not satisfied, but had further reasons, let him come before the Privy Council there to show them."

In the end, however, the Queen felt obliged to soften her words. In her speech at the dissolution on 2 January, she could not forbear returning to her theme of the head and the feet, the necessity for there being a leader to show the way. But it was a gentle rebuke, quite without the passion of her

outburst the previous year. She appeared anxious to show both Houses
that, having recognized their potential strength, she had no wish to undermine their liberties. She could not be sure of being able to prevent them
returning to the disputed ground, but she could for the time being comfort
herself with the thought that she had not committed herself to take a
husband just yet; and, while she had accepted Parliament's petition that
she should – "in what place she liked and as soon as she pleased" – be
"joined by the sacred bond of marriage to the end to have children to help
the Kingdom," she had averted an open debate about her successor.

In Scotland the woman whom she was so reluctant to pronounce her
successor was not finding marriage an enjoyable state. Darnley, or King
Henry as the Scots were now required to call him, was already proving an
intolerably unpleasant husband, drunken, uncouth, vicious, arrogant and
spiteful. On a visit to the house of an Edinburgh merchant, his wife had to
beg him not to drink so much and not to entice his companions to do so.
He "gave her such words," so Burghley was told, "that she left the house
in tears." The more she was outraged by him, exasperated by his stupidity,
his pettish, sulky resentments, the more she came to rely upon her confidential French secretary, David Riccio, the son of a musician from Turin,
who had gone to Scotland on a diplomatic mission in 1561 and had remained as a lute player at court and a singer in the Queen's chapel. Small,
ugly and flashily dressed, Riccio was said to have made a vast amount of
money by taking bribes, to be the instigator of Queen Mary's secret correspondence with Continental papists (which he certainly helped to com-
pose), even to be her lover. When the Queen became pregnant, Darnley
was persuaded to believe that Riccio was the father of the child and just as
easily induced by various Protestant Lords to take part in a plot to murder
him. Riccio was dragged screaming from the Queen's supper table at
Holyroodhouse and stabbed fifty-six times.

The murder – which Burghley was warned to expect a month before it
took place – was welcomed by all those who hoped that it might widen
the breach between Queen Mary and Darnley and promote the Protestant
cause. But Mary was more than a match for the conspirators. She allowed
Darnley back into the bed from which she had lately barred him. Pliable as
always, he was soon induced to betray his fellow-murderers and to join her
in collecting forces to hunt them down and drive them across the border
into England. This was soon achieved and the Pope was fulsome in his
congratulations: "We were struck with horror when we heard of the danger in which you were, owing to the treason of heretics. But the joy we felt

was greater still when we heard of your noted valour, your greatness of soul and admirable constancy."

When the news reached England, Queen Elizabeth expressed her indignation that a monarch – even a monarch who failed to realize that rights entailed obligations – could be so insulted as her cousin had been. She received the Spanish ambassador wearing a miniature of Queen Mary hanging from her girdle by a golden chain, and told him that, had she been in her cousin's place, she would have grabbed Darnley's dagger and plunged it into his own body. She then collected herself and added archly that she would not wish it to be thought that she would behave in such a way were the Archduke Charles to become her husband.

Outraged as she obviously was by the circumstances of the murder, Elizabeth was unwilling to accede to Mary's request that the perpetrators of it should be extradited. It was the second time that such a request had been made of her. Immediately after Mary's marriage to Darnley, the Protestant Lords of the Congregation had risen in revolt, hoping that Elizabeth would support them, which she had reluctantly done with small amounts of money though not with troops. And, when Mary had raised an army and shown her determination to crush the insurrection, the rebels had fled to Newcastle and had sought permission to come south from there to justify their behavior at the English court. Well aware that the French and Spanish ambassadors were keeping keen eyes on the situation so as to be able to report her responses to their respective masters, the Queen forbade the rebels to come to her. However one of their leaders, James Stewart, Earl of Moray, had already left. On his arrival in London the Queen had agreed to see him and had invited the French ambassador to be present at the interview so that he could be a witness to her disowning him.

Moray, clothed in penitential black, had knelt before her and, speaking in French for the ambassador's benefit, the Queen had told him sharply that she could never approve of rebels taking up arms against their anointed sovereign, that he had never received "any aid or countenance" from her in his ill-conceived rebellion. But when Moray, playing his own part in this farce, had explained that he and his colleagues were loyal subjects of Queen Mary and that they had sought only to defend themselves against her advisers, Elizabeth had agreed to take up their case with Mary and in the meantime to allow them to remain in Newcastle.

Towards Riccio's murderers she felt disinclined to be so lenient. She stood firm in her refusal not to grant Mary's request for their extradition, but she refused to allow them to remain in England. James Douglas, Earl of Morton, one of their leaders, sailed for Flanders. He soon crept back to

Newcastle, however, and Elizabeth, learning of his presence there, left him undisturbed until he and most of the other assassins were pardoned and allowed to return home to Scotland. For the moment, then, all seemed quiet again. Elizabeth sent sympathetic messages to Mary which were returned in kind.

12

Traitors and Rebels

*"We do not think it consonant in
nature that the head should be
subject to the foot."*

On 23 June 1566 Sir James Melville, having ridden hard all the way, arrived at Burghley's house in Cannon Row with the news that, four days before, Queen Mary had given birth to a son in Edinburgh Castle. Burghley immediately took a boat for Greenwich Palace where he found Queen Elizabeth dancing in the hall. She sank into a chair as she listened to the message and for a moment sat there in silence, her head in her hand. Then to her ladies she is said to have announced dispiritedly, "The Queen of Scots is lighter of a fair son, while I am but a barren stock."

The next morning when Melville came to give her more details, she disguised her chagrin with a display of sprightliness. She hurried eagerly towards him, congratulated him on the birth of the Prince, agreed to stand as godmother at the baptism, and since it was not the time of year to ask an English lady to go on a journey to Scotland, she suggested that Mary's half-sister, the Countess of Argyll, should take her place at the ceremony, and that the Earl of Bedford, Lord Lieutenant of Northumberland, Cumberland and Westmorland, should take up as a present for her godson a fine gold font.

Soon after accounts reached London of the christening of the baby James, Prince and High Steward of Scotland, there also came reports that his mother was now passionately in love with her Lord High Admiral, the unscrupulous, quarrelsome and masterful Earl of Bothwell. It was then learned that the Queen's husband, Darnley, had fallen ill. He may have had smallpox; he very likely had syphilis. When he began to recover, Mary persuaded him to return from Glasgow, a small village and stronghold of his family, to Edinburgh where he was lodged in a house at Kirk o' Field, just inside the town wall. In the early morning of 10 February 1567 the quiet neighborhood was rocked by a thunderous explosion. Darnley's bedroom floor was blown through the roof, and his body, apparently strangled, was afterwards found forty feet away beneath a pear tree on the other side of the town wall.

As soon as she heard all this Elizabeth wrote to Mary, addressing her formally as "Madame" rather than as "Ma chère soeur," to offer her sympathy on her husband's death and to advise her that she must not "look through her fingers" at what was surely a murder, but must have these responsible sought out and punished. "I should not do the office of a faithful cousin and friend if I did not urge you to preserve your honour," she added. "For the love of God, Madame, use such sincerity and prudence in this case which touches you so closely, that all the world will have reason to pronounce you innocent of a crime of such enormity, a thing which, if you do it not, you would deserve to fall from the ranks of Princesses. I counsel you to take this matter to heart that you may show the world what a noble Princess and loyal wife you are."

Up till now Queen Mary had been showing herself to be neither. She had declined to divorce Darnley, for fear lest her enemies declare her child illegitimate; and, while her incrimination in his murder was never to be established, it was generally held that, unless her complicity was understood, her conduct was inexplicable. All the evidence pointed to her foreknowledge: shortly before the explosion she had left the house at Kirk o' Field, where she had spent the previous night, and had gone back to Holyroodhouse; and after the murder she had made no pretense of sorrow. She had given Darnley's fine clothes to Bothwell; and, claiming that a week's mourning in seclusion had affected her health, she had joined a house-party at Lord Seton's castle near Edinburgh where Bothwell was a fellow guest. Bothwell was put on trial at his own request; but, when he rode into Edinburgh with his armed retainers and then set off from Holyroodhouse for the High Court on Darnley's charger – Queen Mary waving him farewell from an upstairs window – Darnley's father, Lord Lennox, to whom the prosecution had been left, was too frightened to give his evidence. An equally nervous jury acquitted Bothwell "of art and part of the said slaughter of the King." The accused immediately stepped forth to issue a challenge to anyone foolhardy enough to maintain he was guilty.

A week later Bothwell gave a supper party at Ainslie's Tavern in Canongate, Edinburgh, for several nobles and prelates including the Earls of Argyll and Morton and the Archbishop of St. Andrews, the last of these being, in Queen Mary's description, "a poxy priest" who had been recently taking a cure from an Italian specialist in venereal diseases. These men were persuaded to sign a declaration approving Bothwell's marriage to Queen Mary. Bothwell then arranged to abduct her and carried her off to Dunbar Castle where, according to her own account, he raped her. She then married him in a ceremony conducted by the Protestant Bishop of Orkney after he had obtained a divorce from Lady Jean Gordon, sister of the Earl of Huntley, whom he had married little more than a year before.

The Queen's marriage, even more than the suspicion that she might have been implicated in her previous husband's murder, was responsible for the destruction of her reputation in Europe. The Pope, breaking off relations with her, declared that she was quite as bad as the heretic Elizabeth. The people of Scotland were all but united in condemnation of her. In Edinburgh, where placards appeared depicting her naked to the waist as a lascivious mermaid, the mob cried out, "Burn the whore!" The rebellious Protestant Lords rose up against her and her husband. She attempted to oppose them but was forced to surrender; and while Bothwell, pressed by her to do so, fled off the field at Carberry Hill and eventually escaped to Denmark where he died insane, Mary was taken a prisoner to the island fortress of Lochleven in Kinross-shire.

Queen Elizabeth professed herself appalled by this treatment of a queen, however unworthy and disreputable she privately considered her to be. She sensed that Mary's disgrace threatened her own standing in the world and was both shocked and angered by Burghley's declaration that her cousin's behavior justified the rough treatment to which she had been subjected. She wrote to Mary to express her sympathy with her in her plight and to assure her that she could rely upon her support. She sent Sir Nicholas Throckmorton to Scotland to inform the Lords of the Congregation that, while her "cousin and neighbour" may have been at fault, it was highly improper for subjects to hold their rightful sovereign a prisoner or to deprive her of her lawful authority. Throckmorton was later instructed to warn the Lords that if they continued to hold her the Queen of England would take measures to punish them as "an example to all posterity"; and in these measures her Majesty was confident the other "princes of Christendom" would join her. "You may assure them," her instructions continued, "we so detest and abhor the murder committed upon our cousin, their King, and mislike as much as any of them the marriage of the Queen our sister with Bothwell. But herein we dissent from them, that we think it is not lawful nor tolerable for them, being by God's ordinance subjects, to call her, who also by God's ordinance is their superior and Prince, to answer to their accusations by way of force." "We do not," she added, using a favorite image, "think it consonant in nature that the head should be subject to the foot."

The Lords were in no mind to receive such gratuitous advice. They told Throckmorton that he could not visit Queen Mary at Lochleven, that her baby son could not be sent to England, and that it was all very well for him to talk of the help that Queen Elizabeth had given to the Scottish Protestants in the past when she had more recently refused asylum to the Earl of Morton after the assassination of the Papist agent, Riccio. Indeed, Throckmorton soon came to the conclusion that there was little he could do to help Mary. Not only were the Lords determined upon her downfall, so were her people. "It is public speech of all estates," he reported, "that she has no more privilege to commit murder nor adultery than any other private person." She herself, so it was said, steadfastly declined to allow Bothwell to bear the responsibility for her misfortunes; she would rather "leave her Kingdom and dignity to live as a simple damsel with him."

The Lords decided that there was but one course open to them: Queen Mary must either abdicate or submit to an inquiry into her conduct. A delegation left for Lochleven on 24 July to place this alternative before her. She had already been visited there by the Earl of Moray who had found her in a highly emotional state, often in tears, ready to admit to him, if to no one else, that she had made mistakes. "Some things she did confess plainly," Moray said, "some she did extenuate." But she seemed to have resigned herself to the loss of her throne; and she asked him to look after her jewels for her and to act as Regent for her son were she to be forced to abdicate. This she was soon obliged to do. According to her own account, one of the Lords, Patrick Lindsay, grabbed her hand and pushed it roughly towards the deed for signature, though Sir James Melville, who described Lindsay as certainly being in a "boasting humour," said that she subscribed it without demur. Five days later her son, just over a year old, was crowned King James VI. Moray was appointed Regent with the Earl of Morton his Lord Chancellor and principal adviser.

Queen Elizabeth was outraged. She wrote to Throckmorton telling him to deliver a protest in the strongest terms. "And this message we will charge you to do as roundly and sharply as you can," she ordered him, "for sure we be you shall not express it with more vehemency than we mean and intend." After a conversation with Guzman de Silva who, exacerbating her anger, told her that she could not let such an insult to a fellow-sovereign pass unavenged and that she must take firm action against the rebels, she threatened once again to consider the possibility of sending troops to Scotland. She hesitated because she thought that the Scottish Lords would turn for help to France; but she asked Guzman if King Philip might be willing to consider a joint enterprise.

When Burghley came to Windsor for an audience on the evening of 11 August she had made up her mind: she would order an invasion of Scotland to restore her cousin to the throne without delay. Burghley was aghast. He pointed out the dangers of declaring war on the Scottish Lords on behalf of a deposed queen whose behavior had been equivocal to say the least. Unconvinced and evidently distraught, she dismissed Burghley who soon returned with both Leicester and Pembroke, neither of whom had any more success with the indignant Queen than Burghley had had.

Throckmorton's conversations with the Scottish Lords were equally unrewarding. They appeared unimpressed by the threat of war: the English might well ravage their borders, but they would then retaliate by ravaging the English borders. In any case, they could rely on the French to help them if necessary; and Queen Elizabeth would surely not like to provoke a new Franco-Scottish alliance any more than she would want to be responsible for Queen Mary's execution, which an English invasion might well precipitate.

When Throckmorton reported these exchanges to Queen Elizabeth on his return home without the presents that retiring ambassadors usually received, he found the Queen's anger unabated. She had changed her mind about an invasion, yet she was determined to punish the seditious Scotch in some way, and decided to do so by means of a trade embargo. But no sooner had she put forward the idea to King Charles IX – who she hoped would be as anxious to avenge an injury to a fellow monarch as she was herself – another religious war broke out in France, presenting the French King and his mother with more urgent problems than the fate of the deposed Queen of Scots.

Once again Elizabeth had little sympathy for the French Huguenots, whom she still regarded as rebellious subjects rather than persecuted Protestants. Her ambassador in France pressed her to support the Protestants, but she declined to do so, convinced that, were they to be victorious, the French would present an even more dangerous problem than the Scots. Rather than show any sympathy towards the Huguenot leader, the Prince of Condé, she offered her support to the French King in his difficulties; and, while she took no measures to prevent English Protestants "of the common sort" sailing for France to serve in the Huguenot army, she told Guzman that if any gentleman sought permission to go she would have his head.

While offering her support to Charles IX, Queen Elizabeth continued to extend her sympathy to the Queen of Scots who, so she still insisted, should be returned to her throne without undue delay. But Mary, who had a mind to gain more than the crown of Scotland, had made plans of her own.

On the evening of 2 May 1568, with the help of George Douglas, the Laird of Lochleven's brother who was said to be in "a phantasy of love" with her, she escaped from her imprisonment in the castle and called her supporters to arms. She was defeated at Langside, however; and, with her hair cut off to escape detection, she made her way towards England. She had had such a venture long in mind, being, as she put it herself, "in readiness to expose herself to all perils in hope of victory."

Hearing of the warm reception accorded to Mary in Carlisle, Elizabeth began to regret the promises she had made to her. As Burghley said, Mary's undiminished "appetite to the Crown" was a terrible danger to the security of the state. Her demands were becoming more and more insistent. So were her threats: she had gone so far as to say she would seek help from Turkey to regain her throne if no other country came to her support. She asked Elizabeth to receive her at court as soon as possible, and requested clothes in which to appear since she had none but those she had been wearing when she had escaped from Lochleven. At Carberry Hill she had been reduced to wearing an Edinburgh woman's red petticoat which, since Mary was of the "largest size," reached only to her knees.

Burghley warned Elizabeth of the dangers of receiving Mary at court and thereby implying that she was recognizing her as her successor. As to the clothes, and the jewels which might be sent to accompany them, these were a matter for her Majesty to decide.

Elizabeth was disinclined to be generous to Mary both by nature and design. She had already been sent several of Mary's pearls by the Earl of Moray who, from the store placed in his trust, had dispatched a splendid six-row necklace – upon which Catherine de Médicis had once cast a covetous eye – and twenty-five huge black pearls with a message that Queen Elizabeth might buy them for two thirds their value. Elizabeth, who delighted in pearls, was most unwilling to send any of these back. Nor did she relish the idea of parting with any of her own best clothes. She gave instructions to Sir Francis Knollys, now Treasurer of the Queen's Chamber, who was to go to Carlisle Castle to take charge of the fugitive, to get a waiting woman to make up a parcel. The waiting woman, so Knollys afterwards pleaded, misunderstood his instructions and did not realize for whom the clothes were intended. According to rumor she packed no more than two rather tatty chemises, a pair of shoes and a roll of black velvet. Certainly when the clothes were unpacked in Carlisle, Mary looked upon them in telling silence.

She was not usually so discreet. When told by Knollys that, despite her "tragical demonstrations," she was to be removed from Carlisle to the security of Bolton Castle, the seat of Lord Scrope, she burst out angrily, "I have made great wars in Scotland – I pray God I make no trouble in other realms also."

This was precisely what the English government now feared she might do. Elizabeth had announced that she would help Mary regain her rights; but as Throckmorton had pointed out, the Scottish Lords would never allow this, would "not permit her any longer to put the realm in peril by her disorders." Her "misbehaviour, as well in the government of the realm as in her own person," had ensured that she would "never have any more power in Scotland."

Nevertheless her representative in London, Lord Herries, repeated Mary's demands that English troops should be sent into Scotland to restore her to the throne. Failing that, she would have to go to France to enlist the help of Charles IX; and she asked for a passport for Lord Fleming, chatelain of Dumbarton Castle, who was with her at Bolton Castle, to enable him to travel to Paris with a view to preparing for her own visit. No immediate answer was forthcoming to this request, which was naturally regarded in London as both impertinent and alarming. So Mary wrote again in terms even more peremptory. "Madame, I am greatly astonished that you press me so for Lord Fleming's going to France," Elizabeth replied indignantly in the French she always employed when writing to Mary. "You surely doubt my wisdom, in asking me to let the keeper of such a place [as Dumbarton Castle] go there . . . Begging you to have some consideration for me, instead of always thinking of yourself."

Elizabeth's position was, indeed, peculiarly awkward. She had a low opinion of Mary as a person but she regarded with a high, self-protective reverence her rank as queen. She feared that it demeaned her own dignity and authority that Mary should be humbled. Yet her Council and Parliament would never be persuaded to approve an English attack upon the Protestant Lords to restore Mary to the throne. Besides, there was the constant danger of French intervention. "Do not," Throckmorton had been warned by the Lords when an English invasion had been suggested, "do not drive us to France faster than we wish to run."

Mary herself recognized no obstacle to the immediate settlement of her affairs and reacted with disdain to a proposal by the English government that she should submit to an inquiry as to her recent conduct, including her complicity in the alleged crimes of the man to whom, for all her previous devotion, she now referred as the "wicked confederate, the Earl of Bothwell." The Council had a right to demand this inquiry, she was told, because "of ancient right, it appertaineth to the Crown of England [to exercise sovereignty in Scotland], as by multitude of records, examples and precedents may be proved."

Mary eventually consented to the inquiry, which opened its proceedings at York on 4 October, moving to Westminster towards the end of November; but she agreed to it only upon being assured that – once a favorable verdict had been returned – she would be restored to her throne, and that there would be no question of her being judged by her own subjects. "I will never plead my cause against theirs," she insisted to Elizabeth. "I am no equal of theirs and would sooner die than by any act of mine, behave as if I were." "She would rather perish than [abandon her] crown," she repeated later. The last words she would utter on earth "would be those of a Queen of Scotland."

At first the proceedings of the commissioners seemed harmless and inconclusive enough; but as soon as the Earl of Moray began to introduce evidence that threatened to show that Mary had been "privie [to] the murder of the King" – as she had been declared to be in Scotland – Mary's agent, the Bishop of Ross, declared that evidence was now being introduced which the commissioners were not authorized to consider and that he and her other representatives would consequently withdraw. After they had gone, Moray produced a bundle of letters which were alleged to have been found under Bothwell's bed and which, if genuine, appeared to render the Queen's guilt undeniable. These letters had already been shown privately to the commissioners and by William Maitland of Lethington to Mary. Mary had told Maitland to try to suppress them but had not otherwise deigned to comment upon them, except to dismiss them as forgeries. She declined to discuss them. Elizabeth urged her to reply to the charges: "We cannot but as one Prince and near cousin regarding another, as earnestly as we may, require and charge you not to forbear answering." But no answer was forthcoming, then or ever. Unless the English Council was prepared to accept that the accusations of her adversaries were false because she, "on the word of a prince," said they were false, she had nothing more to say on the subject. She required a verdict in her favor without more ado. The inquiry was then brought to a close. Moray returned to Scotland to resume his duties as Regent for the baby King James VI, while Mary, though no charges against her had been "sufficiently proven," was kept in confinement, being transferred to Tutbury Castle in Staffordshire where her guardian, the Earl of Shewsbury, fell under the spell of her charm as so many others had done in the past and allowed her as much freedom, comfort and respect as it was in his power to bestow. He was granted no more than £2,000 a year for the maintenance of her large household; but he was a very rich man and this was one very good reason, apart from his general trustworthiness, why the Queen had chosen him for an arduous and increasingly irksome duty which he was required to fulfill for sixteen years.

In regular communication with Mary at Tutbury Castle was the Spanish ambassador, Guerau de Espés, who had recently replaced Guzman de Silva much to Queen Elizabeth's annoyance, for she had got on very well with Guzman and was never to do so with his sardonic, interfering successor. Espés had come to England with explicit instructions from King Philip to sound out English Catholics dissatisfied with Elizabeth's rule and to encourage them to rise up against her, to establish Mary on the throne in her place and to restore Roman Catholicism as the national faith.

Espés set about his task with energy, enthusiasm and a bluntness of approach that some of his would-be accomplices found disturbing. Pressing upon them the necessity of removing Burghley from office and of bringing back the old Catholic nobility into positions of power, he approached the heads of two of the most important families of the traditionally Catholic north, Charles Neville, sixth Earl of Westmorland – who was married to the redoubtable eldest daughter of Henry Howard, Earl of Surrey – and the ingenuous but staunchly Catholic Thomas Percy, seventh Earl of Northumberland, whose father had been executed after taking part in the Catholic uprising against Henry VIII's government known as the Pilgrimage of Grace, and whose extremely bossy wife was a daughter of Henry Somerset, second Earl of Worcester. Espés also sought out other anti-Burghley magnates, notably the Earl of Westmorland's brother-in-law, the Duke of Norfolk, England's premier and at that time only duke whom he saw as an ideal husband for Mary Stuart.

Norfolk, ostensibly Protestant but with strong Catholic sympathies, was an indecisive and irresolute but proud and ambitious man of no great strength of character and of limited intellectual attainments. His father had been fond of claiming that Plantagenet blood ran through his veins; his mother was Frances Vere, daughter of the Earl of Oxford; his aunt was the dowager Duchess of Richmond. Although he was thirty-four, he had already been married three times, his first wife dying in childbed at the age of sixteen; his third, as rich as the first two, had died in 1567. The richest man in England, all powerful in East Anglia, he lived in almost regal style at Kenninghall at the center of a vast estate. His London house was equally grand. When he moved between the two he was accompanied by five hundred retainers. Rich as he was, the Queen favored him in accordance with his rank and her need of his support, granting him, amongst other lucrative privileges, a license to import Turkey carpets free of duty.

As a member of the commission of inquiry into the behavior of the Queen of Scots, he had confided in Elizabeth his shock at discovering "such inordinate love between her and Bothwell, her loathsomeness and abhorring of her husband that was murdered." Yet when it was proposed to him that he might take Mary as his fourth wife and become her fourth husband, the idea much appealed to him. He consulted the Earl of Sussex, president of the Council of the North, who did not discourage him; he spoke as well to the Earl of Leicester who also gave him grounds for hope. So did Mary herself who addressed to him affectionate and submissive letters which had their desired effect upon his impressionable nature. Queen Elizabeth was not at this stage consulted.

One day Norfolk came upon the Queen in the garden of Richmond Palace. She had always behaved in a kindly manner towards him, calling him her cousin because of the relationship between the Howards and the Boleyns, and overlooking the ill-will he had previously borne towards the Earl of Leicester, whose pretensions he resented as those of an upstart and whose talents he envied. The Queen spoke to him in a friendly way now; but she suddenly and disconcertingly asked him if he had anything to tell her about marriage. Whatever news he might have intended to impart, he decided to withold it. Elizabeth then said that she had heard he was to marry Mary Stuart. Norfolk immediately denied it; his loyalty to his own Queen, he protested, precluded his marriage to another. In any case, he added, alluding to the fate of Mary's second husband, he preferred to sleep on a safe pillow.

It was a remark that Elizabeth remembered. On a later occasion, after the Council had expressed their hopes of the marriage of the Queen of Scots to some English nobleman, Norfolk approached Elizabeth at Loseley near Guildford where she was staying on her way down to Hampshire. He found her sitting in an open doorway in the summer air with the Earl of Leicester kneeling on one side and a child singing to the music of a lute on the other. Leicester stood up and came towards him; and, while the child continued to sing, told him that he had just been talking to the Queen about the proposed marriage. How had she taken it? asked Norfolk. "Indifferent well," Leicester replied evasively. A few days later during that progress, the Queen had asked Norfolk to sit at her table at dinner; and, after the meal, she "gave him a nip, bidding him to take heed to his pillow."

She was still not sure just how far matters had progressed and she remained in ignorance until the court reached Basing House where the Queen's host was the Marquess of Worcester. The Earl of Leicester was staying nearby with the Earl of Pembroke at Titchfield. He had previously been agreeably disposed towards the marriage of Norfolk and Mary, believing that it might improve his own chances with Elizabeth; but when he learned that "some babbling women" at court had been gossiping about it and that the marriage was part of a dangerous plot involving Espés and the northern earls, he made up his mind to divulge as much as he knew. He sent a message from Titchfield to Basing to inform Elizabeth that he had been taken very ill and begging her to visit him. She left immediately and was told how far the marriage plans had progressed by Leicester who contrived to appear on the point of death. The Queen, deeply concerned about Leicester, was furious with Norfolk. She sent for him and upbraided him for his deceit, demanding obedience to her orders and that he break off all negotiations at once. He promised to do as she wished, adding the characteristically inept observation that he had had no thought of improving his own standing in the world by marrying the Queen of Scots for whom he had "a very slight regard": after all, his revenues in England were "not much less than those of the Kingdom of Scotland, and that when he was on his own tennis court at Norwich, he thought himself in a manner equal with some kings."

He had no reason to think himself so now. Not only his reputation but his very life was in danger. The plans that the Earls of Northumberland and Westmorland had put in hand in the north must be stopped. But the conspiracy had already gone too far, and the Queen of Scots was confident of success. Not long before she had written to the Spanish ambassador, "Tell your master that if he will help me, I shall be Queen of England in three months and Mass shall be said all over the Kingdom."

Elizabeth had already crossed swords with the Spanish, and the encounter had not been much to her advantage. Towards the end of 1568 five Spanish ships, laden with money chests containing almost £100,000 worth of coins, had sought protection from storms and pirates in harbors on the south coast. For years pirate ships had been sailing up and down the English Channel with the connivance of the Queen who argued that their crews, fundamentally loyal to England and easily disowned, were a useful weapon against Spanish galleons bringing reinforcements and supplies to King Philip's troops in the Netherlands. Furthermore, so she pointed out to Burghley – who "much misliked" her reasoning – the pirate crews maintained their own vessels, gained valuable experience of the sea in doing so, and on occasions – as on this occasion – brought in valuable plunder.

The plunder now landed at Plymouth and Southampton did not yet belong to the Spanish authorities in the Netherlands. The money had been consigned to the Duke of Alva, but until it was delivered into his hands it remained the property of the Genoese bankers who had agreed to lend it. Representatives of the Privy Council approached the bankers' agent in London who agreed that, provided the terms were equally advantageous to his principals, he could see no objections to the treasure being made over to England rather than Spain. The English government consequently appropriated it.

Reprisals were immediately taken by the Spanish authorities in the Netherlands: English merchants there were arrested and their possessions confiscated. The Privy Council responded in turn by imprisoning Spanish merchants in London and by placing the Spanish ambassador under house arrest. The Spanish then closed the port of Antwerp to English ships, and threatened further reprisals, while the Council received reports that the Duke of Alva was already preparing to land troops on the Durham coast, that the Queen of Scots was to be set free from Tutbury Castle, that the Earls of Northumberland and Westmorland were on the verge of marching south and that the Duke of Norfolk was making ready to support them. As these reports were being examined by the Council, the Marquess of Catena arrived in London ostensibly on some diplomatic mission but in reality to take command of the Spanish army upon its landing in Durham.

Even though the subsequent economic reprisals and counter-reprisals did more harm to Spanish than to English interests, the Queen's appropriation of Alva's gold from Genoa no longer seemed so clever a plan; and, as was now the expected reaction in such circumstances, the Council were berated by her Majesty for having been so foolhardy as to advise the step which at the time she had eagerly taken.

The Duke of Norfolk was told to come to Windsor without delay. He answered that he was unwell, but that when he was feeling better he would respond to the summons. Burghley, modifying the Queen's draft – which angrily complained that she had never been accustomed to receive such "a manner of answer from any person" – repeated the order which the Duke reluctantly obeyed, urging the northern earls to hold fast for the moment. If the uprising broke out now, he told his brother-in-law, it would "cost him his head, for that he was going to court."

Both Northumberland and Westmorland were, however, already on the march towards Durham. The Earl of Sussex, as Lord President of the Council of the North, had been reluctant to take steps to prevent them for fear that he might provoke the uprising it was his responsibility to prevent. He was encouraged in this view by the members of the Council of the North, one of whom advised Burghley that it would be better "to nourish quiet until the winter when the nights are longer, the ways worse, and the waters begin to slip their passage."

But the Queen, distressed by Sussex's inaction and frightened by the seriousness of the threatened uprising, was concerned that, the longer the delay, the greater was the risk of Spanish intervention and the heavier the cost of maintaining the forces that were being assembled. She even felt inclined to believe that Sussex might be a party to the plot. Sussex pleaded with Burghley to believe that he was her Majesty's most loyal subject, fully conscious of the trust she had reposed in him. He had always "hitched his staff to her door." Certainly, he admitted, he had been approached by his friend Norfolk about the proposed marriage to the Queen of Scots, but he had told him that he could give him no advice about it. He had always "written plainly" in the past, he was writing plainly now and would always write plainly in the future. In the meantime he would demand the presence of Northumberland and Westmorland – both of them also close friends of his – at his headquarters in York, although he feared, as he was proved justified in fearing, that the Queen's instructions would precipitate the full-scale rebellion she was so anxious to avoid.

The two earls ignored Sussex's summons, "What a simple man the Duke of Norfolk is," commented the wife of one of them, the Countess of Westmorland, "to begin a matter and not go through with it." Her husband and the Earl of Northumberland would both be "shamed for ever" if they "should now seek holes to creep into." So, announcing their intention of restoring the Roman Catholic religion, an enterprise upon which the Pope had pronounced his benediction, the two earls rode into Durham on 16 November 1569, followed by their retainers and a growing force of sympathizers raised by the local gentry. Soon the rebel leaders were in command of seventeen hundred horsemen and a far less orderly force of four thousand men on foot. They burst into Durham Cathedral where they tore up the English translation of the Bible and the Protestant Prayer Book. The next day they marched south to Darlington; and, having ridden into other towns off the direct route to call the inhabitants to arms, they reached Ripon on 20 November and there – with the managing Countess of Northumberland a most prominent member of the congregation – they celebrated Mass in the Cathedral.

Having detached part of their force to Hartlepool on the coast to hold a bridgehead for the expected Spanish invaders, they then marched on towards Tutbury to rescue the Queen of Scots from her captivity, her release being a pre-condition stipulated by the Duke of Alva for his support. Mary, however, had been removed from Tutbury and been taken further south to Coventry. And the earls, dismayed by her removal, disillusioned by the lack of enthusiasm for their cause the further they moved south and alarmed by reports of large number of the Queen's troops on the march against them, lost heart and began to think of retreat. Several of the other rebel leaders deserted them, much to the indignation of the Countess of Westmorland who "braste owte agaynste them with great curses . . . for there cowerd flyght."

At the end of November the retreating army broke up; and by the middle of December the remnants were dispersed, "every man to save himself as he could." The Earl of Westmorland managed to escape to the Spanish Netherlands, his estates in the diocese of Durham being confiscated and appropriated by Queen Elizabeth rather than the bishop on the grounds that the Crown had had the trouble and expense of defending them. Westmorland's subsequent efforts to negotiate a return home resulted only in attempts by English agents to kidnap him; and, after serving as a colonel in a regiment of other Catholic refugees in the service of Spain, he died at Nieuwpoort, deeply in debt.

The Earl of Northumberland did not escape. Having fled to Scotland, he was handed over by the Regent for the payment of £2,000 and beheaded in the main marketplace in York after proclaiming his faith in the Roman Catholic church and declaring, "I am a Percy in life and death." At Queen Elizabeth's request his contentious widow – who, the Queen said, ought to be burned – was expelled from Spanish territory where she was living on a small pension from the King, and not long afterwards died of smallpox in a convent.

Elizabeth had no wish to lose popularity by appearing to be unfeelingly harsh in her treatment of the lesser survivors of the rebellion which Burghley said had "proved a notable trial of her whole realm." She recognized that, although the uprising had attracted widespread support from men who were not the earl's tenants, most people in the area had shown themselves to be loyal to the Crown. She did nothing, however, to prevent her servants in the north from behaving with exceptional severity, from taking the opportunity of breaking the power of the northern landowners and for punishing those who had threatened the stability of the realm and its hard-won solvency. She bitterly resented the expenses incurred in quelling the

17. Elizabeth in the early 1580s, from a portrait attributed to Cornelius Ketel. Among the Gentlemen Pensioners carrying halberds in the background is Sir Christopher Hatton, Vice-Chamberlain of the Household. The sieve, which the Queen is holding in her left hand, is an emblem both of discernment and of chastity: the Roman vestal virgin Tuccia, when accused of impurity, plunged a sieve into the River Tiber and carried the water back to the temple without spilling a drop.

18. Elizabeth, Countess of Shrewsbury, known as "Bess of Hardwick," wife of the Queen of Scots's keeper and builder of Hardwick Hall, Derbyshire.

19. A valance of Elizabeth's time decorated with applied motifs, at Hardwick Hall.

20. Mary Queen of Scots and her son, then aged seventeen, painted in 1583 by an unknown artist.

21. An embroidered cushion cover from Hardwick Hall, reputedly worked by Mary Queen of Scots, showing her emblems, the thistle and the rose.

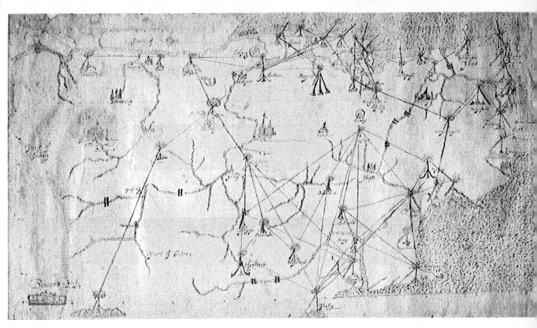

22. The sites of beacons in Kent at the time of the Spanish Armada.

23. The Queen riding to Tilbury to address her troops assembled to resist the Spanish invasion; a painting on wood.

24. A painting by an unknown artist of the launch of the English fireships
against the Spanish galleons in the Calais Roads on the night of 28 July 1588.

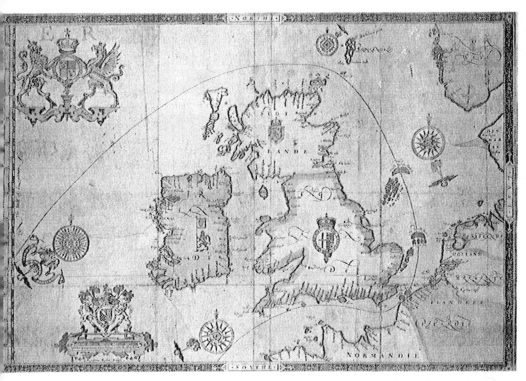

25. A contemporary map of England showing the defeated Armada's route.

26. A painting by Paulus Vredeman de Vries of ladies and gentlemen dancing in the hall of a great house.

27. The aging Earl of Leicester, Captain-General of the Queen's land forces in 1588.

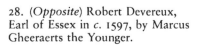

28. (*Opposite*) Robert Devereux, Earl of Essex in *c*. 1597, by Marcus Gheeraerts the Younger.

29. The Queen, resplendent in old age, by Marcus Gheeraerts the Younger.

30. The Queen's funeral cortège, from a contemporary painting showing her crowned effigy being borne on the coffin to Westminster on 28 April 1603.

northern earls' revolt and insisted upon the army that had been raised being largely disbanded before her generals considered it advisable. Her religious policies could not be considered harsh to any sect, so she thought it quite reasonable to make an example of those who had wantonly threatened the stability of the Church settlement. Her efforts to keep the country at peace, and to develop its trade, had cost her much sleeplessness and argument, so she saw no reason on earth to spare those who had recklessly come close to bringing on war with Spain.

Punishments would not, of course, be inflicted at the expense of profit. The property of rebellious subjects who were executed did not necessarily pass to the Crown. For this to happen, miscreants had to be brought to trial and convicted of high treason. It was for this reason that the Earl of Sussex proposed to "imprison principal offenders who might have great lands or wealth . . . to execute some for example . . . and extend her Majesty's mercy to the serving men of meaner sort." The Queen had no objection to the imprisoning of the rich nor to their being required to purchase their pardons for hard cash. But she did object to mercy being extended to the "serving men of meaner sort." No money could be extracted from these rebels; yet they could be made to serve as examples of the fate of all who took up arms against the sovereign's authority. "You may not execeuteth any that hath freeholds or noted wealthy, for so is the Queen's Majesty's pleasure," the Earl of Sussex wrote to one of his subordinates. "By her special commandment, January 10, 1570." At the same time Sussex received her authority to order the hanging of over seven hundred others, mostly poor men of no estate.

For the moment the Duke of Norfolk escaped lightly. Arrested on his way to Windsor, he had been taken to the Tower on 8 October and incarcerated there in the same quarters previously occupied by his grandfather. Two days before this, Burghley had prepared a paper entitled "My Advice to the Queen's Majesty in the Duke of Norfolk's Case," in which he had assured her that she need not "hinder [her] health" since "the matter was not so terrible as [her] Majesty would have it." It had to be admitted that the Queen of Scots was, and always would be, "a dangerous person"; but there were ways of dealing with her, just as there were ways of dealing with Norfolk. Burghley personally was of the opinion that a charge of treason could not be upheld, and that, since an unsuccessful trial would merely increase the Duke's sense of grievance and his danger as a potential rebel, it would be better if he were not put on trial at all. An examination of him in the Tower by Burghley and other Councilors confirmed them all in this view. Once again, the Queen refused to accept the Council's opinion: the very thought of Norfolk and his proposed marriage to the Queen of Scots now horrified her. She was astounded by the Council's attitude. Of course, Norfolk was a traitor. More than once he had denied his intentions regarding the Queen of Scots, hypocritically affirming his loyalty to his own sovereign; yet he was still in touch with the woman. She would have Norfolk's head by her own authority, she declared in a passion of rage; and then she fainted.

Her hysterical behavior was understandable. The Queen of Scots's cause might have suffered a setback through the collapse of the rebellion of the northern earls, but she considered it far from lost and looked to Norfolk to help her escape from her captivity. She wrote to him to say that she would live and die with him, signing himself, "yours faithful to death." She still hoped that she might regain the Scottish throne, and towards the end of January 1570 she heard news from Scotland which led her to believe that she might soon be returning there. Earlier that month the Earl of Moray had been shot dead from a window as he rode through Linlithgow. His assassin was James Hamilton of Bothwellhaugh, whose escape to France was followed by attacks on the Hamiltons and their properties by Moray's supporters acting in the name of the dead man they now described as the "good Regent." The Hamiltons assured Queen Elizabeth of their friendship; but she was unwilling to accept the word of men who, while admittedly for the most part Protestant, continued to regard Mary as their Queen; and she gave orders to the Earl of Sussex to march into Scotland to punish both the Hamiltons and the English rebels who were still causing trouble along the border.

Sussex who had, so he said, been brought up from his earliest youth in the belief that a Scotsman was never to be trusted, set out eagerly on his mission. "I trust, before the light of this morn be past," he declared, "to leave a memory in Scotland whereof they and their children shall be afraid to offer war to England." True to his word, he burned down one of the Hamiltons' castles and laid waste large tracts of land belonging to or occupied by Mary's supporters in Scotland. But he had not progressed far when he was ordered to come back.

The Queen had once more changed her mind. The French government had threatened to intervene unless the English withdrew; and Elizabeth, anxious not to provoke the French, had called a meeting of the Privy Council and, despite the views of some Councilors, had insisted that there must be no quarrel with the French for the moment. To placate them still further, she tried again to come to a settlement with the Queen of Scots who had, while denying any knowledge of Hamilton of Bothwellhaugh's plans, promised to reward him with a pension.

Elizabeth's terms were nevertheless hard: on condition that she was restored to the throne in Scotland, Mary was to ratify the Treaty of Edinburgh, which she had consistently refused to do for the past ten years; she was to agree to the retention of Protestantism in Scotland; she was to send her son, James, to be educated in England; and, during the lifetime of Elizabeth and of "any issue" she might have, she was to renounce her claim to the English throne. To this last condition Mary replied that the words "any issue" should be changed to "lawful issue," an observation that naturally provoked Elizabeth into declaring that, while she might well have regarded the proposed amendment as an insult to her honor, she made allowance for the possibility that Mary might "measure other folks' inclinations" by her own. She was willing therefore, to alter "any issue" to "any issue by any lawful husband." She also agreed to Mary's request to spare the lives of any English rebels who had supported the cause of the Queen of Scots and might be sent back to England for trial.

These points settled, Mary accepted Elizabeth's terms. But the new Regent and the Lords who supported him, concerned by the unrest which they would face were Mary to return to Scotland, prevaricated, eventually excusing themselves from agreeing to the settlement on the grounds that it must first be submitted to the Scottish Parliament. Months passed; the Scottish Parliament was not summoned; Mary, increasingly impatient, began to believe that, however readily she gave way to Elizabeth's conditions, she would never get back to Scotland by negotiations but only by either subterfuge or marriage.

13

Plots and Counterplots

*"If they shall not seem to you to
confess plainly, then we want you
to cause them . . . to be brought to
the rack."*

At this time it seemed to the Queen of Scots's advisers that the most promising marriage for her would be to the brother of the King of France, the twenty-year-old Prince Henry, Duke of Anjou, an "obstinate, papistical" young man in the opinion of Sir Thomas Smith, and "restive like a mule." Yet unsuitable as he might have been considered as a husband, the Queen of England, only too conscious of the trouble to be expected from his marriage to the Queen of Scots, let it be known that she would consider marrying the undesirable young man herself. The hint delighted the Duke's mother. "Such a Kingdom for one of my children!" she exclaimed, as ambitious for them as ever. Wishing to be taken as a serious suitor, which she was not, and concerned to delay the negotiations for as long as possible, at which she was now adept, Elizabeth sent Sir Francis Walsingham to France to conduct them on her behalf. Kept in the dark as to her real intentions, Walsingham undertook his commission with eagerness, advising the Queen from Paris that it would be as well if the negotiations were concluded without delay as the royal family would offer the Duke to the Queen of Scots if the Queen of England did not accept him.

Elizabeth deprecated such haste. She had already told the new French ambassador, Bertrand de Salignac de la Mothe Fénélon, that being so much older than the Duke people might laugh at her for taking so boyish a husband, although when Lady Cobham was tactless enough to suggest to her that "those marriages were always the happiest when the parties were the same age or near about it," the Queen snapped, "Nonsense! There are but ten years difference between us." To her ministers, however, she did talk of the problems of marrying a man who was, in fact, twenty years younger than herself. But Walsingham thought she merely required reassurance; so did Burghley, who wrote, "If I be not much deceived, Her

Majesty is earnest in this." For his part, the Duke of Anjou certainly needed reassurance. He had heard that his intended bride was "not only an old creature but had an ulcer on her leg." He had also been told by the Guises that, if he really wanted to get his hands on the English throne, he would be well advised to marry the Queen of Scots, who was universally acknowledged to be beautiful, rather than an old woman whose morals were highly suspect. Concerned herself that the Queen of England, while undoubtedly unmarried was perhaps far from being a virgin, Catherine de Médicis asked Fénélon for his opinion. "In her own court, she is greatly honoured," Fénélon replied. "All ranks of her subjects fear and revere her, and she rules them with full authority, which I believe she scarcely could do were she a person of ill fame, lacking virtue."

The Duke himself, a painted, scented voluptuary who had in the past never appeared to be particularly concerned about virtue, had by now quite overcome his earlier reluctance in the light of all he had been told about the pleasures and prosperity of the country of which he might become King. But when Elizabeth was pressed for a decision – while maintaining an appearance of continuing enthusiasm and listening approvingly to a recital of the Duke's physical attributes – she cautiously withdrew behind the evasions of her correspondence, ready, if necessary, to produce the ace marked "Calais" from her sleeve. At length, "with some laborious persuasions, her Majesty was induced to agree that the articles [of marriage] be made ready and showed." But, as Burghley told Walsingham on 5 June 1571, "Ere I could finish them I was commanded to conclude them with a request to have Calais restored, a matter so inconvenient to bring forth a marriage as indeed I thought it meant to procure a breach."

Eventually specific terms were put forward by the French: the Duke of Anjou was to be crowned King of England and be the country's joint ruler; he was to receive an annual income of £60,000; he was to be appointed Regent should Elizabeth bear a child and die before him; he was to be allowed to attend Mass in England and in public. These conditions were patently absurd. "Why, Madame," Sir Thomas Smith expostulated when Catherine de Médicis insisted upon her son's attending public Mass in England, "then he may require also the four orders of friars, monks, canons, pilgrimages, pardons, oil and cream, reliques and all such trumperies!" Nevertheless, the talks continued until the whole matter was transformed by an improvement in relations between the French royal family and the King of Spain. Suddenly a marriage to the English Queen seemed no longer so desirable to the French, friendship with England no longer so important. Alarmed, Elizabeth asked Walsingham to bring some urgency into the discussions; but the moment had passed. A marriage of the Duke of Anjou to Mary Queen of Scots now seemed to his mother more desirable.

Mary had other plans in mind. Despairing of her release, she had been persuaded to become a party to the schemes of an ardent Italian Catholic, Roberto Ridolfi, a Florentine banker who had come to London as a business agent and, after involvement in the unsuccessful rebellion of the northern earls, had come to the conclusion that for any revolt to succeed the help of foreign powers was essential. He had outlined his plans to the Pope who had listened to them sympathetically. Pius V, austere and ascetic, the son of poor parents, a shepherd until he was fourteen, had displayed such excessive zeal in pursuing and punishing the unfaithful while employed by the Inquisition in Como that he had been recalled. He had since been promoted Grand Inquisitor and had been even more zealous in his pursuit of heretics everywhere. He had promulgated a Bull excommunicating Queen Elizabeth and absolving her subjects from allegiance. A copy of the Bull – which ended all hopes of the Queen coming to terms with the Papacy and gave encouragement both to rebels in England and to her enemies abroad – had been nailed to the door of the Bishop of London's house. The Catholic who had hammered it there had been arrested, tortured and executed with "the greatest cruelty." Thereafter the Pope was confirmed in his belief that Queen Elizabeth must be disposed of at all costs.

Ridolfi's plan was to free the Queen of Scots, put her on the throne in Elizabeth's place and restore Roman Catholicism. With the help of John Leslie, Bishop of Ross, Mary's agent in London, Ridolfi enlisted the support of the Duke of Norfolk, who had been released from the Tower to house arrest in the Charterhouse after signing a paper declaring his loyalty to Queen Elizabeth, and who was now induced to "affirm his contentation and agreement" to the planned rebellion.

Ridolfi left for Spain by way of the Netherlands. But neither the Duke of Alva nor Philip II was much interested in his overtures. The Duke of Alva was unwilling to spare the ten thousand men for whom the conspirators asked him so long as Elizabeth was alive. If she were to die, "either a natural or any other death," that would be a different matter. The King of Spain, having not only the problems of the Netherlands to consider but the Turks and the Moors as well, concurred with Alva's view.

In coded letters Ridolfi reported his failure to enlist foreign help to the Queen of Scots and the Duke of Norfolk as well as to the Bishop of Ross and to the Spanish ambassador, Guerau de Espés. These letters were taken to England by Ridolfi's messenger, Charles Baillie, who was immediately arrested by Burghley's agents when he stepped ashore at Dover and taken away to the Tower where, in the dungeon reserved for the use of the rackmaster, he was commanded to reveal the names of his superiors. Under torture Baillie revealed that of John Leslie, Bishop of Ross, and divulged the code that had been used in their correspondence. The Bishop, prostrated by worry, was ill in bed when four Privy Councilors came to question him. Declining to submit to their examination as the Queen of Scots's ambassador – and offering his opinion of Ridolfi's letters as "nothing but an Italian discourse, nor yet to be taken heed unto" – he was nevertheless carried next day to the Bishop of Ely's house in Holborn and then to the Bishop's country house in the Isle of Ely.

While he was still in Holborn, other compromising papers had been discovered by the Privy Council's spies. These were contained in bags being taken by the Duke of Norfolk's agents to Mary's friends in Scotland, together with money contributed by the French to her cause. Two of the Duke's secretaries, Higford and Barker, were arrested, as was his steward Bannister, and all were put to torture on the instructions of Elizabeth, who wrote to their interrogators, "If they shall not seem to you to confess plainly their knowledge, then we warrant you to cause them both, or either of them, to be brought to the rack and first to move them with fear thereof to deal plainly in their answers . . . Then [should the sight of the instrument not induce them to confess] you shall cause them to be put to the rack and to find the taste thereof till they shall deal more plainly or until you shall think fit."

The sight of the rack was sufficient to wring confessions from both Bannister and Higford. Barker refused to say anything at first; but he soon succumbed to its pains and disclosed hiding-places in the attics of Norfolk's London house, and "under a mat, hard by the window's side where the map of England doth hang," where various incriminating letters were concealed. Sir Thomas Smith considered that the rack had now extracted all that could be forced from the prisoners, yet he continued with the torture not "in any hope to get anything worthy" but "because it is so earnestly commanded to us." While the racking was resumed, the Bishop of Ross, to whom some of the incriminating letters were addressed by the Queen of Scots, was examined again. He again pleaded his immunity from interrogation as an ambassador until Burghley – who had taken legal advice on the matter and been assured that immunity did not apply in cases of treason – told Ross that he, too, would be delivered to the rackmaster if he did not cooperate with his examiners. He gave way without further ado, confessing all he knew and, in his fearful anxiety to escape the tortures threatened him, he accused Mary of poisoning her first husband, of being a party to the death of her second and of bringing her third to ruin at Carberry Hill. She was "not fit for any husband." The Duke of Norfolk had not done well to become involved with her.

A transcript of the bishop's confessions, hurriedly taken down by Dr. Thomas Wilson, Master of the Court of Requests, was prepared for the Lord Mayor and Aldermen who, at Elizabeth's suggestion, were summoned to the Star Chamber to be shown the evidence of a conspiracy designed to bring a large army of Spaniards into the country.

The minor figures in the affair were soon disposed of: the Bishop of Ross was kept in custody until – after pleading with Elizabeth for his release in a flattering Latin oration – he was permitted to sail to France; Espés, the Spanish ambassador, was expelled from the country; and the Duke of Norfolk was taken to the Tower "without any trouble, save a number of idle, rascal people, women, men, boys and girls, running about him, as the manner is, gazing at him." From the Tower he was escorted to his trial on a charge of treason in Westminster Hall.

It was a show trial intended to intimidate those members of the nobility who might have abandoned Elizabeth for Mary had Norfolk's schemes succeeded. He was not allowed counsel, nor a copy of the indictment; the witnesses against him, whose evidence was read out and commented upon, were not produced for examination in court. He was inevitably convicted, and sentence to a traitor's death was pronounced upon him in all the savage detail required by law. He was taken back to the Tower where he wrote long letters of repentance to the Queen, admitting his offenses yet protesting his essential loyalty and regretting his dealings with the Queen of Scots for whose supporters "nothing never prospereth." The Queen of Scots, for her part, "had nothing to say" about him when approached. He was the Queen of England's subject and must be dealt with as she thought fit. People who tried to connect her with his conspiracy were villains and "lied in their throats."

Although his guilt was evident, although sentence had been passed upon him and the Privy Council and House of Commons were all but unanimous in their demand for his execution, the Queen held back, reluctant to sign the warrant, believing, so Lord Burghley thought, that she might thereby forfeit some of her precious popularity. The Sheriffs of London were still awaiting her signature to the warrant the day before the execution was due to take place. Late that night, Burghley was suddenly summoned by the Queen who told him she had taken "a great misliking that the Duke should die the next day." A new warrant must be issued; the Sheriffs must wait until they received further instructions. "God's will be fulfilled," Burghley wrote resignedly, "and aid Her Majesty to do herself good."

"I cannot write you what is the inward cause of the stay of the Duke of Norfolk's death," he told Walsingham,

> only I find Her Majesty diversely disposed. Some time, when she speaketh of her danger, she concludeth that justice should be done, another time she speaketh of his nearness of blood, of his superiority of honour, etc. . . . Upon Saturday she signed a warrant for his execution on Monday, and so all preparations were made and concourse of many thousands yesterday in the morning. But their coming was answered by another, ordinary execution.

The worry, as was so often the case with her, made the Queen ill, so ill, indeed, that it was feared that she might be poisoned. For five days she was in intermittent agony with a "heavy and vehement" pain that clutched at her heart and made her so breathless that she feared that she might die. Both the Earl of Leicester and Lord Burghley sat at her bedside through long hours of the night. When she recovered the doctors told her that she had been upset by eating some fish that was bad. She denied that possibility: she often ate fish; fish had never upset her in the past; she knew better than that; she had not been purged and bled enough lately. She had been feeling well enough to give up the regular bleeding she had found efficacious in the past; that was the trouble, not fish. The routine must be resumed; she knew better than the doctors.

When she rose from her sickbed, Norfolk's impending execution was still there to fret her. A fresh warrant was drawn up, specifying a new date for the Duke to be taken to the scaffold – 9 April. But again early in the morning before the axe was due to fall the Queen sent an urgent message to Burghley: the execution must be postponed once more. "If they will need a warrant" for this stay of execution, she wrote, "let this suffice, all written with my own hand." Knowing how exasperated Burghley would be, she added placatingly, "Your most loving sovereign, Elizabeth R."

The next month Parliament was due to meet again, and the Queen knew only too well that the House of Commons would not be prepared to tolerate her continued protection of a traitor from the other House. Already, after the publication of the Papal Bull of excommunication, Members had demanded severer measures against Catholics, and they would now be in no mood to spare Norfolk since they could not get at the Queen of Scots. Nor were they: indeed, the speech of one Member who called for the execution of the Queen of Scots as well as the Duke of Norfolk was greeted with shouts of "Yea! Yea!" And when another Member spoke against this drastic solution of their problems the House "misliked so much of his talk that with shuffling of feet and hawking they had well nigh barred him to be heard." There could be no doubt that the general feeling of the Commons was that if they and the Queen were to be safe, Mary must die with Norfolk. As one of them said, they would just as soon be "hanged in resisting the Queen of Scots as hanged hereafter." To these sentiments Elizabeth felt bound to respond: she would not agree to the execution of Mary, however much she agreed with the Member for Barnstaple who described her as "the most notorious whore in all the world"; but she knew she must steel herself to order the execution of Norfolk.

So yet another warrant was issued for his execution; and on 2 June 1572 Norfolk at last walked out onto Tower Hill towards a scaffold which had had to be repaired since no one had suffered there for fourteen years. He met his death with courage. He spoke to the people in a calm, clear voice, protesting his loyalty to Queen Elizabeth, declaring that he "never was a papist" since he knew "what religion meant," and expressing the hope that, although it was no new thing for men to suffer death in this place, he would be the last, as he was the first, to do so in this reign.

The Commons had had their way over Norfolk; but, as one of their number put it, "the axe must give the next warning." An error had "crept into the heads of a number" that the Queen of Scots was above the law; but no one, they insisted, was above the law. Mary Stuart had been shown to be guilty of high treason and she must suffer the consequences. The Commons consequently brought in a Bill for her execution; they also brought in a Bill declaring her incapable of succession to the English throne. Elizabeth agreed to consider the second of these bills; but she would not accept the first. "Can I put to death the bird that, to escape the pursuit of the hawk, has fled to my feet for protection?" she asked the Privy Council. "Honour and conscience forbid."

Burghley, suffering from a particularly painful attack of gout, recognized that for the moment there was no point in discussing the matter with her. "Such slowness . . . such stay in resolution," he lamented to Walsingham. "I am so overthrown in heart, as I have no spark, almost, of good spirits left in me to nourish health in my body."

14

The Queen's Frog

"You may tell his Majesty that the
Prince will be my husband."

"If I were a milkmaid with a pail on my arm, whereby my private person would be little set by," the Queen once told Parliament, "I would not forsake that poor and single state to match with a monarch. . . . Yet for your behalf, there is no way so difficult that may touch my private person which I will not well content myself to take."

Some time before it had been suggested that she might consider taking as a husband the youngest brother of her former suitor, the Duke of Anjou, Francis, Duke of Alençon. He was reported to be very short and extremely ugly, with a face not only scarred by smallpox but with a nose so large as to appear to be worn for a joke. He was also not yet nineteen while the Queen was by then thirty-nine and it had for some time been widely supposed that her talk of marriage was merely carried on for reasons of diplomacy. Certainly when negotiations had seemed to be progressing well in the past, she had been quick to point out her suitor's disadvantages. There seemed little reason any more to doubt her earlier declaration to an envoy from the Emperor: "If I am to disclose to you what I should prefer if I followed the inclination of my nature, it is this: beggar woman and single, far rather than queen and married." Moreover, if she were to marry, she would be far less remarkable as a woman than she had always represented herself as being. Ordinary women might marry; a virgin queen was in a different position altogether.

Yet the Duke of Alençon was said to be intelligent, to talk well and, on occasions, amusingly; and unlike his brother he was believed not to be so staunch a Catholic that the Huguenots found him objectionable. As for his ugliness, this had been much exaggerated, so Fénélon assured the Council. It would certainly not present an insuperable problem even to one "with such a delicate eye as she." Besides, the Duke would soon grow a beard and that would help to hide such defects as there were. Burghley was in favor of the match, considering even the possibility of calling in specialists for the removal of the marks of smallpox from the Duke's face. Yet from past experience he had cause to believe that her Majesty would not be brought to settle her mind to any marriage. It was, therefore, with doubt that it could ever be brought to pass that on 22 August 1572 he wrote to Coligny to say that he thought the marriage "more important for the good of this realm and of Christendom in general, and for the advancement of religion, than I fear our sins will suffer us to receive." Two days after this letter was written Coligny was slain in the massacre of Huguenots in Paris on St. Bartholomew's day; and public opinion in England was outraged by the evident involvement of the French court in the murders.

The Queen, however, appeared quite kindly disposed towards the marriage to Alençon, considering that friendship with the French court and government was more important than a display of righteous indignation over the St. Bartholomew's Day Massacre. But she told the French ambassador when she saw him that summer that she would not be able to commit herself until she had met the duke and been able to judge of his merits for herself. In the meantime she was clearly anxious to show the duke's representatives at her court, de Bocqueville and his suite, that the Queen of England was a prize well worth striving for. The court was on progress in East Anglia and was staying for a few days at Long Melford in Suffolk, where her host was required to entertain the French entourage as well as her Majesty's household. At dinner the Queen inquired why there was so little gold plate on the table, evidently concerned that the French visitors should not presume that the display at Long Melford was to be compared with the splendor of the settings to be seen at Whitehall or Hampton Court. The Lord Chamberlain, the practical and straightforward Earl of Sussex, disobligingly answered that he had been on progress in Henry VIII's time and had never seen so much gold on a table when the court was on the move. The Queen turned on him in fury, complaining that men like him were unworthy of regard or reward and, turning to Lord North, she asked him for his opinion. North, thus forced to choose between telling the truth and saying there was little gold on display, prudently chose to say that her Majesty was quite right: there was, indeed, not much gold plate to be seen, a submission which later prompted the Lord Chamberlain to attack North for his servility and to berate him so severely that Leicester had to come between the disputants to calm them down.

There were further unpleasant scenes after dinner when the dancing began and the Queen, eager to show how gracefully an Englishman could perform, sent the young Earl of Oxford a message asking him to join in. Annoyed by the Queen's public berating of the Lord Chamberlain, Oxford declined to dance. The Queen repeated her request; Oxford still refused to move, adding that he saw no reason why he should do anything to please the French. The page, perhaps, delivered a more mollifying message, for the Queen did not persist.

The negotiations for the French marriage continued, however, unpopular though they were in the country at large and opposed as they were by Leicester and most other Councilors apart from Sussex and Burghley. Another envoy from France, Jehan de Simier – "a most choice courtier, exquisitely skilled in love-toys, pleasant conceits, and court dalliances" – arrived in England at the beginning of 1579 to represent the interests of his master who had become Duke of Anjou since his brother's accession as Henry III and who had plans to invade the Netherlands, defeat the Spanish there and take over the government in their place. Soon after his arrival, so the Spanish ambassador heard, Simier consulted doctors as to the possibility of the forty-five-year-old Queen bearing a child. Apparently reassured on this important point, he paid court on the duke's behalf to the Queen. She was obviously captivated by his charm, his insinuating flattery, his lively sense of humor, his daring in creeping into her bedchamber to steal a nightcap to send to his master. His ready response to her intelligence and wit was such that both Hatton and Leicester were reported to be "growing much annoyed." Hatton told Sir Thomas Heneage that he loved the Queen quite as much as he who "by greatness of a kingly birth was deemed most fit to have her." Leicester maintained that Simier's hold over the Queen, his convincing her of the ill-favored and dissolute Duke of Anjou's worthiness to be considered a suitable husband, was due less to his skills as an advocate than to the drinks he gave her and the "unlawful arts" he practiced upon her. She was clearly fascinated by him. She called him her "Monkey"; and there were reports that she had burst into his bedroom very early one morning and told him to talk to her "with only his jerkin on."

Indeed, Leicester feared that so besotted by Simier had she become – and so intrigued by his accounts of the Duke – the Queen would disregard the people's revulsion against the match, that she would even agree to the conditions the French had demanded, conditions quite as unreasonable as those formerly required by the duke's brother. Leicester went to see the Queen and begged her, if she had the wishes of her people at heart, not to grant a passport allowing Anjou into England.

At any other time Leicester's plea might have been effective. But not long before he had contracted a secret marriage to Lettice Knollys, the widowed Countess of Essex. This was now common knowledge at court, though it had not yet reached the ears of the Queen. Simier ensured that it did so one day at Greenwich, with predictable results. The Queen's fury was boundless, her sense of betrayal overwhelming. She demanded Leicester's immediate arrest; she would have him sent to the Tower; for the moment he was to be incarcerated in the Tower Mireflore in Greenwich Park. As he had done in the past, the Lord Chamberlain, the Earl of Sussex, conscientiously took it upon himself to calm her down, to prevent her from taking steps which she would afterwards regret. After all, Sussex suggested, the Earl of Leicester had done nothing wrong; he was free to marry; his arrest could scarcely be justified in the eyes of the world. The Queen was gradually soothed by Sussex's sensible and sympathetic words. Leicester was released; and, not for the first time relying upon the Queen's readiness to visit sick friends in her alarm that they might die and leave her, he gave it out that he was ill. The Queen, as he had hoped, hurried to his bedside at Wanstead and all was made right again. Provided that his wife did not appear at court, he might return there himself when he was better. The Queen stayed two days at Wanstead; and, when she left, Leicester knew that he had been forgiven and was once more in her confidence.

All the same, the Duke of Anjou was given his passport and prepared to sail. His visit to England was meant to be a secret; but it was spoken of everywhere, not just at court, where two ladies, notorious for their gossip, were confined to their rooms until it was over. In the country at large news of it was received with much indignation. Simier was fired upon as he walked through a London street; and, some time later, as he was being rowed down to Greenwich in the royal barge with the Queen, Sir Christopher Hatton and the Earl of Lincoln, a serving-man named Appletree let off two or three shots from a gun in what seemed to be attempted murder. The Queen and Simier, Hatton and Lincoln all escaped; but a boatman was wounded in the arm, and Appletree, who turned out to be a clumsy simpleton with no evil intent, was sentenced to death and was about to be hanged in the courtyard of Windsor Castle when, to the cheers of the crowd, the Queen sent a reprieve which was contrived to arrive within minutes of his death.

The auspices for Anjou's visit could hardly have been less favorable. But the Queen appeared to be as charmed by him as Simier had led her to expect she would be. He was certainly very small and very ugly; but he was also most entertaining and disarmingly eager. He arrived on the morning of 16 August 1579, so early that Simier was still in bed; and he requested to be taken to the Queen at once. Only with difficulty was he persuaded to lie down himself for a time to recover from the effects of his journey. "At last

I persuaded him to take some rest," Simier wrote to the Queen, "and soon got him between the sheets and I wish to God you were with him there as he could then with greater ease convey his thoughts to you."

When he arose and was taken to her, the Queen, although his presence in England was still meant to be a secret, delighted in the attentions he paid her and did all she could to ensure that they were well observed by the court. Bestowing upon him one of those epithets which it was her habit to give to her favorites and servants, she called him her "frog," a nickname which, while appropriate enough, might have been considered unwelcome but which he seems to have accepted with pleasure. A week after his arrival there was a ball at court. The Queen joined in the dancing with enthusiasm, glancing at her "frog" from time to time as he stood watching her from behind a tapestry, making gestures in his direction, playfully acknowledging the presence of a man who was supposed not to be there and whom the courtiers, joining in the game, pretended not to notice.

Four days after this ball, Anjou was recalled to the country he had not officially left by the death of a friend who had been killed in a duel. But before sailing from Dover he sent messages to the Queen assuring her of his love and couched in terms of such fiery passion that the French ambassador described them as being hot enough to set water aflame.

After his departure the Queen introduced his name into her conversations as frequently as she had once introduced that of the Earl of Leicester, remarking upon his wit, his elegant manners, his astute grasp of political realities if not, as in Leicester's case, his handsome face and beauty of form. And even those who did not recognize in the Duke the exceptional qualities to which the Queen so often referred had to agree that a close alliance with France, if it could be arranged on favorable terms, would be highly desirable. This was particularly so now that Philip was on the verge of becoming King of Portugal as well as of Spain on the death of the Portuguese Cardinal–King, the last ruler of the house of Aviz, and now that the religious wars in France had been brought to a temporary halt by the Peace of Bergerac.

It was at this time, in the month of the Duke of Anjou's departure from England, that there appeared in London a pamphlet entitled *The Discoverie of a gaping gulf whereinto England is like to be swallowed by another French marriage if the Lord forbid not the banes [banns] by letting her majestie see the sin and punishment thereof.* The author was John Stubbs, a Norfolk landowner who had been to Cambridge, had studied law at Lincoln's Inn and had become a Puritan zealot. His pamphlet was respectful and complimentary towards "our dear Queen Elizabeth," who was being "led blindfold as a poor lamb to the slaughter," but virulent in its attack upon the motives of the Roman Catholic Duke of Anjou. And, to her Majesty's fury, it not only suggested that a French husband would have an undue influence over her but that, now she had passed her forty-fifth birthday, it was unlikely she would bear "her first child at these years." Surely the Queen, having this improbability in mind, and having so frequently in the past voiced her "constant dislike" and "indisposed mind" towards marriage, could not really wish to lose her virginity now to a man who, apart from being a Roman Catholic, was wholly unworthy of her, who came from a family notoriously diseased by "God's punishment on flesh and bones," and who could not have other than devious reasons for wanting to marry a woman so much older than himself. Stubbs prayed to God to grant "honourable, healthful, joyful, peaceful, and long sovereignty" to her Majesty "without any superior over-ruling commander, especially French, namely Monsieur."

Stubbs's protestations of loyalty to the Queen were as nothing to her when weighed in the balance against his remarks about her age, and his typically Puritan condescension towards her as a woman, his suggestion that she could no longer have children, his implication that the courting and planning, the flattery and attention of suitors, which she had so much enjoyed in the past, could never be enjoyed again, his suggestion that the complimentary overtures of the Duke of Anjou must have been insincere, his bringing into open day the unacceptable belief that the Queen, as a potential wife and mother, was no longer an important piece on the chessboard of European diplomacy. Besides all this, the pamphlet was a blatant insult to the brother of a friendly king and an impertinent Puritan attempt to influence government policy. If the Queen were to marry, she wished it to be seen as a sacrifice in the interests of her country, not as a gratification of self-indulgence.

On 27 September a royal proclamation was issued prohibiting the further distribution of Stubbs's pamphlet, copies of which had now reached towns all over southern England; and a fortnight later the author, the publisher, William Page, and the printer and bookseller, Hugh Singleton, were put on trial at Westminster on a charge of disseminating seditious writings under an Act passed in 1555 to protect Queen Mary and her husband Philip from "libellous attack." Following the guidance of the Lord Chief Justice, the jury returned a verdict of guilty, and the defendants, as was usual in such cases, were all sentenced to have their right hands cut off. The verdict was questioned by several lawyers, who maintained that the 1555 Act had been passed specifically to protect Philip and Mary and had been abrogated at Mary's death; but the Lord Chief Justice firmly held that the Act was still operative because the rights and privileges of monarchy were immediately transferred upon death to the monarch's successor and that, in any case, this particular piece of legislation had been re-enacted by Elizabeth's first Parliament. One lawyer who continued to insist that the verdict was illegal was sent to the Tower; another who agreed with him, was sent to the Fleet Prison and, on refusing to retract his opinion, was ordered to resign his office and to leave London.

The publisher was pardoned but the printer, Hugh Singleton, and Stubbs himself were brought from the Tower to a scaffold erected in Westminster marketplace, although both the Duke of Anjou and the French ambassador had asked her to pardon them too.

"I pray you all to pray with me that God will strengthen me to endure and abide the pain that I am to suffer," Stubbs said in his address to the crowd, "and grant me this grace that the loss of my hand do not withdraw any part of my duty and affection toward her Majesty . . . My masters, if there be any among you that do love me, if your love be not in God and her Majesty, I utterly deny your love."

When his speech was over, he placed his right wrist upon the block and the executioner took up a butcher's cleaver and a mallet and struck off the hand at a blow. "I can remember standing by John Stubbs," wrote John Stow, the antiquary, "and as soon as his right hand was off [he] put off his hat with his left, and cryed aloud, 'God save the Queen!' The people round about stood mute, whether stricken with fear at the first sight of this kind of punishment, or for commiseration of the man whom they deputed honest."

After uttering "God save the Queen!" Stubbs fainted; but Page endured the pain of his bleeding stump being seared with a hot iron and exclaimed, "I have left there the hand of a true Englishman." Both men were carried back to the Tower, Stubbs being set free from imprisonment eighteen months later, his plea for an earlier release on the grounds of his wife's ill health having been refused.

The Queen had expressed the opinion that Stubbs ought to be hanged and had burst into tears when the Council gravely informed her that they would take the responsibility of breaking off negotiations with the Duke of Anjou if that was what she wanted to do. She told the Councilors that she had not yet made up her mind; she had expected, she said, that they would have wanted her to marry and have children. Why was it, she asked them, that she, and she alone, was denied the right to a husband and children?

Eventually, after a wearisome meeting at which Burghley himself took down the minutes – the clerks being dismissed from the room for the eleven hours of delicate discussions – the Privy Council sent her word that they reserved judgement until her own wishes were known. She replied crossly that she was asking for advice. They then let it be known that they would approve the marriage if it pleased her. This was not sufficiently positive. Eventually the Council decided cautiously to recommend that she should refuse the Duke of Anjou's offer because there was such strong objection to the marriage in the country. She accepted their advice with apparent reluctance, although clearly influenced by references to public opinion. But she refused to write to Anjou with a definite rejection of his proposal.

The Spanish ambassador heard that the decision had made her extremely gloomy, that she had told her ladies how much she had wanted to marry and have children, that she had castigated everybody who had opposed the marriage, reserving particular scorn for Walsingham, who had made it clear that he now disapproved of the match. She made her own feelings plain by sending the rejected suitor a present of jewels worth eight thousand crowns.

The affair, however, was not yet quite over. In June 1581 the Duke of Anjou once again came to England in secret. Worsening relations between the English and Spanish governments had made a French alliance desirable once more. So had the Duke of Anjou's acceptance of an offer to become their ruler which had been made to him by the rebels in the Netherlands, as well as the overthrow and execution of the anglophile Regent of Scotland, the Earl of Morton.

Anjou's visit had been preceded by that of an embassy sent from France to discuss with the Privy Council the terms of the settlement. One of the members of this embassy, Marchaumont, had accompanied the Queen to Deptford where Sir Francis Drake's *Golden Hind* lay at anchor after its return from its voyage round the world with a hold packed full of Spanish treasures. As they were walking across the gangplank into the ship the Queen's garter came undone, as it did not infrequently, and trailed along beneath the hem of her skirt. Marchaumont asked if he could keep it to send to his master, the Duke. The Queen replied that for the moment she had no other means of keeping up her stocking and replaced it there and then, allowing Marchaumont to see her leg as she did so. When they had been rowed back to Westminster she gave him the garter for presentation to the Duke, a memento of whom Sir Francis Drake had already given her, a frog made of diamonds to go with one of her favorite ornaments, "a little flower of gold with a frog thereon," and "therein Mounseer his phisnomye."

The Queen's dress was covered with these and other jewels when, a fortnight later, she welcomed the French delegates to a grand reception in a huge painted marquee with nearly three hundred glass windows which had been erected in the riverside gardens of Whitehall Palace at a cost of over £1,700, its roof painted to resemble the sky and hung with wreaths of evergreen and baskets of fruit sprinkled with gold leaf. The subsequent celebrations and entertainments were of remarkable grandeur. Magnificent dinner parties were given for the French guests by Leicester and Burghley as well as by the Queen. There were bear-baitings and river pageants and a splendid allegorical spectacle in which four knights, brilliantly accoutred and mounted, made an attack upon the Castle of Perfect Beauty, which serenely withstood their assault. A few days after this display, the French delegates were invited to call upon Burghley at Cecil House to discuss the purpose of their visit.

Several Councilors who had already made it clear that they disapproved of the proposed marriage repeated their objections. The Earl of Leicester's nephew, Sir Philip Sidney, wrote a letter to the Queen which, with a boldness that led to his absence from court for a time, emphasized how strongly her subjects disapproved of a match with a "Frenchman and a Papist . . . the son of a Jezebel of our age." The Queen's own feelings were well concealed. She had been delighted to receive from the Duke of Anjou a sympathetic letter with one of her favorite jewels, an emerald, stuck into its seal, and she sent him in return a letter with a diamond attached. But she would still give no certain answer regarding her intentions. "She wants nothing in the world so much as you," one of Anjou's agents in London told him; "and there is no one in the world she would rather have near her," provided *"il se pouvait faire sans enfants . . . Il semble que par la disposition de son corps, elle aye peur de mourir."* She told Anjou herself that if she married him she feared she would not have long to live.

From Paris – where as a known opponent of the match the Queen had deviously sent him to promote it – Walsingham wrote to her, urging her to make up her mind since, by hesitating, she lost "the benefit of time which (your years considered) is not the least thing to be weighed." At the same time Walsingham strongly expressed his exasperation to Burghley: "I should repute it a greater favour to be committed into the Tower, unless her Majesty may grow more certain . . . I would to God she would resolve one way or the other." The King, he said, was losing all patience.

Yet the Queen continued to prevaricate. When the French commissioners arrived at Cecil House, they were astonished to be told that, whereas a formal alliance with France was perfectly agreeable to the Queen and the Privy Council, there was no need to cement it by a marriage. A few months later, however, marriage seemed once again on the cards when the Queen authorized Burghley to send Anjou £30,000 in silver to help him further his plans to become ruler of the Netherlands.

His mother, Catherine de Médicis, had never liked the idea of an alliance without a marriage; and when the Duke of Anjou himself arrived in England on an official visit in November that year, the Queen also seemed to have rejected the plan. She appeared to be more devoted to the Duke than ever, though still careful to keep everyone unsure of what her real intentions were. Shortly before Anjou's arrival she sent a message to Lord Burghley, who was ill with gout, asking him what he wanted her to do. Yet within a short time of the Duke's appearance she seemed to have made up her own mind. She persuaded him to go with her to St. Paul's Cathedral and there kissed him in sight of the congregation; and on Accession Day she and the Duke were seen walking in the gallery of Whitehall Palace after dinner. The French ambassador, Michel de Castelnau, Sieur de Mauvissière, who had replaced Fénélon, went up to them and, encouraged by their evident affection for each other, asked if he might tell his master, the King, that they were to be married. The Queen kissed the Duke on the mouth, took a ring from her hand, placed it on his finger and declared unequivocally, "You may tell his Majesty that the Prince will be my husband." Anjou "gave her a ring of his in return," Mendoza, the Spanish ambassador reported, "and shortly afterwards the Queen summoned the ladies and gentlemen from the Presence Chamber into the gallery, repeating to them in a loud voice in [Anjou's] presence what she had just said."

The Queen could scarcely have made a more astounding pronouncement. Soon the whole court knew of it and the Privy Council were appalled. Her ladies were instructed to bewail the fearful state of marriage, its unpleasantness and the dreadful restrictions and duties it imposed. Hatton, with tears in his eyes, told her that however much her people loved her, they would not be able to forgive her this. Leicester more roughly asked her whether she were a woman or a maid. She answered them both calmly and patiently: they need not be disturbed; nothing had been said which could not be unsaid. And very soon they were unsaid.

After a sleepless night, the Queen sent a message to the Duke: she was frightened that if she married him, she told him again, she might not long survive the ceremony; she knew he would not want to take that risk; she would always be his friend. He snatched the ring which she had given him from his finger and cast it furiously to the ground. He would rather they both died, he later declared, than not marry her; and when the Queen said that she hoped he was not threatening an old woman in her own realm, he burst out, "No, no, Madame, you mistake. I meant no hurt to your blessed person. I meant only that I would sooner be cut in pieces than not marry you and so be laughed at by the world."

He began to weep; she handed him her handkerchief. It was arranged that he should leave for France but come back in six weeks and then, perhaps, they would get married after all. Already, however, terms had been proposed which put a marriage quite out of court. Demanding as they were, the stipulations put forward by the Privy Council had been accepted by the French King and his mother. But then the Queen once again insisted that they must include the return of Calais. Later she said that if the Duke of Anjou's intervention in the Netherlands involved her in war with Spain, the French must bear the cost of all her military operations. Since these outrageous demands might not only bring the marriage discussions to an immediate halt but lead to diplomatic relations being severed altogether, the Council suggested that the Duke should be given £200,000 to take away with him by way of compensation. As might have been expected, the Queen was appalled at the thought of parting with so much, and commented that if the Duke would consider accepting it instead of herself, she would certainly not marry him, nor give him the money either, and he could do what he liked about it. To the Earl of Sussex she confided at this time that she was coming to dislike the idea of marriage more and more. She had good reasons to do so, she added, but she would not reveal what these were, even to a twin had she one.

Then, while the Duke of Anjou was waiting for a favorable wind to take him across the Channel, a messenger arrived at court from the King of France to say that if the Queen still held out for marriage on the impossible terms she had proposed, the French would have no alternative but to enter into alliance with the Spaniards. On receipt of this ultimatum, the Queen spent another wakeful night, constantly calling upon her Mistress of the Robes for one petty purpose or another. She felt ill the next day, stayed in bed, and in the evening sent for the Earl of Sussex to say that she imagined that she must now pay no heed to her own inclinations but marry Anjou after all. Exhausted by her changes of mood and mind, Sussex wearily asked her not to talk to him about it any more. Would she please just tell him what she had decided to do when she had made up her mind to do it.

Burghley was more patient. He told her, when they were alone together, that she must decide between two alternatives: she must marry the

Duke or agree to allow him a sum even larger than that already proposed, together with the promise of a naval escort to take him to the Netherlands where the people were waiting to create him Duke of Brabant. Making over so huge a sum was a dreadful prospect to her; but the imminence of marriage was even worse. She went down to Kent with the Duke and said goodbye to him with emotional affection. They exchanged loving letters, and although she had brought herself to part with £60,000 towards the cost of his campaign, his confession of desolation at their parting brought from her the declaration that she would willingly give a million to see her "Frog" swimming in the Thames again. She instructed Leicester to accompany him to Antwerp and subsequently made a great display of anger when Leicester was reported to have said that he left him there "like an old hulk run ashore high and dry . . . stuck upon a sandbank."

The news of the ending of the marriage negotiations came as no surprise to Philip II, who had known the Queen for longer than nearly all her Councilors. He told Mendoza that he had always felt sure she would break them off in the end; and there were those who believed that she had never really intended to marry the Duke anyway, that her protestations of regard for him and her ostentatious parade of affection were merely meant to convince the French and Spanish that the prolonged negotiations were in earnest, that the whole purpose of the enterprise was to gain time and to keep the peace by the prospects of close alliance, that the Protestant party at court led by Leicester would be as sure to prevent the marriage as Burghley had prevented her marriage to Leicester himself years before. Some of her ladies said that she danced for joy in her bedchamber when she was given the news that the Duke had sailed at last from Sandwich. Yet when news reached England in June 1584 that he had died – after proving himself a most inefficient commander in the Netherlands – she made a public display of her grief and ordered the court into mourning. "Now melancholy doth so posses us," said Walsingham, "as both public and private causes are at a stay for a season."

There were to be no other marriage negotiations of any serious intent. Elizabeth was, as she had more than once said was her desire, to die the Virgin Queen. "I know the truth of that, madam," Sir James Melville, the Scottish diplomat, claimed to have been bold enough to suggest years before in response to her own declaration that she would not marry unless obliged to do so. "Ye need not tell me. I know your stately stomach. Ye think, gin ye were married, ye would be but Queen of England, and now ye are King and Queen baith. I know your spirit. Ye cannot suffer a commander."

15

"This Most Wicked and Filthy Woman"

"These treasons will be proved to
you and all made manifest."

On 23 November 1583 Francis Throckmorton, a nephew of Sir Nicholas and an ardent Catholic who had not long since returned from a continental tour, was brought down from his cell in the Tower of London and tied upon the rack. It was known that he had visited several leading English Catholics in exile during the course of his tour and, as the Privy Council's spies reported, that he had subsequently paid frequent visits to the house of the Spanish ambassador in London, Don Bernardino de Mendoza. In his own house had been discovered not only various treatises in defense of the Queen of Scots's title to the English throne and "six or seven pamphlets against (her Majesty Queen Elizabeth) printed beyond sea," but also plans of English harbors where foreign troops could be landed and a list of Catholics living in England who were believed to be ready to rebel against Queen Elizabeth in the Queen of Scots's cause.

Throckmorton withstood the pain of his first racking; but when he was twice tortured again on 2 December and threatened with further agonies he confessed that an invasion of England was, indeed, planned and that the Queen of Scots was privy to the plot. The ropes and straps were undone and he was lifted onto the seat beside the rack. "Now," he said, "I have betrayed her who was dearest to me in this world." He wished he were dead, he added; and soon he was. Executed at Tyburn the following summer, he called upon God from the scaffold to witness that his confession had been drawn from him in the hope of pardon. One of his fellow conspirators, the Earl of Northumberland, shot himself through the heart in the Tower; another, Lord Paget, fled abroad and soon afterwards died at Brussels.

Deeply concerned for the Queen's safety and, by inevitable extension, for their own, the Privy Council drew up a Bond of Association by which, in the dreaded event of her Majesty's assassination, they undertook to destroy both those responsible for her murder and all in whose interests the crime had been committed. Copies of the Bond were distributed far and wide and thousands of loyal subjects signed them, to the great pleasure of the Queen who saw in the Bond a most satisfactory way of dealing with the Queen of Scots while evading all responsibility herself for her punishment. Parliament also took steps to secure the safety of the Queen as best its Members could, decreeing that any claimant to the throne who could be shown by a committee of Councilors, bishops and judges to have had foreknowledge of her Majesty's assassination, should be excluded from the succession, and that all Jesuits and seminary priests who had entered the country within the past twenty-five years should be expelled within forty days, anyone sheltering them to be treated as a felon.

Sir Christopher Hatton, Member for Northamptonshire, informed the House of Commons that he had been given a prayer which had been written by a worthy man for the Queen's preservation and asked permission to read it out. He did so, pausing after each sentence, so that the Members could repeat the words, which they did, kneeling down before the benches.

The common people, too, knelt down before the Queen to demonstrate their sympathy and their support of her in her present trials. The Spanish ambassador was riding with her a few days before Christmas on the way from Hampton Court to London. The roads were muddy as they always were at that time of year when they were not frozen or slippery with ice; but the people sank to their knees all the same, calling out blessings upon herself and curses upon her enemies. The Queen remarked to Mendoza that, as he could see, not everyone wanted her dead.

Mendoza's days in England were almost at an end. At the beginning of January he was summoned to a meeting of the Privy Council at which, so that there should be no question of his misunderstanding, he was addressed in Italian since his English was poor and most Councilors' Spanish was equally limited. Walsingham, who had undertaken to do the talking – his Italian, so he claimed, being better than anyone else's – told Mendoza that his complicity in the Throckmorton plot had been established and that he was to leave the country within fifteen days; he should consider himself lucky to be merely expelled and not otherwise punished. The words were spoken "so impertinently," Mendoza reported to King Philip, that he dared not repeat them to his Majesty verbatim. He replied to Walsingham that he would need more time to make the necessary arrangements for his departure; and when told by the now standing Councilors that he would not be granted any more time, he added that, as he had failed in his endeavors to please Queen Elizabeth as a minister of peace, he would now endeavor to satisfy her in war. "The insolence of these people so exasperates me," Mendoza concluded his report, "that I desire to live only to be revenged on them."

Transferred to Paris, Mendoza kept in touch with dissident English Catholics and maintained his secret contacts with Mary Queen of Scots, against whom no action had been taken following the Throckmorton revelations. Mendoza's continuing correspondence with Mary came as no surprise to the Council; nor did reports of the trouble she was causing in the household of her guardian, the Earl of Shrewsbury.

Shrewsbury had carried out his unwelcome duties with tact and care, moving his charge from one house to another as the situation demanded and his orders required, from Tutbury to Coventry, from Chatsworth to Sheffield Castle, foiling plots to release her and dealing as best he could with the spies in her household and the conspirators amongst her attendants. He had asked from time to time to be relieved of his post, but all his requests had been turned down; and in 1579 his already inadequate allowance as Queen Mary's keeper had been reduced by about a quarter. He was plagued not only by Queen Mary but also by his wife, who had once been an over-intimate friend of his charge but was now on the worst possible terms with her, having, in her rampantly ambitious way, arranged for a marriage between Elizabeth Cavendish, one of her daughters "by her second husband, and Charles Stuart, Earl of Lennox, a younger brother of Lord Darnley. Soon after the marriage Elizabeth Cavendish gave birth to a girl, Arabella, who, as a direct descendant of Henry VII, represented a threat both to the claims of the Queen of Scots and to the peace of mind of the Queen of England. Elizabeth had the mother sent to the Tower for a time for having dared to marry and to give birth to so inconvenient a child, while Mary grew increasingly resentful of the child's grandmother, of whom she had once been fond. In order to make life as unpleasant for her as she could, she wrote to Queen Elizabeth to pass on scandalous gossip which she claimed to have had from Lady Shrewsbury's own lips.

Mary had heard from the Countess, so she said in one of her letters, that Queen Elizabeth had been to bed with the Duke of Anjou; she was also reported to have slept with Jehan de Simier, his envoy, to whom she had passed on state secrets. Sir Christopher Hatton had felt obliged to leave her court because he was made so uncomfortable by her fawning love for him. Her ladies dared not look at her from fear of laughing because of her absurd delight in the most fulsome flattery. She lost her temper with them so uncontrollably that she attacked one with a knife and broke another's finger. Her body was so deformed that a husband, if she were ever so fortunate as to find one, would be unable to consummate the marriage. A marriage was most unlikely, though, since she did not have long to live. Lady Shrewsbury had said much more than this; but Mary would keep the rest in reserve until a meeting with Elizabeth could be arranged.

Although Elizabeth seems not to have seen this letter, which was found amongst Burghley's papers after his death, she did learn of the rumors being circulated by Lady Shrewsbury, her Cavendish sons and her agent, Henry Beresford, to the effect that her husband, who was on increasingly ill-natured terms with his wife, was conducting an adulterous affair with the Queen of Scots. The Countess and her sons were required to present themselves before the Privy Council to whom they admitted having repeated the slanders which they had been told, but maintained that they themselves did not believe them. The Queen herself, anxious to heal the breach between husband and wife, offered to act as mediator, and suggested that the family papers should be handed over for examination. This was done but no settlement could be reached; and eventually Lady Shrewsbury left her husband, settled at Chatsworth and devoted her great wealth to building other houses, including Hardwick Hall in Derbyshire where she died. By then her husband had at last managed to give up the charge of his prisoner into the hands of Sir Ralph Sadler, profoundly relieved to have been delivered from "those two demons," his wife and the Queen of Scots.

Mary, however, was still in a position to make trouble for Elizabeth. Since the Throckmorton plot her freedom to use her dowry from France to pay her agents and to keep constantly in touch with Paris and Edinburgh had been curtailed. But she was still, by her own very existence, able to endanger that of the Queen. "So long as that devilish woman lives," wrote Walsingham who for ten years and more had been trying to get incontrovertible proof of her guilt through his network of spies, "neither her Majesty must make account to continue in quiet possession of her crown, nor her faithful servants assure themselves of safety of their lives." It had long been recognized that Elizabeth's death was a prerequisite of any successful rebellion or invasion launched to place Mary on the throne, and the problems of the Queen's security were constantly discussed by her Councilors. They suggested that she should no longer ride or walk anywhere unattended, that she should be accompanied at all times by an armed bodyguard; yet the idea of cutting herself off from the sight and reassuring admiration of her people was appalling to her. She would rather be in her grave than in such restraint, though to her grave, as she had good reason to know, there were conspirators enough eager to consign her.

Soon after William Parry had plotted with the Queen of Scots's friends to murder Elizabeth and had been hanged, drawn and quartered, another conspiracy was unearthed. By now Queen Mary was under the watchful eye of Sir Ralph Sadler's successor, Sir Amyas Paulet, a zealous and conscientious Puritan who had succeeded his father as Governor of Jersey and had become British ambassador in Paris where he had reported on the activities of the Huguenots with marked approval. Although the Earl of Leicester found him too unbending a character for his taste, he had much impressed Walsingham, who warmly recommended him for his new post. He was instructed to treat his charge far more strictly than she had been in the past: she was to be severely circumscribed in her activities, to be kept, indeed, in carefully guarded seclusion, no longer allowed to live as though presiding over a court; her correspondence was to be examined without her knowledge. Paulet agreed to observe these rules to the letter, undertaking to treat the Queen with respect but firm authority. Were an attempt made to rescue her, he said, he would not shrink from killing her with his own hand. His diligence was not, however, to be financially rewarding. He was not a conspicuously rich man and could not afford to bear the expense that the Earl of Shrewsbury had borne. Queen Elizabeth nevertheless required him to spend much of his own money in maintaining the Queen of Scots's attendants, who were more than fifty in number, as well as his own household, which included thirty soldiers.

Soon after his appointment, Paulet was told to arrange for his charge's transfer from Tutbury Castle to Chartley, a house in the same county belonging to the Earl of Essex where the expenses of keeping her were much increased. Having with great difficulty supervised a removal that necessitated the hire of eighty carts, Paulet was told that there were to be further alterations in the manner of the Queen of Scots's supervision. The strict watch that he was keeping on her activities was preventing her corresponding as freely as she had done before with the agents of foreign powers and much useful intelligence was thereby being lost. Walsingham had discussed the matter with her Majesty and it had been decided therefore that one of Walsingham's spies at Chartley, Gilbert Gifford, a young renegade Catholic with the appearance of an exceptionally cherubic chorister, should arrange for the prisoner's secret letters to be taken out of the house in a waterproof bag inside a beer barrel and for letters intended for her eyes only to be smuggled to her in the same way. The barrels were to be carried to Paulet, the letters extracted, their contents deciphered by the Privy Council's cryptologist and the translated versions sent to Walsingham and to Queen Elizabeth.

In May 1586 there began slowly to emerge the outlines of a serious conspiracy, once more involving the murder of Elizabeth. Among the conspirators were John Ballard, a Catholic priest, Thomas Morgan, the Queen of Scots's agent in Paris, Don Bernadino de Mendoza, the Spanish ambassador there, and Anthony Babington.

Babington was a charming, extremely rich young man from an ancient family. His father was "inclined to papistrie," and Babington himself was brought up in the Catholic faith to which he was to display the most fervent attachment. He had served as a page to the Queen of Scots, for whom he had conceived a passionate devotion; and afterwards in London he had joined a secret society of fellow Catholics committed to her cause and to the support and maintenance of Jesuit missionaries in England. These young men met frequently in various London taverns to discuss their plans, including the assassination of Queen Elizabeth – a task that Babington eagerly undertook to perform himself – as well as the release of the Queen of Scots, whom he was anxious should be fully informed about the part he personally was to play in her salvation.

He was blithely confident of success. He had his portrait drawn with his friends – "the Pope's white sons for divers pieces of services" – and he wrote a long letter to the Queen of Scots, describing how he intended to release her and how "six noble gentlemen" had undertaken to be responsible for the "tragical execution" of her "usurping competitor."

All this became known to Elizabeth who – frightened though she was by the prospect of the six noble gentlemen shooting or stabbing her at any moment – agreed that Babington should not be arrested for the time being, that Walsingham should hold his hand until more details of the plot had been revealed, until more of the conspirators had been identified, and until the Queen of Scots's reply to Babington's letter had been extracted from the beer barrel.

On 17 July Mary sat down to write her answer. She approved the plan in general, made various criticisms of it in particular, asked when help from Spain was to be expected, and concluded, "the affair being thus prepared and forces in readiness both within and without the realm, then shall it be time to set the six gentlemen to work, taking order, upon the accomplishment of their design, I may suddenly be rescued from this place."

The Queen of Scots was now fully implicated, and the Queen of England did not scruple to refer to her as "a wicked murderess" in a letter thanking Sir Amyas Paulet for having "so well discharged" his troublesome duty. But the names of the six gentlemen were still unknown. So Walsingham, with Elizabeth's approval, had one of his calligraphers forge a postscript to the Queen of Scots's letter asking for their identities to be divulged.

Days passed and Elizabeth walked in constant danger. She had been shown by one of Walsingham's spies a copy of the picture of Babington and his friends: and while strolling in Richmond Park, surrounded by her ladies and several gentlemen, she recognized one of the men in the portrait, Robert Barnewell, who stole quickly away when she stared at him. Every day further details of the developing plot were gathered, and on 4 August 1586 Walsingham struck at last. The priest John Ballard was arrested without warning after a meeting of the conspirators in one of the London taverns that they frequented. Babington went into hiding, having cut off his hair and dyed his skin with walnut juice. He was discovered before the end of the month and taken to the Tower where, "with a mild countenance," he readily confessed his part in the plot, placing the blame upon Father Ballard. Their fellow conspirators were soon rounded up and brought to trial for crimes for which the decreed punishment was hanging. But hanging, said Elizabeth in a fury of resentment such as she had experienced at the time of the rising of the northern Earls in 1569, was not punishment enough. Enraged by the treason of these contemptible young men who had put her life and the realm at such risk, she wrote to Burghley the day before their trial to command him to tell the judge to deliver the usual sentence but to add that "such is the form usual, but considering the manner of horrible treason against her Majesty's own person which hath not been heard of in this kingdom, it is reason that the manner of their death, for more terror, be referred to her Majesty and her Council." Burghley jibbed at this: the ordinary penalty was quite cruel enough, he maintained; it was, in fact, so cruel that it was usually seen to that the victim was dead before the disembowelling and emasculation took place. "I told her Majesty," he informed Hatton, "that if the execution shall be duly and orderly executed by prolonging the same both to the extremity of the pains in the action, and to the sight of the people to behold it, the manner of death would be as terrible as any new device could be. But herewith her Majesty was not satisfied but commanded me thus to write to you to declare it to the judge and others of the Council there."

In the cases of Ballard and Babington, and those who suffered with them on 20 September – on a scaffold erected in a "fielde at the upper end of Holbourne" – the executioner was obedient to the instructions upon which the Queen had insisted, taking care "to protract the extremity of their pains in the sight of the multitude." Father Ballard was hanged first, while Babington awaited his turn, not kneeling down to pray as was customary, but standing with his hat on his head, "as if he had been but a beholder of the execution" and displaying "a signe of his former pride." He was still alive when taken down from the gallows and as the executioner took up his knife and began to cut open the stomach and pull out the entrails he was heard to murmur, *"Parce mihi, Domine Jesu."*

When she heard of the butchery of this day's executions and the uproar of the crowd, disgusted by the spectacle, Elizabeth thought it as well that when the next lot of prisoners were executed they should be left hanging until they were dead. She gave orders accordingly.

It was now to be decided how to proceed against the Queen of Scots. There was no doubt that her deep complicity in the plot could be proved in court. But when evidence of her guilt had been available in the past, Elizabeth had been reluctant to bring her to trial. She had taken no action, for instance, when a London stationer had divulged on the rack the methods used to convey secret letters to and from the prisoner, nor when it was revealed that Mary was implicated in the landing of Catholic troops in Ireland, nor even when, at the time of the Throckmorton affair, an intercepted letter from Mary clearly implicated her in the plot and assured the conspirators that she would "never forget their affection" for her "and their great suffering" in her cause. Now that Queen Elizabeth's crown had once again been threatened and her life, too, placed in the gravest danger, her Councilors hoped that she might be induced to take the steps from which she had previously shrunk.

Even so it was difficult to persuade her to take the first step, to confirm the Council's arrangements to have her brought to trial; but her agreement to this could not well be refused once she had been induced to have the Queen of Scots's name mentioned in the indictment of Babington.

The prisoner had already been removed from Chartley to Sir Walter Aston's house at Tixall. This change of residence, she was told, had been arranged so that she could enjoy the pleasures of a stag hunt. While she was away from Chartley her coffers and the drawers of her cupboards were searched for further incriminating letters. The next month she was taken to Fotheringhay Castle in Northamptonshire, where she was put on trial before a commission including Sir Amyas Paulet, Walsingham, Burghley, Hatton and over thirty other Councilors, peers and judges, two of them known Catholic sympathizers. Queen Elizabeth remained in London where she sorely missed at such a time her two principal advisers. She instructed Walsingham's assistant, William Davison, a firm Puritan and experienced diplomat, who had been left behind with her, to write to them, telling them how greatly she longed to hear how her "Spirit" and her "Moor" found "themselves after so foul and wearisome a journey."

She had been in a fearful state of indecision ever since she had had to face the prospect of a trial. Her hurriedly written messages to her ministers became virtually illegible. Some of them only Burghley could decipher; one, addressed to the Lord Chancellor, drove him to complain that he could not make out "one half line of it." At first she had thought it might be as well to hold the trial in London, but then she decided against it. Hertford Castle was suggested, but this was too near the capital. She had eventually decided upon the more remote Fotheringhay; but the commissioners must not give their verdict there or pronounce sentence upon Mary until she had been consulted. Orders were sent to Fotheringhay to this effect together with a private letter from Davison to Walsingham expressing the vain hope that the messenger would not reach Fotheringhay with the Queen's instructions in time to prevent a verdict being reached.

The Queen of Scots was behaving as her accusers had expected her to do. At first she had refused to attend the trial on the grounds that she was not subject to jurisdiction in an English court and had, in any event, done nothing wrong.

"You have in various ways and manners attempted to take my life and to bring my kingdom to destruction by bloodshed," Elizabeth had angrily responded to this characteristic protest. "These treasons will be proved to you and all made manifest. It is my will that you answer the nobles and peers of the kingdom as if I were myself present . . . Act plainly without reserve and you will then sooner be able to obtain favour of me."

Even her most ardent supporters could not maintain that Mary acted plainly: she was as devious in her answers as she was dignified in her demeanor. She was brave and passionately eloquent, it could not be denied, and most skillful in avoiding giving direct answers to questions she would prefer not to have been asked. Yet she could not convince her accusers that she was innocent; and, when driven into a corner, having denied a fact subsequently proved, she could only insist that her word must be accepted since it was the "word of a princess."

It was a contention that Elizabeth herself might well have put forward; so she was particularly annoyed when the French ambassador officiously expressed to her the views of Henry III who considered that there was "no special law in England" which could make his sister-in-law subject to any jurisdiction in that country. She had "been born a sovereign princess" and, "by the privilige common to all kings," was "exempt from human jurisdiction and subject only to the judgement of God." Her execution, Mauvissière added, would outrage every king in Christendom.

Elizabeth was herself outraged by this interference. She told Mauvissière, in effect, that his master should mind his own business; if he continued to meddle in her affairs their friendship would not stand it. Besides, the trial could not be stopped now. She gave orders to the commissioners to come to London to give their verdict. This was pronounced in the Star Chamber in Whitehall on 15 October: the Queen of Scots was declared guilty of "imagining and encompassing her Majesty's death."

Fourteen days later Parliament reassembled, much to the annoyance of the Queen, who nervously anticipated the pressure its Members would put upon her. They had been summoned to meet on 15 October; but Elizabeth had postponed their meeting to the 27th and then to the 29th, anxious to put off their demands for the Queen of Scots's death for as long as possible. When she could delay the assembly no longer, her answer was as her Council had feared it would be. She received a delegation from both Houses at Richmond, where she had retired so as to be as far away as reasonable from the debates at Westminster. She was, she said, "loath to hear so many foul and grievous matters revealed," to have Members speaking of Mary in terms insufferably insulting to a queen, calling her "this most wicked and filthy woman," this most "detestable traitor," an "enemy to us all." She thanked the delegates for their loyalty to herself, explained the difficulties of the position in which she had been placed, and assured them that she would willingly die, for the sake of her people, if by her death a better monarch would be found. She lived only to keep them "from a worse." Parliament had "lain a hard hand" upon her by requiring her to give directions for her cousin's death. She would need time to consider what would be "just and honourable" to do. But they would have "with all conveniency" her resolution as soon as her mind was made up. Several delegates were deeply affected by her response. Burghley said some were in tears when she finished. Yet others were concerned that her promised answer would not be soon forthcoming, and their fears were confirmed when Sir Christopher Hatton brought them a message requiring them to suggest means of dealing with the Queen of Scots other than by execution.

The unanimous opinion of both Houses was that the prisoner must die; and the delegates returned to Richmond with this answer on 21 November, when the Queen addressed them in another long and in parts disjointed speech. She asked them to consider that she had just cause to complain that she, who had in her time pardoned so many rebels, "winked at so many treasons . . . or altogether slipped them over with silence," should now be forced to this proceeding against her cousin, the Queen of Scots. During her reign, she went on, she had seen or heard of many opprobious books and pamphlets accusing her of being a tyrant. "I thank them for their alms," she said. "I believe therein their meaning was to tell me news; and news it is to me indeed." What would the authors of these books and pamphlets now say when it was "spread that, for the safety of her life, a maiden queen could be content to spill the blood even of her own kinswoman?

"If I should say I would not do what you request," she added in a conclusion that left more than one of her audience completely in the dark as to her meaning, "it might peradventure be more than I thought, and to say I would do it might perhaps breed peril of that you labour to preserve, being more than in your own wisdom and discretions would seem convenient, circumstances of place and time being duly considered. As for your petition, your judgement I condemn not . . . but pray you to accept my thankfulness, excuse my doubtfulness, and take in good part my answer answerless."

The delegation ruefully returned to London more than ever unsure of her Majesty's intentions, although in no doubt that she dreaded appearing both before her own people and in the eyes of Europe as a vengeful woman or as one who would sacrifice a fellow queen for her own safety. After arriving in London from Richmond the delegates learned to their dismay that she had decided to prorogue Parliament, leaving the question of the proclamation against Mary still undecided. The next day they heard she had changed her mind: Parliament was not to be prorogued but to be adjourned for a week's recess; then, on 2 December, it was announced that Parliament was to be adjourned until 15 February 1587. On 4 December the proclamation adjournment was published. But the warrant for the execution had still to be signed; and the Council could not get it signed.

Early in January Councilors began to hope that they might soon obtain her Majesty's signature. But in the third week a long letter arrived for her Majesty from the Queen of Scots. In it Mary protested against the injustice of her condemnation, pleaded her constant loyalty to the "apostolical Roman church," and made various requests for her servants and for her own body after her death. The Earl of Leicester reported that the reading of its pathetic contents "wrought tears" from the Queen. He told Walsingham that he hoped it would do no more mischief than that; but the delay was dangerous, particularly in her Majesty's present state of mind. Often she sat unwontedly speechless.

On 1 February, while the court was at Greenwich, one of her trusted advisers came to see her. This was Lord Howard of Effingham, the Lord Admiral, who had been one of the commissioners appointed for the Queen of Scots's trial. A courtly man, himself a cousin of the Queen and married to the daughter of her cousin, Lord Hunsdon, he spoke to her as others dared not, telling her that her delay in dealing with the warrant was angering both her Councilors and her subjects. Further procrastination might be fatal.

After Lord Howard had gone the Queen sent for William Davison. For some time she herself had been coming to the conclusion that she could delay no longer. Importunate French and Scottish demands that the warrant should on no account be signed were hardening her resolve. So were rumors of attempts to release the Queen of Scots from her confinement and the discovery of yet another murderous plot, in which the brother of the English ambassador in Paris was involved. But, according to Davison, it was Howard's intervention which was crucial.

Davison was out walking in Greenwich Park when the summons from the Queen reached him. He hurried into the palace, went to his room for the papers, then sent in his name to the Queen. She made some remark about the fine weather, then asked him if he had brought the warrant; he produced it and she asked for pen and ink and signed it, dropping it on the floor at her feet and asking him if he were not sorry to see her signature upon it. He said he was, indeed, sorry for the necessity of it, and the Queen smiled. She then signed the other papers. Davison picked them up and was about to leave when the Queen sardonically suggested that he should show the warrant to Walsingham, who never enjoyed good health and was at that time confined to his bed, since the sight of it would "go near to kill him outright." Davison again turned to go, but she called him back to ask him if it might, even now, be possible to find someone to murder the Queen quietly so that her signature on the warrant would not be necessary after all.

The Archbishop of Canterbury, when consulted in the matter, thought that this might well be the answer to their problems, on the grounds that it was better to dispose of a queen in private than in public. But most other Councilors did not approve of her Majesty's proposal. Even so, she ordered an approach to be made to Sir Amyas Paulet, who immediately declined to make "so foul a shipwreck" of his conscience, to commit an "act which God and the law forbideth." Sir Drue Drury, who had been sent to assist Paulet at Fotheringhay, was also approached and also declined the role of assassin, much to the annoyance of the Queen, who inveighed against the "daintiness" and "niceness" of these two "precise fellows," commenting crossly that they, like other members of the so-called "Bond of Association," were evidently unwilling to fulfill their oaths to kill all those involved in any plot to assassinate the Queen.

The day after she had signed the warrant, so Davison said, she asked him if it had been sealed by the Lord Chancellor. When he told her it had, she asked sharply, "What needeth that haste?" Alarmed by these words, Davison consulted Sir Christopher Hatton and asked for the support of the Privy Council. Davison and Hatton then went to Burghley, who assembled as many members of the Council as he could at such short notice and proposed to them that the warrant should be sent to the Lord Lieutenant of Northamptonshire immediately, without seeking any further instructions from the Queen. After all, when she had signed the warrant the Queen had said "that she did not want" to hear any more about it. The Council agreed with Burghley, so the warrant was dispatched to Fotheringhay in the care of Robert Beale.

The next morning the Queen, in Burghley's presence, told Davison that she had had a dream that the Queen of Scots was executed and this had made her so angry that she did not know what she could have done with him. Davison asked if she intended that the orders in the warrant should be carried out. "Yes, by God," she replied; but she wished the business could have been dealt with in some other way so that all the blame would not fall upon her. Neither Burghley nor Davison told her that the warrant had already left London.

Three days later, on the morning of 8 February, in the great hall at Fotheringhay the victim – by now a corpulent figure, dressed in a dark red petticoat, playing her part with the utmost courage and grace – Mary Queen of Scots was beheaded.

Riding through the night, a messenger brought the news to Greenwich, where the Queen was staying. She was on the point of going out into the park when he arrived, and so missed him; but when she returned to the palace church bells for miles around were being pealed in celebration. She was told why they were ringing and received the news without apparent emotion. Later in her rooms she burst into tears, protesting that she had given no orders for the execution to take place and that those responsible must be punished. For weeks she had been under an emotional strain that had several times brought her close to hysteria. She was near to break-down now, eating little, sleeping badly. She would have blamed Walsing-ham had he not been ill at home when the Council agreed to dispatch the warrant, and had he not been quite capable, as the Clerk of the Council said, of telling the whole truth as he knew it without fear or favor. Burgh-ley, who was now also ill, with gout, she shrank from blaming, though she banished him from court for a time, having the letters which he wrote to her offering his resignation endorsed "Not received." So she decided – after furiously haranguing the Council for betraying her and bringing her name into disrepute throughout Europe – to blame Davison who had, af-ter all, taken the warrant to the Lord Chancellor for sealing. According to her own account, which differed materially from Davison's, she had told him not to release the warrant after she had signed it, not to let it out of his sight until he had received further instructions from her about it.

Davison too was ill, by now, suffering from palsy. He was advised by several of his fellow Privy Councilors to stay in bed, out of immediate range of the Queen's ever increasing anger. But he could not so easily escape her. She ordered his arrest. His doctor said he was too ill to be moved. Even so, on 14 February he was taken to the Tower where he was closely questioned by Sir Christopher Hatton, who was instructed to ob-tain from him an admission that he had disregarded the Queen's instruc-tions and known wishes. Davison denied the charges without suggesting that the Queen was unjust in bringing them or revealing that she had proposed assassination rather than execution though, when still unwell, he was brought before the Star Chamber to be charged with "misprision and contempt" he did tell the court that he had felt justified in not seeking further instructions about the warrant after her Majesty had told him "she would not be troubled any more with it."

His judges were sympathetic. His past services were acknowledged, his honesty admitted and the Queen's prevarications well known; but he was sentenced all the same to a fine of ten thousand marks and to imprison-ment in the Tower during the Queen's pleasure. The Queen's pleasure, so an alarmed Burghley was told, would really have been to see the man hanged, whether or not he were sentenced in a court of law. She would like, she added, to tell the entire Privy Council that they would be hanged as well. She might pardon them, or at any rate most of them, but she would certainly like to see them hanged, and she was sure the law allowed her to order their hanging. She sought the opinion of the lawyer most likely to give her the answer she wanted to hear, Sir Edmund Anderson, Chief Justice of the Court of Common Pleas, an energetic supporter of the

Crown's authority. He had demonstrated his severity during the proceedings against Babington and his accomplices, and was renowned for his brutal interrogations, as well as the "strange fierceness of his countenance" when questioning Puritans. After some hesitation, Anderson agreed that the Queen's prerogative as sovereign was absolute and that she could have any of her subjects hanged at will whenever she wanted to, without due process of law. With this opinion to encourage her, she now intended, so Burghley heard, to ask the opinion of other judges. Burghley, of course, was appalled. He wrote a letter in cipher to a trusted intermediary asking him to warn the judges what was expected of them and to be extremely wary in their answers. "I would be loath to live," he wrote, "to see a woman of such wisdom as she is, to be wrongly advised, from fear or other infirmity . . . with an opinion gotten from the judges that her prerogative is above the law . . . I am fearful of the harm may grow to her reputation if it should be known."

It did not become generally known. The judges did not support Anderson's view; and both the Attorney-General and the Solicitor-General threatened to resign. Several Councilors warned they would do the same if the Queen persisted. So no more was heard of this.

While she was still in a state of barely suppressed hysteria, few Councilors dared approach her and those who did were liable to be savagely berated. When her cousin, Thomas Sackville, Lord Buckhurst, a much favored poet, diplomat and courtier, made so bold as to advise her that her prerogative did not extend to having her subjects put to death without trial, she shouted at him in her rage. Some Councilors, nevertheless, did what they could to procure Davison's pardon and release. Lord Burghley, for his part, had written a protest against Davison's arrest but, on reflection, he had decided to rewrite the letter in a more cautious tone. And when it was proposed that Davison, as the principal Secretary of State's faithful and efficient assistant, might be allowed to succeed him, Burghley, anxious to secure the office for his son, Robert Cecil, did not go out of his way to press the claims of other candidates, however worthy. Davison himself petitioned the Queen to forgive him and to allow him to return to some office in her service. But she declined to receive his letter, and, on his release from the Tower, he was obliged to retire to a modest house in Stepney where, though he was still allowed his salary and his fine was remitted, he was reduced to living in severe poverty.

The Queen's anger with her Councilors for what she took to be their failure to relieve her of a burden that she had found intolerable did not soon subside. "Our sharp humours continue here still," Walsingham reported on 3 April. "The Lord Treasurer remaineth still in disgrace and behind my back her Majesty giveth out very hard speeches of myself . . . If her Majesty could be otherwise served I know I should not be used."

Walsingham, however, was indispensable; and so was Burghley. He continued in disgrace throughout April, the Queen making "marvellous cruel speeches" about him as "traitor, false dissembler and wicked wretch." But by the summer she had come to accept that she could not well manage without him. She seems not to have told him that she was sorry to have used him so ill, never to have indicated that she recognized he had acted for the best; but at least he was received back into her favor. That summer she spent a longer time at Theobalds than she had ever done before.

Elizabeth's fury had been exacerbated by reaction on the Continent to the Queen of Scots's execution. In Spain, King Philip – pressed by Cardinal Allen to restore England to its "ancient glory and liberty" and to punish its ruler, "a woman hated of God and man" – expressed outrage at what she had done to her pitiable enemy. In Paris, the English ambassador was spat at in the street and denied an audience by King Henry III who, with his mother, openly and in defiance of protocol and precedent, attended a requiem Mass for Mary in Notre Dame.

"I must needs write unto your Lordship the truth," Sir Edward Stafford wrote to Burghley, "that I never saw a thing more hated by little, great, old, young, and of all religions than the Queen of Scots's death, and especially the manner of it . . . Today I find all men here in a fury, and all that love not Her Majesty in a great hope to build some great harm to her upon it."

Stafford and other ambassadors were advised by Burghley and Walsingham either to gloss over such accounts of sympathy for her dead rival in the reports they sent to the Queen or to send them to the Privy Council instead. The Queen herself assured foreign monarchs that she was not responsible for the Queen of Scots's death, that the secretary, Davison, had sent the death warrant without her authority. They did not believe her.

16

"The Enterprise of England"

"I myself will be your general."

While William Davison was still languishing in the Tower, Sir Francis Drake was given command of a powerful squadron and, on 2 April 1587, ordered to prevent the King of Spain's fleets from "joining together out of their several ports, to keep victuals from them, to follow them in case they should come forward to England or Ireland."

An attempted invasion of England by the Spaniards had long been expected. Detachments of Spanish soldiers had already been landed in Ireland, and Philip II had congratulated his ambassador in London for being firm with Elizabeth when she had objected to it. "You have acted prudently," he had told him. "It will do no harm for her to be alarmed, and you are doing well in fostering this fear." Relations between the two countries had grown worse in 1580 when Drake – after a three-year voyage during which he had sailed round the world – brought the *Golden Hind* into Plymouth loaded with quantities of silver and jewels. This plunder had been taken from Spanish ships in the Pacific and carried for safe-keeping to the Tower after some of the best diamonds and emeralds had been entrusted to a jeweler for making up into a gorgeous and irresistible present for the Queen, who had compounded Drake's provocation by attending a banquet aboard the *Golden Hind*. Anxious to deliver a protest against Drake's action and the Queen's evident approval of it, the Spanish ambassador had asked for an audience. He found her sitting on a couch from which she did not rise as she usually did, complaining of a painful hip. The ambassador perfunctorily expressed his regret at her indisposition, then came immediately to the matter of the Spanish treasure whose restitution he demanded. The Queen answered him, so he said, with "terrible insolence," to which he responded with the challenge that if she would not listen to his words, no doubt his master would try cannon. The Queen appeared uncharacteristically and unnervingly unmoved by the rudeness of this threat. Speaking so coolly that she might have been "repeating the words of a farce," she said that if ever he addressed her like that again he would be thrown into a place where he could not speak at all. Endeavoring to extricate himself by flattery, the ambassador said that no one could contradict so beautiful a lady before whom even lions would crouch in adoration; and at these words, so he maintained, her vanity overcame her anger. She smiled and preened – "so absurd is she." Then, despite the hip of which she had complained, she got up from the couch, walked across to the window and murmured these words, which, spoken in Italian, he caught before he took his leave, "Would to God that each had his own and all were content."

Since then the danger of war with Spain had rarely receded and never for long. Philip had hesitated to attack while Mary Queen of Scots was alive, for she would, in the event of victory, have taken over Elizabeth's crown; but now that the crown was his own for the taking he had made up his mind to strike. He was assured by William Allen, leader of the exiled English Catholics, that he would be welcomed in England as a savior from a hated Queen, that the English would rise up in support of an enterprise blessed by the Pope, and refuse to take up arms on behalf of "an infamous, depraved, accursed, excommunicate heretic, the very shame of her sex, and princely name," the issue of an "incestuous copulation of her supposed father" and the "infamous courtesan, Anne Boleyn."

Drake's attempt in 1587 to delay the Spanish attack was only partially successful. Scarcely had he sailed than the Queen drew back from the enterprise and – together with a letter explaining that the King of Spain's preparations were not so advanced as had been thought, and that there was still hope that an accommodation could be reached with him – had counter-orders sent to Drake to "forbear entering any of the ports or havens of Spain or to do any act of hostility by land," in effect "to confine his operations to the capture of ships on the open sea." These orders did not, however, reach Drake before he had reached the Spanish coast and had destroyed much of the shipping in the harbors of Cadiz and Corunna. Yet, as he put it himself, he had done no more than "singe the King of Spain's beard," and while his action succeeded in postponing what became known in Spain as "the Enterprise of England," it had not prevented it. The main strength of the Spanish fleet was still anchored at the mouth of the Tagus and, persistently as he argued that it should be attacked there – "which will be the better cheap for your majesty and much the dearer for the enemy" – the Queen held Drake back so long as there seemed the possibility of negotiating a settlement.

To her Councilors such a peaceful settlement appeared impossible; and they did as much as they could to prepare for war, making arrangements for raising men and providing ships, defending likely landing places, barricading roads and giving orders for the blowing up of bridges when the necessity arose. A bridge of boats was built across the Thames so that troops could march quickly to oppose the Spaniards should they land in Kent. Lord Howard of Effingham was in command of the fleet as Lord High Admiral – since it would not have been appropriate for the son of a poor Devon tenant-farmer to serve in such a capacity – but it was understood that Drake as Vice-Admiral would be the executive commander.

The ships of the navy were, at least, in good condition. William Allen, created a Cardinal by Pope Sixtus V in August 1587, and eager to encourage a Spanish invasion of England, assured King Philip that they were mostly rotting tubs; but, according to Lord Howard of Effingham, not one of them knew what a leak meant. Certainly the Queen, like her father, had always taken great interest in the navy, both in the maintenance of ships and the welfare of sailors, whose pay she had overcome her parsimony to increase. She took immense pride in the dockyards at Chatham and liked to impress foreign visitors – as she had impressed the Duke of Anjou – by taking them to see the numerous vessels in all stages of construction lying there against the wharfs and in the docks. She had appointed John Hawkins, an experienced naval commander from an old seafaring family, her Treasurer of the Navy, and under his direction Europe's most efficient fleet had been built. Smaller ships were preferred to large galleons since, as Sir Walter Ralegh, Vice-Admiral of Devon and Cornwall, observed, "the greatest ships are least serviceable, go very deep to water and [are very expensive to construct]. A ship of 600 tons will carry as good ordnance as a ship of 1,200 tons and . . . the lesser will turn her broadsides twice before the greater one can [wind] once."

Yet now that it was essential for the navy to be kept at its highest possible strength and in constant readiness the Queen, still hoping for a peace treaty, exasperated her Councilors by declining to spend money in keeping her ships fully crewed and well supplied with stores and ammunition. It was Lord Howard of Effingham's maxim that "sparing and war" had "no affinity together"; but the Queen – keeping an eye even sharper than usual upon expenditure so that there should be neither waste nor any of the usual peculation – could not bring herself to be unsparing. She did, however, see to it that Francis Walsingham was allowed more than he could generally expect for his network of spies; and she did not hesitate to resort to expedients to raise money by means which she knew would be unpopular, it being impracticable to call Parliament at a time of such emergency. She asked for a loan from the rich, who were made aware that it was their patriotic duty to contribute; she borrowed money at low rates of interest from the merchants of the city of London; she imposed taxes on coastal towns; she called upon all whose rank required the duty "to attend upon her with such a convenient number of lances and light horse as might stand with their ability." In obedience to this last request, Sir Christopher Hatton paid for 400 men, the Earl of Warwick for 360, Burghley for 350. Even Walsingham, by no means a military man, agreed to come forward, dressed in full armor, at the head of 50 lancers, 10 carabineers and 200 foot soldiers. Other courtiers, noblemen and gentlemen undertook to provide similar bodies of troops and to appoint suitable commanders if they could not lead them into the field themselves.

The Queen supervised the high command personally, giving her most experienced ministers responsibility for various areas. The Earl of Derby, for example, was to exercise full authority in her name in Lancashire and Cheshire, Hatton in Northamptonshire, Burghley in Lincolnshire, Hertfordshire and Essex. The commanders in the field in these counties were to be the deputy lieutenants. The Earl of Leicester, whose main force was stationed at Tilbury, was appointed the Queen's Lieutenant and Captain-General. Lord Hunsdon, who was charged with the Queen's personal safety, was to command the troops encamped around Windsor. In all, by the end of July, about 50,000 infantry and 10,000 horsemen had been mustered, most of them in the coastal counties. Within their ranks, as the Queen had confidently predicted, were many Catholics in defiance of a papal Bull demanding that they rise up to depose her and ignoring the constant exhortations of Cardinal Allen who – as Burghley, in his snobbish way, reminded a meeting of justices of peace before they took up their posts in their respective counties – was, after all, only a "base companion" from a Lancashire family of little merit.

The great Spanish Armada of 130 ships carrying almost 17,000 soldiers under the unwilling command of the Duke of Medina-Sidonia sailed from Lisbon on 30 May 1588, resolved upon stopping England interfering in the Netherlands and upon winning freedom of worship for English Catholics. Storms were soon encountered in the Bay of Biscay, and Sidonia, his ships scattered, was obliged to seek shelter at Corunna for a month until its passage could be resumed. He left Corunna on 22 July with the intention of sailing up the English Channel to the Flemish coast and of escorting 16,000 more troops under the command of the Duke of Parma, Philip's Regent in the Netherlands, across to England. A week later, early in the afternoon, the sails of his ships were sighted off the Cornish coast. Beacons were lit and soon news of the Armada's approach was being signaled from hill to hill across the length of southern England. Drake sailed out of Plymouth to attack the enemy fleet; but although the Spaniards, astonished by the maneuverability of the English fleet and the range of its guns, lost three ships, the rest sailed slowly on towards the rendezvous with Parma. It did not get further than Calais Roads. Here it was attacked again, and after hard fighting and scattered by high winds, it was "driven like a flock of sheep," as Drake said, past Parma's men waiting in their barges off Nieuwport and Sluys and up the English east coast, the sailors throwing mules and horses overboard into the waters of the North Sea.

It was not yet known in England that the immediate danger was passed; and, when the first reports came in, the Council feared that the Spanish ships might yet regroup and bring the Duke of Parma's army across the Channel. They could, at least, comfort themselves that the country was ready to resist them.

Despite William Allen's predictions, even the most prejudiced Catholic observers were forced to conclude that the Spaniards could expect little support in England, except perhaps in the north. Most Englishmen, from the highest Anglican to the strictest Puritan, were prepared to resist the invaders. So, indeed, were many if not most Catholics; and, although the heads of several leading Catholic families were taken into custody and interned in Wisbech Castle, this action was taken more for their own protection than because it was feared that they would turn traitor. The country, in effect, was united behind the Queen. Now that there was nothing for her country to do but to fight, nor any matters of policy to vex her, she rose to the occasion with invigorating spirit, giving the lie to the Lord Deputy of Ireland, who maintained that at the time of the Armada she "pissed herself with fear."

She expressed a desire to visit her land forces and suggested she might ride down to the south coast where it was expected the enemy might land. But Leicester as Captain-General told his "most dear Queen" he could not consent to that. She might however, like to come to Tilbury and review the troops there. She accepted the invitation; she came downriver from Whitehall Steps by barge, accompanied by Yeomen of the Guard, went up to the camp and, after spending the night at Arderne Hall, rode out to address the troops, mounted on a fine white horse that was preceded by the Earl of Ormond carrying the sword of state and a page bearing a plumed helmet. Another page held the reins of her horse. She herself carried a small silver staff. She wore a steel corselet over her white velvet dress but otherwise disregarded the advice given about her safety. She rode through the ranks of soldiers, then dismounted and walked up and down among them, sometimes with her usual gait, at others with "the countenance and pace of a soldier." On occasions such as these she always spoke well; and her words had been well chosen now. They had been written down and were read out to the companies by their officers.

> My loving people, we have been persuaded by some that are careful of our safety, to take heed how we commit ourselves to armed multitudes, for fear of treachery. But I assure you, I do not desire to live to distrust my faithful and loving people. Let tyrants fear . . . I have always so behaved myself that, under God, I have placed my chiefest strength and safeguard in the loyal hearts and good will of my subjects, and therefore I am come amongst you as you see at this time, not for my recreation and disport, but being resolved, in the midst and heat of the battle, to live or die amongst you all, to lay down for my God, and for my kingdom, and for my people, my honour and my blood, even in the dust. I know I have the body of a weak and feeble woman, but I have the heart and stomach of a king, and of a king of England too, and think foul scorn that Parma or Spain or any Prince of Europe should dare to invade the borders of my realm, to which, rather than any dishonour shall grow by me, I myself will take up arms, I myself will be your general, judge and rewarder of every one of your virtues in the field. I know already for your forwardness you have deserved rewards and crowns, and we do assure you, in the word of a Prince, they shall be duly paid you . . . By your valour in the field, we shall shortly have a famous victory over these enemies of my God, of my kingdom and of my people.

The Queen was still at Tilbury when a messenger came with reports that the Armada had been overwhelmed and dispersed. Its ships were sailing north past Newcastle and the crisis was over. On the afternoon of 9 August the Queen returned to London, where the citizens crowded the streets, shouting for joy. She announced that next St. Elizabeth's Day, 19 November, would, like the day of her accession, be a public holiday; and on that day, and for three days thereafter, there were festivities and pageants throughout the country, bear-baitings and cockfights, dancing and tug-o'-wars, plays and tableaux. In London on Sunday 24 November the Queen went in procession to a service of thanksgiving in St. Paul's Cathedral, riding in a chariot drawn by two white horses, like the Goddess of Victory. She halted the procession before entering the cathedral, stepped down from the chariot and, outside the West Door, knelt down to pray aloud before the assembled crowds. Inside the cathedral she repeated her prayers and, after a sermon delivered by John Piers, Bishop of Salisbury, she addressed the congregation herself, giving thanks for the nation's victory.

She had never been so admired, so revered. Whenever she appeared in the streets, multitudes gathered to see her pass, to express their devotion. Godfrey Goodman, later Bishop of Gloucester, then a boy of five living in the Strand near the Church of St. Clement Danes, remembered being told that the Queen was on her way to a Council meeting and he must come quickly if he were to see her.

> Then we all ran [Goodman wrote]. When the court gates were set open, no man did hinder us from coming in . . . [And after] we had stayed there an hour and a half and the yard was full, there being a great number of torches, the Queen came out in great state. Then we cried again, "God save your Majesty." Then the Queen said again unto us: "God bless you all, my good people!' Then we cried again: "God save your Majesty!" Then the Queen said again unto us: "You may well have a greater prince, but you shall never have a more loving prince." And so, looking one upon another a while, the Queen departed. This wrought such an impression upon us, for shows and pageants are ever best seen by torch-light, that all the way long we did nothing but talk what an admirable Queen she was, and how we would adventure our lives to do her service.

Yet not everyone could share the joy of the time. Appalled by the costs of the Armada's defeat, the Queen saw to it that no more money was now spent than was strictly necessary. The men of the land forces were discharged immediately the danger was over so that they could go home to help with the harvest; but, as so often in the past, they had to wait for several weeks before they received their pay; and then they did not get all they had been promised. Sailors, many of whom had been kept on short rations and had to rely on captured powder for their guns, were also kept waiting for their money. Drake as Vice Admiral and Hawkins, Treasurer of the navy, felt obliged to find the money from their own pockets to buy necessaries for seamen who were brought ashore in Kent suffering from dysentery.

The Queen hoped to recoup at least part of her expenditure by exacting ransoms from the Spanish for the prisoners taken. Thousands of survivors of ships wrecked off the coast had struggled ashore in Ireland, where most had been killed either by loyal Irish chiefs on orders of the English authorities, or by local inhabitants who robbed them or delivered them up for money. Officers and men whose clothes betrayed their relative wealth were, however, usually spared. In England, too, senior Spanish officers who had been captured in the earlier engagements off the Devon coast were retained in custody while Elizabeth entered into negotiations with the Duke of Parma for ransoms. Other prisoners were given to English merchants whose employees had been arrested in Spain, or whose goods had been impounded there, so that they could negotiate on their own behalf for the release of their men or the return of their confiscated property.

Nor could the Earl of Leicester enjoy the general happiness. He was fifty-five years old when the Queen came to Tilbury. The handsome features had coarsened, the smooth dark skin roughened and reddened, the hair grown white, the lithe body uncommonly fat. He was suffering from "sore pains in the stomach," perhaps from a cancerous tumor. The days when it was claimed by jealous enemies that, "seeking pasture among the waiting gentlewomen of her Majesty's chamber, he hath offered them £300 for a night" were long since over. His duties as Captain-General now over too, he traveled north to Derbyshire to take the waters at Buxton, writing on the way to beseech her Majesty to pardon her "old servant to be thus bold in sending to know how [his] gracious lady doth." "For my own poor case," he went on, "I continue still your medicine and it amends much better than any other thing that hath been given me . . . I humbly kiss your foot."

The Queen read the words and later wrote on the sheet, "His last letter." She placed it in a jewel-box that she kept in her bedroom. Leicester died almost alone, according to Edmund Spenser, with "scarce any left to close his eyelids near," his "greatness vapoured to nought," his name "worn already out of thought." The Queen's grief was private: she rarely afterwards spoke of him; and, occupied with affairs of state, she let others make arrangements for his funeral.

She did, however, spare time to ensure his debts to the crown were repaid: she gave orders for the seizure of Kenilworth Castle and all his estates in Warwickshire. Already, so it was said, she had eyes for none but his stepson, Robert Devereux, second Earl of Essex.

17

The Earl of Essex

*"I shall break him of his will, and
pull down his great heart."*

Their earlier meetings had not been propitious. He had first been presented to the Queen at Christmas 1577 soon after his eleventh birthday, when she had leaned forward to kiss him but he had turned his face away. He had also forgotten to take off his cap, a breach of etiquette upon which the Queen commented with some playful, but to a boy embarrassing, remark. He was already exceptionally good-looking, with shining auburn hair and striking black eyes, but he had not yet acquired the self-confidence that his contemporaries were later to find overbearing. He had become Earl of Essex on his father's death in 1576. His mother was the Queen's cousin, Lettice Knollys, Sir Francis's daughter, who afterwards – to Elizabeth's intense fury – had married the Earl of Leicester. In his ancient pedigree were most of the great families of medieval England; his guardian was Lord Burghley; one of his tutors was the Archbishop of Canterbury; he could scarcely have enjoyed better advantages in life and he made the most of them. Reckless and vain, heedlessly extravagant, though very poor, something of a scholar as well as a sportsman, high-spirited, forthright and a "great resenter," he burst through life as though in a constant hurry. He ate so quickly and abstractedly he seemed not to care what was put before him, rushing from the bed of a mistress to sit in his study or chapel contemplating some mystery before dashing off again upon another quest, impatiently offering his limbs to his servants to dress him, so Henry Wotton said, accepting the clothes without heed, giving "his head and face to his barber, his eyes to his letters, and ears to petitioners."

He had an arrogant charm of manner which the Queen found at first intriguing and then, as she had found Sir Walter Ralegh's, compelling. "When she is abroad," wrote one of his servants soon after Essex's twentieth birthday – the Queen then being fifty-three – there is "nobody with her but my Lord of Essex, and at night my Lord is at cards, or one game or another with her, that he cometh not to his own lodging till birds sing in the morning."

From time to time there were scenes and squabbles. Essex did not disguise his jealousy of other men at court to whom the Queen showed favor, of Burghley's son, Robert Cecil, of "that knave Ralegh" and of Charles Blount, an ambitious soldier of "very comely proportion," perhaps the subject of Nicholas Hilliard's celebrated *Young Man Among Roses*, whose skill at a tilting match one day was rewarded by Elizabeth with a richly enameled gold chess queen which he wore tied to his arm with a crimson ribbon. Resentful of the ostentatious way in which this emblem was worn, Essex remarked to Sir Fulke Greville, "Now I perceive every fool must have a favour." The remark was repeated to Blount, and in the ensuing duel Essex was slightly wounded. "By God's death," the Queen exclaimed when she heard of the affair, "it were fitting some one should take him down and teach him better manners, or there were no rule with him."

There were other more serious quarrels when Essex, eager to distinguish himself and bored by life at court, slipped away without permission to join military expeditions. He already had some experience as a soldier: at the age of eighteen he had been given by his stepfather, the Earl of Leicester, the high-sounding though not responsible appointment of General of the Horse in an army sent to the Netherlands. He had returned from that expedition unharmed, but there was no telling how his impetuosity might endanger his life in future. The Queen sent messages after him, summoning him to come home. He ignored them; she wrote again more insistently, warning the commanders of the expedition that if they did not send him back, "Ye shall look to answer at your smart; for as we have authority to rule, so we look to be obeyed." Essex came to heel sullenly; more angry scenes ensued; but he was always forgiven. She made him Master of the Horse, an office worth £1,500 a year; she allowed him £300 a year from the see of Oxford, which she kept vacant at least partly for his benefit; she gave him a further £300 a year from an equally reprehensible manipulation of church revenues; she lent him money – and he had to sell one of his manors "of ancient inheritance" when she demanded repayment of the loan.

She granted him the profitable right to exact tax on the importation of sweet wines. But then, again without seeking permission, he married Sir Francis Walsingham's daughter, the widow of Sir Philip Sidney; and the Queen was predictably more angry than she had ever been with him. She insisted that his wife should live "very retired in her mother's house." He agreed to this and after a time he and the Queen were seen to be "in very good favour" once more.

Eventually she agreed to give him a military command in France, where the then Protestant Henry of Navarre had asked for English help. His friends had told Essex he would do much better for himself seeking "a domestical greatness like to his father-in-law," Walsingham. But it was military glory he chiefly desired and the Queen most reluctantly indulged him after he had knelt before her for two hours, beseeching her to appoint him her commander.

She knew the risk she was taking. When her ministers and servants were under her own eye in England she was generally able to ensure that they were submissive and obedient and that, although they often tried to hoodwink her and sometimes pursued policies in opposition to hers, she usually had her own way in the end. She was, however, able to exercise no such control over her naval and military commanders who considered that as a woman she could not possibly know anything about warfare. Once they had escaped her presence and were in possession of a command overseas they disregarded her orders in a way that would be unthinkable at home. They attacked places they had no orders to attack; they ignored objectives upon which they had been told to concentrate; they recklessly sought victories before the Queen's hatred of warfare's extravagance brought about a negotiated settlement; or they prolonged campaigns unnecessarily so that they could make more money from their conduct of them.

Essex's behavior, as might have been expected, was quite as reprehensible as that of her other commanders. Admittedly he behaved with "true valour," according to Sir Henry Wotton, who was then on a prolonged tour of Europe, but the Queen expressed her dissatisfaction with his generalship, his reckless impetuosity, his failure to keep her informed as to what he intended to do. "Where he is," the Queen complained crossly, "or what he doth, or what he is to do, we are ignorant." After an unsuccessful attack on Rouen in which his brother, Walter Devereux, was killed, she wrote to complain of the bravado of his action, although she had previously urged an assault without delay. Not only had he failed in the attempt but – as a consequence of his "unadvisedness" – he had lost his only brother. He had also, to the Queen's furiously expressed annoyance – for she herself continued to bestow such honors with great circumspection – knighted no fewer than twenty-one of his followers. She recalled him for a dressing-down; but, having once reprimanded him, all was "jollity and feasting" again, and he was allowed to return to France on the strict understanding that the "rash and temarious youth" would never be allowed unnecessarily to expose himself to danger. The Queen was in tears at his departure.

Nevertheless she agreed four years later to his being appointed commander of an expedition that had been raised for an attack on Spain, whose power to wound England had been little damaged by the defeat of the Armada. The Queen had changed her mind even more often than usual over this expedition and its command. She eventually decided that Essex and his rival, the Lord Admiral, Lord Howard of Effingham, should be made joint commanders; but then Sir Walter Ralegh returned from the West Indies and rumors flew about the court that he was to be appointed instead. It soon transpired, however, that he was to be given a subordinate command as Rear-Admiral, leaving Essex and the Lord Admiral to argue about their respective precedence. The Lord High Admiral was certainly a higher post than that of any of the offices held by Essex, but Essex was an earl and Howard of Effingham a mere baron. Essex attempted to settle the argument by signing a document so high up on the page that there was no room for the Lord Admiral to place his signature above his own. But before the document was dispatched the Lord Admiral snatched up his penknife and cut the offending signature off the sheet.

For weeks it seemed that there would be no expedition for either general or admiral to command. "The Queen wrangles with our action for no cause but because it is in hand," Essex complained. "I know I shall never do her service but against her will." If she called the attack off at this stage he would "become a monk upon one hour's warning."

She did decide to call it off. She sent orders to Plymouth for the commanders to return. They were both so "dear to her" and such "persons of note" that she could "not allow of their going." This was followed by instructions for the attack to go ahead and for a prayer composed by her Majesty to be read out to the soldiers and the sailors aboard the ships:

> Most omnipotent and guider of all our world's mass! We humbly beseech, with bended knees, prosper the work and with best forewinds guide the journey, speed the victory, and make the return the advancement of thy fame and surety to the realm, with least loss of English blood. To these devout petitions, Lord, give thou thy blessed grant! Amen.

The prayer was answered. Cadiz was captured in an assault led by Essex whose bravery, the Lord Admiral admitted, was inspiring. On their way home, having destroyed Cadiz's defenses and taken prisoner several rich Spaniards as hostages, the victorious English forces raided the Portuguese town of Faro. Here they looted its treasures and seized the valuable library of its bishop, which Essex claimed as his share of the plunder and later gave to his friend, the scholar and diplomat, Thomas Bodley, founder of the Oxford library that bears his name. Essex returned to England the national hero he had always sought to be. A thanksgiving service was held in St. Paul's; and, when the preacher praised the skill and bravery of his command, the congregation burst into applause.

This was not at all to the Queen's liking. Francis Bacon warned him that it was bound to be so; her Majesty would have no one presuming to eclipse her own popularity. She had been told of the St. Paul's preacher's extravagant praise of the hero's conduct and had immediately forbidden any further thanksgiving services. She had also heard that the plan of operations at Cadiz had been Ralegh's, and that had Essex had his way a far more hazardous attack would have been attempted. Where, she asked, was the treasure that the army commanders should have brought home with them? The Spanish conceded the loss of millions, yet the plunder brought back from Cadiz and Faro for the royal coffers was nothing like enough to meet the cost of the expedition and, to cap it all, she was being asked to find even more money for the overdue pay of the sailors. Well, she would have to reimburse herself by demanding the ransom money due upon the return of the hostages. Essex took issue with her over this, pointing out that the soldiers would thereby lose their prize-money. She retorted that they had no one to blame but themselves.

Slowly, the Queen's anger cooled; and, as so often in the past, Essex, her "wild horse," was received back into favor once more. His friends and relations basked in the warmth of her Majesty's approval. His uncle, Sir William Knollys, was appointed Comptroller of the Household. His former guardian, the aged Lord Burghley, who had previously done his best to impede Essex's progress in the interests of his son, Robert Cecil, deemed it time to moderate his opposition to the Earl's rise; and at a Council meeting he went so far as to support Essex in the matter of the Spanish ransoms. For once he miscalculated. The Queen rounded on him, blazing with rage. "My Lord Treasurer," she stormed, "either for fear or favour, you regard my Lord of Essex more than myself. You are a miscreant. You are a coward!" This was too much for Burghley, now in his seventy-seventh year. He considered seeking permission to leave court and live the rest of his days as "an anchorite or some such private life" which would be "meetest for [his] age, infirmity and daily decaying estate."

Taking advantage of his reinstatement as the Queen's favorite, and eager to increase his popularity, Essex let it be known that he was an uncompromising enemy of the Spaniards, determined to offer them a challenge from which more cautious Councilors held back; and, in defiance of his oath of secrecy, he made public the forceful opinions he expressed in Council whenever he attended its meetings. Lord Burghley warned him not to be so bellicose; and one day, after Essex had let forth some particularly aggressive sentiments, the old man silently pushed across the table towards him a psalter open at the words of the 55th psalm: "The bloody and deceitful men shall not live out half their day."

Disregarding such prescient advice, Essex made it known that he must have the command when another attack upon Spain was contemplated and that, if he were not given that command, he would leave the court immediately. "I shall break him of his will," the Queen expostulated, "and pull down his great heart!" Instead she gave him the command with Sir Walter Ralegh and Lord Thomas Howard under him. Much gratified by this he wrote to assure her of his undying devotion to his dear, beautiful and "most admired sovereign." He humbly kissed her "royal, fair hands"; he poured out his soul "in passionate jealous wishes for all true joys to the dear heart" of her Majesty; he was her Majesty's "humblest and devoutest vassal." She returned his messages in kind; she sent him presents; she sent him her picture; and, after a fierce gale had dispersed the fleet and driven the surviving ships back to harbor, she remained disposed to have all her ministers love him, Robert Cecil assured him. "She and I do talk every night like angels of you."

But the delayed expedition was a disaster. After a successful assault on Fayal by Ralegh – who, to Essex's anger, attacked upon his own authority before the commander-in-chief had arrived to give him his orders – Essex sailed for the island of San Miguel, intent upon a similar triumph, while the Spanish treasure-fleet sailed undisturbed into the impregnable harbor of Terceira.

Essex returned home to the fierce remonstrations of the Queen, who blamed him for having allowed the expedition to go forward after the disaster of the gale. She would never have consented to it, she said, had she been given proper advice. Dejected and dismayed, Essex retired to his country house Wanstead Park, which he had inherited from his stepfather. Here he took to his bed and wrote to tell the Queen that he was "conquered by beauty." She soon relented, but Essex sulked: he was not well enough to travel back to London; he might come if it were shown to the world that his reputation was considered untarnished; he would come if the Queen asked him outright to do so. To this she replied in effect that she did not care whether he returned or not. Then, again, she relented. She appointed him Earl Marshal, giving him precedence, unquestionably, once and for all, over Lord Howard of Effingham, the Lord Admiral. Essex went back to court.

Although undeniably attractive, capable of exercising an almost hypnotic charm, Essex was far more popular in the country at large than he was at court where, with the advice and help of the two clever brothers, Francis and Anthony Bacon, sons of Sir Nicholas and of Lord Burghley's sister-in-law, he was emerging as the principal rival to Sir Robert Cecil, the Queen's secretary. Impulsive and self-opinionated, exasperatingly conscious of his talents which were, indeed, as Elizabeth recognized, considerable, Essex marched about the palace, his tall figure leaning forward like the neck of a giraffe, as though he were a prince of the blood. He was rumored to be having affairs with various of the Queen's ladies, and to have his eye on several profitable and influential appointments both for himself and for unsuitable friends whose claims he pressed with persistent importunity, on occasions so irritating the Queen that she lost her temper with him. "In passion she bade me go to bed if I would talk of nothing else," he reported to Francis Bacon for whom Essex was trying to obtain the Solicitor-Generalship. "Wherefore in passion I went away, saying while I was with her I could not but solicit for the cause and the man I so much affected, and therefore I would retire myself till I might be more graciously heard. And so we parted."

For a time rebuffed, Essex soon returned to the attack which he maintained for well over a year until at last the Queen, sometimes seemingly to be on the point of agreeing to the appointment of Bacon – who she acknowledged was beginning "to frame very well" – gave the office to someone else.

With requests made to the Queen on his own behalf, Essex was often no more successful, for, while she enjoyed Essex's company as a handsome young admirer, she was reluctant to trust his judgment as she trusted that of the Cecils. In the past her favorites, Leicester and Hatton among them, were employed in responsible offices as well as indulged flirtatiously. But for the Queen Essex was essentially a courtier, not a statesman. He asked to be made Lord Warden of the Cinque Ports, a post given to Lord Cobham who was immediately added to the list of his enemies. There was "no worth" in Cobham, he protested to the Council; and, since her Majesty took it upon herself to grace the man with honor, Essex had "right cause to think [himself] little regarded by her." He protested also directly to the Queen, who soon afterwards appointed him Master of the Ordnance, the kind of military post that Francis Bacon had advised him to avoid, anxious for him to concentrate his energies on appointments at court. Essex then complained about the Lord Admiral, Lord Howard of Effingham, being created Earl of Nottingham, particularly since the patent mentioned Howard's services at Cadiz, for which Essex considered that he himself should have the greater if not the only credit. He said that he had been gravely dishonored by the creation and challenged the new earl or any of his sons to single combat. The Queen again endeavored to placate him. She tried unsuccessfully to persuade Nottingham to forgo his rights; then, hoping that the work might encourage him to become the useful royal instrument that Leicester had been, she employed Essex as her secretary while Robert Cecil was away on a diplomatic mission in France.

But it was not in Essex's nature to let sleeping dogs lie for long. Nor did he understand, as Leicester had understood, that however indulgent the Queen might appear, she was not to be coerced or bullied, that susceptible as she might be to flattery, she was not to be pressed into raising any man higher than his merits warranted or occasion required. Nor was Essex willing to be considered a mere pen-pusher. He longed to be accepted as a military hero, a cynosure for the populace, ambitions that the Queen, always desiring to be at the centre of the stage herself, naturally deplored. "I demand whether there can be a more dangerous image represented to any monarch living," Francis Bacon asked, "much more to a lady, and of her Majesty's apprehension?"

Essex was soon causing trouble and offense again by encouraging the clandestine marriage of his friend, the homosexual Earl of Southampton, to one of Elizabeth's maids of honor, the pregnant Elizabeth Vernon, and by giving grounds for the rumor that he himself was still sleeping with certain of the Queen's ladies despite the warnings given him and despite the disapproval of his former guardian's sister-in-law, the formidable and pious Lady Bacon, who urged him to read I Thessalonians 4:3, where he would see that it was "the will of God that [he] should be holy, and abstain from fornication."

Essex was also becoming increasingly outspoken in the Council, demanding a more forceful foreign policy, constantly attacking Burghley, who was trying to reach some peaceful accommodation with Spain, and loudly protesting against appointments of which he disapproved. Sometimes he was supported, sometimes opposed by the Queen, who seemed to change her mind from day to day. When Sir William Knollys, Essex's uncle, was proposed for a command in Ireland, he objected to the appointment, unwilling to lose the support of an ally in his rivalry with the Cecils. He suggested that the post should be given instead to Sir George Carew, a friend of the Cecils, whom he wanted to get out of the country. The Queen, however, decided against him. She announced that Knollys should go, whereupon Essex lost his temper and, with a gesture of furious insolence, he turned his back on her. The Queen, provoked beyond measure by his petulance, jumped up, struck him a violent blow on the side of his head and told him to go and be hanged. His hand flew to his sword, and he seemed on the point of drawing it from the scabbard when the Earl of Nottingham leaped forward to restrain him. Crying out that he would never have submitted to such treatment even from King Henry VIII, he rushed from the Queen's presence and rode hard to Wanstead where he alternately sulked and raged at the injustice that had been done to him, refusing to seek forgiveness, protesting that it was he who had been wronged. When at last he was persuaded to write a letter of apology to the Queen, he addressed her with conventional flattery but as though it were she who should be extending a hand of forgiveness to him:

> I was never proud till your Majesty sought to make me too base . . . When I think I have preferred your beauty above all things, and received no pleasure in life but by the increase of your favour towards me, I wonder at myself what cause there could be to make me absent myself one day from you . . . Your Majesty hath by the terrible wrong you have done both me and yourself, not only broke all laws of affection but done against the honour of your sex.

Hearing that there was renewed trouble in Ireland, Essex returned to London soon after this letter was written to offer his services. But the Queen would not receive him. "He hath played long enough upon me," she said, "and now I mean to play awhile upon him." Essex persisted. "I do confess," he wrote, "that as a man, I have been more subject to your natural beauty than as a subject to the power of a king." This gained admittance but not forgiveness. He returned to Wanstead where, ignoring the advice of his friends, he declined to make the unqualified apology for which the Queen was waiting. "I have received wrong and feel it," he protested. "My cause is good, I know it." He also knew that he was still a popular hero, that the failure of his most recent expedition against the Spaniards was generally laid at doors other than his own. In London he was extolled for his firm stand against his country's Catholic enemies, for his supposedly ardent Protestantism. In Cambridge he was chosen as Chancellor in 1598.

Soon afterwards Elizabeth gave way, as most observers at court had expected her to do eventually, and on Twelfth Night that year she and Essex were seen dancing together again. It was considered, though, that the reconciliation was not an entirely happy one, and when Essex was appointed to the command of an army being sent to Ireland in 1599 it was widely felt that he would not have been her choice had there been other suitable contenders for the appointment. But Sir Walter Ralegh, who had been granted twelve thousand acres in Ireland, did not want it. Nor did Sir William Russell, the Lord Deputy of Ireland; while Sir Richard Bingham, Governor of Connaught, a "man eminent both for spirit and martiall knowledge" and with wide experience of suppressing rebellious subjects, was suffering from a complaint of which he was soon to die. Sir Charles Blount, now Lord Mountjoy through the death of an elder brother, was considered an ideal choice and would certainly have been that of the Queen. He was a brave and talented soldier, had been present at the battle near Zutphen where Sir Philip Sidney had received his fatal wound, had commanded a company in France and had fought bravely against the Spaniards in the Azores. But, according to Essex, Mountjoy was not of sufficient standing in the world, besides being, as an Oxford graduate and former student of the Inner Temple, "too much drowned in book-learning." The command required "a prime man of the nobility, strong in power," one "in favour with military men who had been before general of an army" – in fact, himself. He well knew what it might cost him were he to fail, but success would give him the full glory he sought.

And if he performed "in the field what he hath promised in the Council" all would indeed be well, a courtier, Robert Markham, observed. "But although the Queen hath granted forgiveness for his late demeanour in her presence, we know not what to think hereof. She hath, in all outward semblance, placed confidence in the man who so lately sought other treatment at her hands; we do sometime think one way, and sometime another."

Essex also w...s in two minds. Gratified though he was to be given the command, he dreaded leaving court where "practising enemies" might conspire to do him mischief in his absence. Besides, the Queen exasperated him by her tergiversations, tinkering endlessly with the details of the force's composition and its armaments, complaining of its cost, repeatedly reminding him of the prescribed limits of her commanders' authority.

Yet when at last he departed for Ireland towards the end of March 1599, he seemed in good spirits, riding through London to the tumultuous cheers of the crowd, content to have persuaded the Queen to allow him to return to England at any time he chose.

Serious trouble had long been threatening in Ireland, whose problems caused the Queen the gravest concern in the last years of her life, worried as she always was by the thought of how endangered her throne and country would be were a large Spanish army to be welcomed there. She "grew weary," it was said, reading the Irish dispatches; and Sir Thomas Smith observed that she seemed never more uncertain of herself, never more liable to change her mind than when there were Irish troubles to be resolved.

The English settlers despised the natives, whom they considered little better than savages, while the Irish in turn detested the English and, provoked by their rapacious seizures of land, burned their houses and massacred the occupants. The Queen would have preferred to have as little as possible to do with Ireland, to leave the country to be governed by the old Irish and Anglo-Irish families who would be directly answerable to her, a hierarchical form of government that always appealed to her and would certainly be a great deal less expensive than the administration by conquest and settlement favored by several of her Privy Councilors and by a majority of the English officials in Dublin.

Royal officers like Sir Richard Bingham, Governor of Connaught, contended that it was impossible to govern a beggarly and barbarous people without recourse to the sword, while the rebellious people thus oppressed retaliated with a savagery that provoked ferocious reprisals. In the north Hugh O'Neill, Earl of Tyrone, a rebel leader who had been in touch with Philip II, had defeated a royal force near the banks of the Blackwater River, much to "Her Majesty's sense of dishonour," as the Earl of Nottingham informed the Council in Dublin in a letter of strong rebuke; and it was largely to fight Tyrone's rebels that the Queen's formidably expensive army had been raised. Mercy would be shown to all who deserved it, a proclamation from the Queen informed the Irish people, but, as for the rest, they would be extirpated as "enemies to God and traitors to our Crown and dignity."

When he arrived in Dublin, however, Essex was induced by the Queen's officials there not to attempt an attack on Tyrone in Ulster but to march against the rebels in Munster. This he did, and did successfully, hanging all the rebels he captured. But he had not been sent to Ireland to attack Munster and the Queen wrote to tell him so, complaining that he should have directed his forces against the "Northern traitor" and that, repeating his misbehavior in France, he had created in the field a large number of highly unsuitable knights. Furthermore, though well aware that she would strongly disapprove of it, he had given the appointment of Lord-General of Horse to his friend the Earl of Southampton who, having gone out to Ireland as an unofficial observer, was alleged to be sharing a tent with a captain whom he "would cull and hug in his arms and play wantonly with." Essex was forcefully told that his permission to return home was withdrawn – he "was not to come out of that Kingdom by virtue of any former licence whatever" – he must immediately put a stop to his marching about Ireland, as though he were on a royal progress – at a cost of £1,000 a day – indulging in a succession of maneuvers which might well please the Anglo-Irish but which certainly did not please the Queen.

Pressed in subsequent angry and, for her, unusually concise letters to invade Ulster, and upbraided for allowing the rebels to establish themselves there, Essex persuaded his officers to sign a document listing the reasons why such a move against Tyrone was inadvisable. On receipt of this letter, Elizabeth – already outraged by reports of the gross peculations of dishonest captains and officers of the commissariat – was naturally furious. She wrote again to Essex ordering him to do as he was told, reminding him again how much money his expedition was costing, and how little was being gained by such large expenditure:

> If sickness in the army be the reason [for not marching north into Ulster], why was not the action undertaken when the army was in a better state? If winter's approach, why were the summer months of July and August lost? If the spring were too soon, and the summer that followed otherwise spent . . . then surely we must conclude that none of the four quarters of the year will be in season for you.

Essex sullenly marched north at last, grumbling that "unfortunate news" could only be expected from this "accursed country." But instead of fighting Tyrone he agreed to meet him at the River Lagan to discuss an armistice. He rode alone to the bank of the river; Tyrone, also unattended, rode down from the north and into the water; and there the two men spoke to each other for half an hour, agreeing to a truce.

Essex then went home, again ignoring the Queen's orders, trusting that once he was with her his vital presence would exercise its usual charm, that the loss of over 10,000 men and nearly £300,000 would soon be forgotten. He had intended to sail from Ireland with a large force to support him in what he knew must be a difficult interview with the Queen and Privy Council, and to enable him to remove, if necessary, those of the Queen's advisers ill-disposed towards him. But, warned that this might be regarded as tantamount to treason, he decided to go accompanied by a small escort only and arrived in London early on the morning of 18 September 1599. Learning that the court was at Nonsuch near Ewell, Essex rode straight there, galloping into the courtyard at ten o'clock, his face and clothes splashed with mud. Leaping from his horse, he ran up the stairs, through the Presence Chamber and the Privy Chamber and into the

Queen's bedchamber where her Majesty sat among her ladies, still un-
dressed, her grey hair loose, waiting to be attended to at her dressing-table.
Essex sank to his knees before her, and took her hands in his and kissed
them fervently, the mud still spattered on his cheeks.

The Queen, astonished by the sudden appearance of a man she had
supposed to be still in Ireland and unsure as to whether or not he had
brought his army with him, received him with guarded pleasantries and in so
reassuring a manner that when he was sent away so that her Majesty could
be dressed, he confessed his relief to one of his companions, thanking God
he had "found a sweet calm at home" after all the "trouble and storms" he
had suffered abroad. Home was not, however, to remain calm. When next
he saw the Queen her behavior towards him was not nearly so pleasant. He
found her mood much changed, Lord Talbot was informed, "for she began
to call him to question for his return, and was not satisfied in the manner of
his coming away and leaving all things at so great hazard."

At a Privy Council meeting later on that day, it was decided that Essex,
who was required to stand bareheaded at the end of the table, must be
placed under house arrest while his conduct was closely examined. In the
meantime even his wife, who had just given birth to their daughter, Frances, was forbidden by the Queen to see him.

Those close to her understood how difficult it would be for her to
forgive her wayward favorite now. His former bad behavior had been that
of an over-indulged child, confident that sunshine would follow a brief
storm, that his punishment would be neither severe nor protracted. But on
this occasion he had flagrantly disobeyed the Queen's orders and wasted a
great deal of her precious money. Although he declined to acknowledge
any misconduct and blamed Ralegh and other Councilors whom he
classed as his enemies for his present misfortunes, he could scarcely expect
to be trusted with high command or important duties again. For the moment the Queen refused to see him, describing his behavior as "full of
scandal to our realm and future peril to the state." Even when he fell ill
with one of those sudden attacks that incapacitated him from time to
time, she did not hurry to his bedside as he might well have hoped, and as
she usually did when those she loved were ill, but contented herself with
messages of qualified sympathy.

In order to discover the nature of his complaint, the Queen sent eight
doctors to report on it. They concurred that he was suffering from some
serious internal disorder that was likely to cost him his life. Still highly
popular in London, he received numerous letters wishing him well; prayers
were offered in churches for his recovery; slogans in support of him and in

derogation of his supposed enemies were splashed across the walls of
Whitehall Palace. All this hardened the Queen in her determination not to
forgive him too readily. On his slow recovery, he sent her a present, which
was returned to him; when his favorite sister, Penelope, wife of Lord Rich
and mistress of Lord Mountjoy, asked to be allowed to see him, her
request was refused; and when Sir John Harington, whom Essex had
knighted in Ireland, came to her with a message from him, she seized him
by the belt, bursting out angrily, "By God's son, I am no Queen. This man
is above me. Who gave him command to come here so soon? I did send
him on other business. . . . By God's son, you are all idle knaves and Essex
worse." Her choler, Harington said, "did outrun all reason." Walking
"fastly to and fro," she commanded him to go away at once. He did not
"stay to be bidden twice," Harington admitted. "If all the Irish rebels had
been at my heels, I should not have had better speed."

Later, however, she made it up with Harington and told him so graciously that he was forgiven that he declared he would never have "a
statelier judge" again until he "came to heaven." Essex, however, she
would not forgive. Determined not to restore him to the favor from which
he protested he was so unjustly excluded, she flew into a rage or fell into
silent petulance whenever his name was mentioned. And when she received a letter from his sister, Lady Rich, condemning Essex's enemies at
court, expressed in terms so outlandishly flattering of the Queen as to
appear an impertinent lampoon, she complained to Robert Cecil of the
woman's "insolent and saucy" presumption, ordering her to be placed
under house arrest as well as her brother.

In October she dismissed Essex from all his offices and required the
Privy Council to issue a statement itemizing his various offenses. He was to
remain a prisoner at her pleasure and to be sent to Grafton, the Oxfordshire house of his uncle, Sir William Knollys. A few weeks later he was
released; but he was not allowed to return to court, though he kept writing for permission to do so in letters sprinkled with the compliments she
still so much relished, even from him. "Till I may appear in your gracious
presence," one of these letters ran, "time itself is a perpetual night and the
whole world sepulchre unto your Majesty's humblest vassal." In another
he wrote, "Haste paper to that happy presence whence only unhappy I am
banished. Kiss that fair correcting hand . . . Say thou comest from pining,
languishing, despairing Essex." In yet another he asked for a renewal of his
right to receive the taxes imposed on sweet wines which she had granted
him years before and which constituted the larger part of his income. But
the Queen decided he had got through quite enough of her money already,

and she turned down his request with the observation that "an unruly beast must be stopped of his provender." "My Lord of Essex has written me some very dutiful letters," she told Francis Bacon, "and I have been moved by them. But what I took for the abundance of the heart, I find to be only a suit for the farm of sweet wines."

For Essex the sudden stoppages of most of his income was the last straw; and in outbursts alternately of injured innocence and violent anger, he spoke out against the Queen to everyone who came to Essex House in the Strand to which he had been permitted to return. He raged like a madman, Harington said, uttering "strange words, bordering on such strange designs" that made his friend "hasten forth and leave his presence . . . He hath ill advisers and much evil hath sprung from this Source." One day he was heard to exclaim that "the Queen's conditions were as crooked as her carcase." The insult was repeated to Elizabeth, and Ralegh believed that the words would constitute Essex's death warrant were he to err again.

He was, indeed, ripe for error. Exasperated by the Queen's rejection of him and of the services he was only too anxious to perform, infuriated by the loss of his income, and egged on by Southampton and a succession of impoverished dissidents and troublemakers who strolled in and out of Essex House, he planned an uprising. He would round up his rivals at court, seize control of London by occupying the Tower and Whitehall, take possession of the person of the Queen and force her to give him and his friends the offices and influences that she now seemed intent upon reserving for Cecil and his supporters. To arouse enthusiasm for the deposition of a vengeful and despotic monarch, some of Essex's friends went to the Globe Theatre to pay forty shillings to the Lord Chamberlain's players, Shakespeare's company, to perform their play about Richard II, a monarch deposed.

The excited comings and goings at Essex House and at Drury House – where Southampton mistakenly thought the conspirators' discussions could take place more secretly – soon came to the notice of the Council's spies; and on 7 February 1601 Essex was summoned to court to explain himself. He pleaded that he was too ill to go, and gave orders that the insurrection should take place the next day, a Sunday, while he was still at liberty to lead it and while the City apprentices, who, he believed, would rally to him, were not under the immediate eyes of their masters.

Early that morning several members of the Privy Council, including Sir William Knollys and the Lord Chief Justice, arrived at Essex House demanding to see the Earl of Essex. They were admitted to the house, which

was crowded with the Earl's followers, among them several Welsh swords-
men who had returned with him from Ireland. The visitors were refused an
interview and locked up in the library by Essex, who sallied out with two
hundred men down the Strand towards Fleet Street and the City whose
inhabitants, so Puritan preachers had assured him, would join the apprentices and rise up as one man to support him. There was no such response.
The progress of Essex and his adherents towards Fenchurch Street was
watched in silence; their shouts were not returned; their claims that the
Queen's principal Secretary of State had sold her crown to the Spanish
court were derided. Francis Bacon reported that in all the populous city
where Essex "thought himself so dear" there was not one man "from the
chiefest citizen to the meanest artificer or prentice that armed with him."
The Queen had always supposed that this would be the case. She had been
on edge throughout the crisis, so Harington said. "These troubles waste
her much. She disregardeth [the food] that cometh to the table, and taketh
little but manchet [fine wheaten bread] and succory pottage [chicory soup].
Every message from the city disturbs her, and she frowns on all her ladies."
Yet she had never really doubted the Londoners' fundamental loyalty.
Even when a false report was brought to her that the City was in revolt,
she remained quite calm, so Robert Cecil said, displaying no more concern
than she would have done at talk of an affray in Fleet Street.

When Essex came to the house of a City sheriff who, he had been told,
would welcome him and call out trained bands in his support, he went
inside. He was covered in sweat, so it was noticed, though it was a very
cold day. The sheriff, wanting nothing to do with him, made his escape by
a back door and hurried off to the Lord Mayor, convinced that the insurrection had no chance of success.

Essex had by now realized this himself. After a meal in the sheriff's
house he and his remaining companions withdrew towards Ludgate Hill,
others of his supporters having made off when Essex was declared a traitor
by royal proclamation and a pardon was promised to those who abandoned his cause. Near Ludgate Hill a band of soldiers, called up by Richard Bancroft, the fiercely anti-Puritan Bishop of London, later Archbishop
of Canterbury, fired upon him and shot him through the hat.

Running away to Queenhithe, Essex took a boat there for the watergate
of Essex House. He dashed up to his room where he set about burning
some incriminating private papers until interrupted by another company of
soldiers sent to arrest him. Soon after the soldiers' arrival in the courtyard
several Privy Councilors, including the Earl of Nottingham, joined them
there and called upon Essex to surrender. He answered them from the

17. A miniature of the Queen aged thirty-eight, the earliest known likeness of her by Nicholas Hilliard.

18. Greenwich Palace from the north bank of the Thames, by Anthonis van den Wyngaerde.

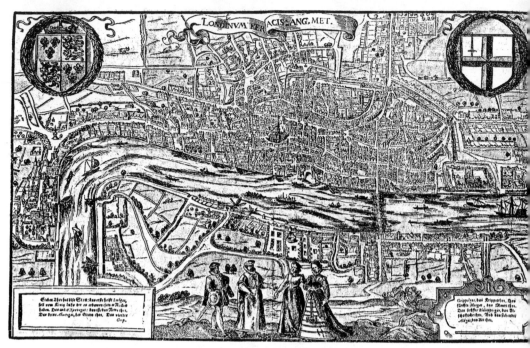

19. London in 1572, from the *Civitates Orbis Terrarum* by Braun and Hogenbergius, showing the "Bearebayting" ring in the foreground and old St. Paul's Cathedral and the Tower of London on the far side of London Bridge.

20. When the Queen left Norwich on one of her progresses she departed with "the water standing in her eyes."

21. A portrait believed to be of Mary Queen of Scots, attributed to Jean Clouet.

22. The Queen of Scots facing trial by a commission of peers and Privy Councilors in the hall at Fotheringhay Castle in 1586.

23. Charles Howard, Baron Howard of Effingham, later
first Earl of Nottingham, the Queen's cousin and Lord
Admiral, by an unknown artist.

24. Sir Nicholas Bacon, the Queen's
Lord Keeper, father of Francis Bacon
and brother-in-law of William Cecil,
by an unknown artist.

25. Robert Cecil, Lord Burghley's
son, who was appointed Principal
Secretary of State in 1596, from a
portrait by John de Critz the Elder.

26. The Queen *c.* 1592 by Marcus Gheeraerts the Younger, the so-called Ditchley portrait, it being first recorded by Thomas Hearne, the early eighteenth-century antiquary, on a visit to Ditchley House, which belonged in Elizabeth's time to Sir Henry Lee, her Champion.

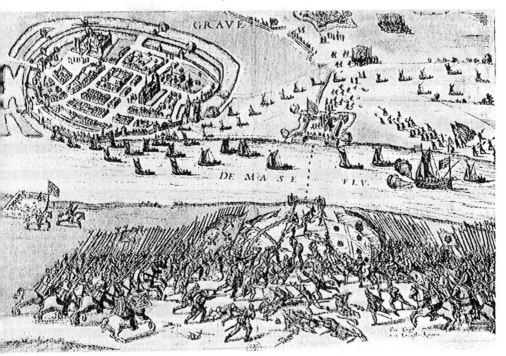

27. The Earl of Leicester, in command of the Queen's troops in the Netherlands, was no match for the Spaniards under the Duke of Parma, who captured Grave on the Maas in 1586.

28. Sir John Hawkins, the naval commander from an old sea-going family, was Treasurer of the navy at the time of the Spanish Armada.

29. Sir Francis Drake, the greatest of Queen Elizabeth's seamen.

30. English ships engage the galleons of the Spanish Armada in the Channel.

31. The white marble effigy of the Queen in Westminster Abbey was made by John de Critz and Maximilian Colt.

roof, shouting at first that he would go out fighting, then demanding an audience of the Queen. Nottingham, having allowed the ladies of the household to leave unharmed, sent to the Tower for cannon and powder and threatened to blow the house up. As the armament was being landed at the watergate, Essex appeared with Southampton. They handed over their swords in token of surrender and were escorted to Lambeth Palace and thence to the Tower.

From the Tower, the two prisoners were brought to face their judges in Westminster Hall on 19 February. One of these judges was a man whom Essex considered to be among his most inveterate enemies, Lord Grey de Wilton; and when this man's name was called, Essex gave a sardonic laugh. The verdict, indeed, was never in doubt. Ralegh spoke in support of the charges; so did Essex's former friend, Francis Bacon, who had sought permission not to attend the earlier meetings of the Council where the misdemeanors of the accused had been discussed but whose presence had been required by order of her Majesty.

Sentence of death was passed on Essex at seven o'clock that evening. When he was marched back to the Tower, crowds gathered around the prisoner and some of them spoke to him; but he did not reply, walking quickly in the torchlight in the midst of the guards, his face bent towards the ground. It was supposed by many that he would be pardoned, as Southampton and all but six of their fellow-conspirators were; but the Queen had made up her mind that no mercy could be shown to a man who had threatened to take up arms against her. She told the French ambassador with deep emotion that she had put up with too much disrespect to her person to spare him. "In such cases," she added later, we must lay aside clemency and adopt extreme measures." Even so, she showed a familiar reluctance when the time came to sign the warrant; and, after bringing herself to put pen to paper, she recalled the document. The following day, however, she signed a fresh warrant, and it was taken away before she could change her mind.

Dressed in a black coat and with a black cap on his head, Essex was taken from his quarters to a scaffold within the Tower precincts. He knelt down at the block, so Robert Cecil said, with "great patience and humility." He prayed aloud for several minutes, asking forgiveness for his sins, repeating the Lord's Prayer, and – prompted by one of the attendant clergymen – forgiving his enemies. He took off his black coat, then his black doublet and lay down with his neck upon the block in a bright scarlet waistcoat with long sleeves. "Lord, be merciful to thy prostrate servant!" he called before stretching out his arms as a sign for the headsman to strike. The axe was brought down in so clumsy a stroke that two other blows were required before the head was severed. The executioner held up the head by its hair, shouting, "God save the Queen!"

The Queen was playing the virginals when a messenger brought confirmation of the traitor's death. She received it in silence. No one else spoke. After a time she began to play again.

18

Lords and Commons

*"I count the glory of my crown that
I have reigned with your love."*

The disgrace of the Earl of Essex had cleared the path to power for his rival Robert Cecil, the younger son of Burghley and of his second wife, the clever Mildred Cooke, daughter of Edward VI's tutor, Sir Anthony Cooke. His mother had a shallow dent on the left side of her forehead, and Cecil, too, suffered from this slight deformity. She was also rather hunchbacked as was her son, though more noticeably so; and he was very small, not more than five feet in height. He walked flat-footedly, with a shuffling movement, his long thick hair brushed back from his wide, pale brow, his small pointed beard neatly trimmed. He was once described on his way to discuss some problem with the Queen treading across the floor "like a blind man, his hands full of papers and head full of matter." His malformed appearance and solemn, businesslike, rather cold manner were misleading guides to his character. Some of his friends, to whom he wrote delightfully indiscreet letters, were most genial men and he himself was both quickly humorous and affectionate, with many varied interests, and a taste for gambling and convivial dinner parties at which his pet parrot would strut upon the table. His wife, Elizabeth Brooke, daughter of Lord Cobham, Lord Warden of the Cinque Ports and later Lord Chamberlain, had not been at all reluctant to accept his proposal as he had thought she would be. She was a kindly, domesticated, chatty woman, much concerned with the price of ribbons and damask. They were devoted to each other. When she died he mourned her deeply; and when Cecil met her brother after her death both men, it was observed, were close to breaking down. It was said that his hair turned white overnight. Six months later one of his aunts urged him to emerge from his melancholy, otherwise he would forever be "a surly, sharp, sour plum."

Sickly as a child, he had studied hard as though determined to do well in his lessons, since he could play few games and hawking and shooting were the only sports he could practice. After studying at home under tutors and in his father's well-stocked library, he had gone to St. John's College, Cambridge, then to Gray's Inn, then to France where he had attended disputations at the Sorbonne. After his return to England he had been elected to Parliament as one of the Members for Westminster, and had soon come to the Queen's attention. Upon his departure on a diplomatic mission to the Duke of Parma, she asked him to report directly to her. She called him "Pygmy," which he naturally did not like, and "Little Elf," a less disdainful nickname that acknowledged the existence of high spirits behind the pale mask of his solemn demeanor.

His father had high hopes of him. Burghley's son by his first wife, Thomas, although no longer a drunken ne'er-do-well, remained something of a disappointment. Thomas was his heir. The barony was to go to him as well as Burghley House in Lincolnshire and Cecil House in the Strand. He would also have inherited Theobalds in Hertfordshire had not his father altered his will at the end of his life in Robert's favor. Thomas was quite content with these arrangements. He seems not to have in the least resented his father's favoritism, accepting that Robert was much cleverer than he was, more worthy of the respect the Queen had for his talents. He warmly supported his brother whenever called upon to do so, and appeared perfectly happy to remain in the background, fulfilling without notable distinction the office of Lord President of the Council of the North. It was not until after the Queen's death that he was to become a Privy Councilor and first Earl of Exeter.

Despite his father's patient and persistent advocacy, Robert Cecil's advancement was not as rapid as both men might have hoped. While recognizing his merits, his shrewdness, his mastery of detail and his usefulness as an unofficial spokesman of the government in the House of Commons, the Queen was reluctant to grant him the office of Secretary of State, for which his father had destined him and whose duties he had been helping to perform since the death of Sir Francis Walsingham. She admitted Robert to the Privy Council after what he called "a princely, prudent admonition," but so long as Essex – who saw Robert Cecil as a principal rival – stood high in her regard she declined to commit herself. It was not until he had shown his exceptional gifts by his work in helping to organize the expedition to Cadiz in 1596 that the Queen honored him by the appointment he had already done so much to deserve. Even then there was a long delay, during which Essex challenged him to a duel, before he was handed the seals of his new office.

Thereafter, while the fortunes of Essex declined, Robert Cecil made himself ever more indispensable and ever richer, his appointment upon his father's death to the office of Master of the Court of Wards – as well as the profits derived from his patronage as Secretary of State, his subsequent grant of the right to receive dues on various imported luxury materials, such as silks and satins, and his investment in privateering expeditions – enabling him to indulge what became a passion for buying and building houses. He had a large house in London where the Queen was a guest at a housewarming party in 1602; and, by means sometimes less than honest, he acquired properties in Cornwall, Wiltshire and East Anglia as well as the Cranborne estates in Dorset and the Brigstock Parks in Northamptonshire.

As a token of his gratitude to the Queen for his influence and newfound riches he gave her a splendid topaz and a very fine ruby jewel. But, although he had become "the greatest Councillor of England," in the words of one of Sir Robert Sidney's correspondents, "the Queen passing the day in private and secret conference with him," she never grew especially fond of him, was never fully at ease with him as she had been with his father, her dear "Spirit." She suspected that he kept information from her; and so he did, continuing what had long become an accepted practice. "And so hoping, by your next despatch," he wrote to the Lord Deputy of Ireland in a characteristic letter, "you will write that which is fit to be showed her Majesty, and that which is fit for me to know . . . in which kind all honest servants must strain a little when they will serve princes."

Yet the Queen acknowledged Cecil's capacity for unremitting hard work, the soundness of his advice, as well as his valuable help in her dealings with Parliament in which he sat as Member for Hertfordshire. She did, however, have cause to be dissatisfied with his handling of the arrangements for the last Parliament of her reign, in 1601.

The Queen had become adept in handling Parliament herself, alternately rebuking Members for what she considered to be their misconduct and flattering them by the exercise of her charm, making them mollifying, flattering speeches, singling out Members for special attention and compliments, praising their talents to others in words intended for repetition, afterwards showing that she remembered their names and the towns and counties they represented. In listening to their collective addresses, she would nod her head in approval or raise her hand in graceful salutation or even curtsy to them. Yet it was evident that she considered them rather a nuisance, and summoned them as rarely as she could, only thirteen times in forty-five years. "Let this my discipline stand you in stead of sorer strokes," she reprimanded them on one occasion. "Never tempt too far a prince's patience." They must not presume, she told them during a later session, "to meddle with matters above their capacity, not appertaining unto them."

If she did not rebuke them herself, she told one or other of her ministers to do so – as she did, for instance, in 1584 when the Lord Chancellor was sent to the Commons to tell them they must not consider religious matters, a subject the Queen had expressly forbidden them to discuss. Indeed, there were very few important subjects which they could discuss without the Queen complaining that they were impinging upon her prerogative. She called Parliament for the specific purpose of authorizing taxation; and, when its Members had given the required vote, she expected them to disperse as soon as possible, usually seeing that they were given good reasons, such as the onset of plague, why they should do so. Fortunately, many Members were as unwilling to hang about in London as the Queen was to have them there; and, as the session wore on, attendance invariably declined, despite fines imposed by their leaders upon absentees.

At the beginning of the Queen's reign it had not been too difficult to persuade Members to vote according to her wishes, since the incompetence of her predecessor's rule could be blamed for the poor state of the country's finances; but, when this excuse could no longer be made, ministers were sometimes hard put to it to explain that, while the new reign was as eminently successful as they maintained it was, unforeseen circumstances had combined to make an additional subsidy necessary.

When Parliament was particularly recalcitrant, the Queen herself appeared to charm Members into submission, to make them promises which were as often as not unfulfilled, to remind them that, as her Lord Keeper put it, she granted them "liberal but not licentious speech, liberty with due limitation," and that, as their anointed Queen, she could "never be constrained to do anything" against her will. She was confident that as her "loyal subjects" they would never attempt to coerce her or to encroach upon her prerogative. She had no doubt, she said when they were proving difficult, that they were being led astray by a few troublemakers. She took great pains in preparing these speeches, at once hortatory, conciliatory and complimentary, rewriting them more than once and having them copied and distributed not only for the benefit of Members who might have missed hearing her words but also for the public at large.

From time to time she reminded Members that her prerogative entitled her to veto Bills of which she disapproved and that it might well be in the nation's interest that she should sometimes do so. In fact she vetoed few of the more than five hundred Bills presented to her in the forty-five years of her reign, and consent to these was usually refused because she wished to please interested parties who might have been harmed by them, not because she considered that they were infringements of her prerogative. Discussions of Bills that threatened her prerogative were nearly always nipped in the bud.

The Queen's successes in her dealings with Parliament, her skillful avoidance of legislation distasteful to her, were all the more remarkable since she often had not only the Members of the Lords and Commons to deal with but also her own Councilors, who often used Parliament as an ally in furthering those policies that were not of the Queen's choosing and who frequently persuaded Members to bring forward for discussion subjects that she was anxious should not be debated.

In 1601, however, the issue uppermost in most Member's minds was one which Councilors would have preferred not to be discussed either. On this occasion Parliament assembled in a peculiarly rebellious and discontented mood. There was widespread dissatisfaction over the high rates of taxation, over real and suspected abuses in the Exchequer, above all over her grants of monopolies to various Councilors, courtiers and friends.

When the Queen passed a crowd of disgruntled Members on her way from the Lords, there was "little room to pass," one of them reported. "She moved her hand to have more room, whereupon one of the gentlemen ushers said openly, 'Back, masters, make room,' and one answered stoutly behind, 'If you will hang us we can make no more room,' which the Queen seemed not to hear, though she heaved up her head, and looked that way towards him that spake."

Although her stand caused much discontent and "muttering in corners," she declined to give way on various financial matters which, she maintained, were for her and the Council to consider undisturbed and alone. But she recognized the necessity of making concessions in the matter of monopolies which aroused such deep resentment both in Parliament and in the country at large. These monopolies, which provided the Queen with a most useful means of rewarding men from whom services were expected, included those on salt, tobacco, various wines, brandy, starch and so many other commodities that a Member, on listening to a recitation of the list, called out, "Is not bread there?" Robert Cecil had never seen the House in "so great confusion." Members fell into silence when Sir Walter Ralegh, "the gentleman with the bold face," who held the monopoly for playing-cards – a monopoly described by a bishop as being "in the fore-rank of abuses" – stood up to defend monopolies in general. But the speeches of other Members who agreed with him were almost drowned by the uproar in an unusually crowded chamber. It was clear that the overwhelming feeling of the House was that no measure of the Queen, in the words of one Member, was "more derogatory to herself or more odious to the subject or more dangerous to the Commonwealth than the granting of these monopolies." It was also clear that the Commons would not even debate the matter of a subsidy before the question of monopolies had been settled.

The Queen realized she must appease the growing anger by surrender and by an admittance that there had, indeed, been "error, troubles, vexations and oppressions" which, now she had heard of them and realized how serious they were, she would rigorously root out.

She offered to see a delegation of Members at Whitehall Palace. No, not a mere delegation, "all, all!," some of them shouted. Her Majesty replied that she would be glad to see them all. They came and knelt before her and she addressed them in what became known as her "Golden Speech," an oration so well phrased and so well delivered in clear, precise tones so different from their own more or less broad country accents, that several Members were seen to have tears in their eyes. The words seemed to come from her heart extempore, as they did in all her most effective speeches, which were so much better phrased than the elaborately mannered convolutions of her more labored writing style, a style which some considered occasionally so tortuous as actually intended to render her meaning unclear so that she could escape responsibility for giving orders that might prove unwise.

> There is no jewel [she said], be it of never so rich a price, which I set before this jewel: I mean your love. For I do esteem it more than any treasure or riches . . . And though God hath raised me high, yet this I count the glory of my crown that I have reigned with your love . . . My heart was never set upon any worldly goods, but only for my subjects' good. What you bestow upon me I will not hoard it up, but receive it to bestow on you again. Yea, mine own properties I account yours, to be expended for your good . . . There never will Queen sit in my seat with more zeal to my country, care for my subjects, and that will sooner with willingness venture her life for your good and safety than myself . . . And though you have had, and may have, many princes more mighty and wise sitting in this seat, yet you never had, nor shall have, any that will be more careful and loving. . . . And I pray you, Mr Comptroller, Mr Secretary and you of my Council that before these gentlemen go into their counties, you will bring them all to kiss my hand.

At the dissolution of Parliament the Speaker felt able to praise the benefits of her reign in the most fulsome terms, to express thanks for the "happy, quiet and most sweet and comfortable peace" that the country had long enjoyed and – "blessed be God and your Majesty" – still did enjoy.

19

"A Lady Shut in a Chamber"

*"Tush, Browne, tush! I know more
than thou dost."*

At the time of the meeting of this last Parliament, Queen Elizabeth was sixty-seven years old, and she hated to be reminded of the fact. Four years before, the Bishop of St. David's had ill-advisedly chosen as his text for a Lenten sermon the twelfth verse of the 90th Psalm: "So teach us to number our days, that we may apply our hearts unto wisdom." This was bad enough; but then the bishop, Anthony Rudd, a hale Yorkshireman of forty-seven, compounded his folly by turning to mystical numbers, to seven and to nine, and to seven times nine, the Great Climacteric, a particularly critical stage in human life. The Queen, listening to him through the window of an upstairs gallery, was seen to be growing ever more restless and cross. So Rudd quickly left these numbers for others less contentious, citing, for example, 88, a figure that had been thought by some to be unfortunate for the Queen yet had brought the defeat of the Spanish Armada. But the damage had been done and, instead of thanking the preacher for his sermon as was her customary habit whenever she approved of one she had bothered to listen to, the Queen called down to him that he should have kept his numbers to himself. "I see," she added, "the greatest clerics are not the wisest men." She had once told Whitgift that Anthony Rudd, whom she had previously found perfectly agreeable, ought to be his successor as Archbishop of Canterbury. Whitgift, as Thomas Fuller said, was not a man "intentionally to lay a train of powder to blow up this archbishop-designate," yet he had in fact done so by offering him a piece of advice: the Queen best liked "plain sermons which came home to her heart." Now this was the result. Rudd's chances of preferment were ruined: he ended his episcopal days, as he had begun them, as Bishop of St. David's.

Had he lived more at court, Rudd would have known that the Queen, far from being edified by the 90th Psalm, liked always to be told how young she looked, that she was, indeed, often so told and never tired of the compliment. And it was generally admitted that when her grey hair had been covered by a wig, her wrinkled face painted and her body gorgeously and skillfully attired, she did not look as old as she was. In the year after Rudd had preached his ill-conceived sermon a German visitor, Paul Hentzner, saw the Queen at Greenwich and was much impressed by the sight of her majestic appearance in a low-cut, white silk dress, covered with jewels, a red wig on her head. He remarked upon her small hands and long fingers, her thin, slightly hooked nose, her white skin and her small, black eyes. Her remaining teeth were black, too, he noticed, "a defect the English seem subject to from their too great use of sugar." "She had in her ears two pearls with very rich drops," Hentzner added. "Upon her head she had a small crown . . . and she had on a necklace of exceeding fine jewels."

Hentzner watched her as she walked to chapel, the train of her dress carried by a marchioness, pausing to talk to one or two people in the crowds on either side, those whom she addressed kneeling when she spoke to them:

Now and then she raises some with her hand. While we were there a Bohemian baron had letters to present to her; and she, after pulling off her glove, gave him her right hand to kiss, sparkling with rings and jewells . . . Whenever she turned her face, as she was going along, everybody fell down on their knees. The ladies of the court followed next to her, very handsome and well-shaped and for the most part dressed in white. She was guarded on each side by the gentlemen pensioners, fifty in number, with gilt battle-axes . . . While she was still at prayers, we saw her table set out with the following solemnity: A gentleman entered the room bearing a rod, and along with him another who had a table cloth, which, after they had both kneeled three times with the utmost veneration, he spread upon the table, and after kneeling again, they both retired. Then came two others, one with the rod again, the other with a salt-seller, a plate and bread; when they had kneeled, as the others had done, and placed what was brought upon the table, they too retired with the same ceremonies performed by the first. At last came an unmarried lady (we were told she was a countess) and along with a married one, bearing a tasting-knife; the former was dressed in white silk, who, when she had prostrated herself three times in the most graceful manner, approached the table, and rubbed the plates with bread and salt, with as much awe as if the Queen had been present: when they had waited there a little while, the yeomen of the guard entered, bare-headed, cloathed in scarlet, with a golden rose upon their backs, bringing in at each turn a course of twenty-four dishes, served in plate most of it gilt; these dishes were received by a gentleman in the same order they were brought, and placed upon the table, while the lady taster gave to each of the guards a mouthful to eat, at the particular dish he had brought, for fear of any poison. During the time that this guard were bringing dinner, twelve trumpets and two kettle-drums made the hall ring for half an hour together. At the end of this ceremonial, a number of unmarried ladies appeared, who, with particular solemnity, lifted the meat off the table, and conveyed it into the Queen's inner and more private chamber, where, after she had chosen for herself, the rest goes to the ladies of the Court.

In the inner chamber the servants knelt when presenting the dishes at the Queen's table, the food in them – mostly sweet things now, cakes and puddings and sugary custards – being tasted by one of her ladies before being taken to her own lips.

Another observer, the French ambassador, André Hurault, Sieur de Maisse, who also saw her at about this time, reported:

She was strangely attired in a dress of silver cloth, white and crimson . . . [with] slashed sleeves lined with red taffeta, and was girt about with other little sleeves that hung down to the ground, which she was constantly twisting and untwisting. She kept the front of her dress open, and you could see the whole of her bosom, and passing low, and often she would open the front of her dress with her hands, as if she were too hot . . . On her head she wore a garland of rubies and pearls, and beneath it a great reddish-coloured wig, with a great number of pearls, not of great worth. On either side of her ears hung two great curls of hair, almost down to her shoulders and within the collar of her robe, spangled like the top of her head. Her bosom is rather wrinkled . . . As for her face it is . . . long and thin, and her teeth are very yellow and irregular . . . on the left side less than on the right. Many of them are missing, so that you cannot understand her easily when she speaks.

On his way to her de Maisse passed through rooms whose walls were covered with linenfold paneling and brightly colored tapestries, beneath molded plasterwork ceilings and across thick carpets from Turkey and Persia, past huge stone chimneypieces gaudy with heraldry and cabinets filled with treasures in silver and crystal, mother of pearl and ivory. On every side were courtiers in their extravagantly embroidered clothes, their padded doublets, their breeches stuffed with wool, their stockings tightly drawn around their calves, wide ruffs at neck and wrists, rings in their ears, their beards dyed, their feet encased in diamond-studded, high-heeled shoes of silk and velvet.

The clothes the Queen herself wore in old age, except when there was no need for display, were as gorgeous and striking as they had ever been, with "innumerable jewels on her person," as de Maisse recorded, "not only on her head, but also within her collar, about her arms and on her hands, with a great quantity of pearls around and on her bracelets."

She expected all those about her to dress as impressively as befitted their rank. Bishops were told to pay no attention to the silly opinions of Puritans on the subject of ecclesiastical dress. The aged Bishop of London who preached a sermon against the vanity of arraying the body in costly clothes was told off quite as sharply as Anthony Rudd had been.

No one, however, could wear clothes which betokened a higher rank than that to which the wearer could properly lay claim or which outshone the glory of the Queen's own splendid dresses; and when Lady Mary Howard, a young lady whom Essex had greatly admired, appeared at court with a sumptuous velvet dress embroidered with pearls, upon which others bestowed the most fulsome compliments, the Queen called her up and asked if she could borrow it. She then put it on herself; but, as she was taller than Lady Mary, it did not fit her. Was it not too short for her? she asked Lady Mary, who had to agree that it was. "Why then, if it become not me as being too short," said the Queen, "I am minded it shall never become thee, as being too fine. So it fitteth neither well." Eventually the dress was returned to its owner, but Lady Mary never dared to wear it in the Queen's presence again.

Her ladies had long become accustomed to being demeaned and embarrassed by her, as well as to being shouted at or being given a few sharp blows about the ears. At Oatlands she once caught sight of a locket not very well concealed in the bodice of a dress worn by the Earl of Oxford's daughter, who had not long been married to the sixth Earl of Derby. When the Queen asked to look at it, Lady Derby begged to be excused from showing it. The Queen insisted; and, on being handed it, opened it and found inside some verses written to Lady Derby by an admirer. She praised the verses, then tied the locket first to her shoe, then to her arm, and ostentatiously walked about with it.

Her ladies had also to grow used to her increasingly unpredictable tantrums, which would suddenly break out without warning and on the slightest pretext as when, for instance, she heard that a certain lady had been taking a physician's medicine for some complaint instead of the herbal cordial of ancient recipe which she herself had recommended. She was more than ever liable to erupt in fury when she heard of a marriage, planned or accomplished, of which she disapproved or when she suspected her maids of honor of any sexual impropriety. Frequently she would ask her younger ladies if they wished one day to marry; and they, well aware of the kind of answer expected of them, answered that they had no such thoughts in mind or that the very idea appalled them. Newcomers to court soon learned the rules of this particular game; but one who did not was the young daughter of Sir Robert Arundell, of whom this story was told: Mary Arundell was in love and when the Queen asked her the familiar question she was shy and hesitant in her answer. The Queen, arranging for them to be alone together, pressed her to confide in her. The girl told her her secret and confessed that she and the man she loved had not yet dared to ask her father for his permission. She was told to leave the matter in the hands of the Queen who summoned Sir Robert Arundell, told him everything and asked him if he had any reason to object to the match. Arundell replied that if the Queen had no objection he certainly had not; and he gave his permission in writing. Elizabeth then sent for the girl and told her that she had succeeded in obtaining her father's permission. "Then I shall be happy, and please your Grace," the girl said.

"So thou shalt," the Queen told her. "But not to be a fool and marry. I have his consent given to me and I vow thou shalt never get it into thy possession. So go to thy business. I see thou art a bold one to own thy foolishness so readily."

Yet for all the stories that were told of her pettiness, irritability and vanity, some true, others invented, no one could deny that the Queen still retained her ability to charm when she chose to exercise it, as she did upon Sir William Browne, a general who had been campaigning abroad, and who came to court to deliver his report. The Queen made the other people in the room stand back so that she could speak to him in private. She sat on a stool and he knelt before her; but she told him, as "an old faithful servant," that she would not talk to him unless he got up. She certainly had much to say and twice interrupted him when he attempted to speak himself. "Tush, Browne, tush!" she said bossily, "I know more than thou dost." But when he left her, Browne felt an inestimable honor had been bestowed upon by him by the Queen's easy, friendly, confidential manner.

Nor could anyone deny that the Queen still retained much of her invincible authority, even though her ladies sometimes laughed at her now behind her back, mocked her for "trying to play the part of a woman still young." "I know not one man in this kingdom," wrote Robert Cecil, "that will bestow six words of argument to reply, if she deny it." Cecil himself well knew that, old as she now was, she remained determined to keep all affairs of state under her direct control, none more so than the affairs of

Ireland, which she set her heart upon settling – insofar as Irish affairs ever could be settled – before she died.

Since Essex's death the situation in Ireland had become critical: Spanish troops had landed in large numbers and the Earl of Tyrone's rebel troops were marching to join forces with them. Fortunately the Queen had now found a commander in Ireland whom she believed she could trust, Charles Blount, Lord Mountjoy. "Tell our army from us," she wrote to him, "that every hundred of them will beat a thousand . . . I am the bolder to pronounce it in His name, that hath ever protected my righteous case, in which I bless them all. And putting you in the first place, I end, scribbled in haste. Your loving sovereign, E.R."

Her trust was not displaced. Skillfully using the cavalry which Essex had to the Queen's dismay placed in the incompetent hands of Southampton, Mountjoy attacked and defeated the Irish army so decisively that the Spaniards, already at odds with their allies, entered into negotiations with the English. "The contempt and scorn in which the Spaniards hold the Irish," Mountjoy wrote contentedly, "and the distaste which the Irish have of them [should ensure] that hereafter it will be a difficult thing for the Irish to [get help from] Spain."

For the moment there was the problem of what to do about Tyrone, who was still at large. Both the Council and Mountjoy considered that his offer to surrender provided his life were spared should be accepted. The Queen, however, wanted him captured and executed, and, "as God in Heaven doth know," Cecil reported to Mountjoy, "even in these great causes, she is pleased to proceed more absolutely than ever, by the rules of her own princely judgement." She was known to be nearing the end of her life, but neither Cecil nor any of her other ministers cared openly to question that "princely judgement." Eventually she was persuaded to agree that Tyrone's life should be spared if he submitted. But she insisted upon conditions that he was most unlikely to accept; and, in sending her instructions to Mountjoy, Cecil made it clear in a separate letter for his eyes only that, while he was to do all he could to obtain Tyrone's agreement to her conditions, he was not to lose this opportunity of obtaining Tyrone's surrender. Above all, the Queen must never learn that her orders were not being followed to the letter; nothing must be written in official dispatches that might lead her to suppose that her "princely judgement" was being questioned. A separate, confidential letter should be sent to the Secretary of State personally to explain the exact situation; Cecil's own letter must be returned to him. For, as Harington said, she could even now, "put forth such altercations when obedience was lacking as left no doubtings whose daughter she was."

Determined though she was to appear as much in command of events as she had ever been, the Queen's control over the court was no longer as sure as it had been in the past. In earlier days she had contrived skillfully to balance rival factions; and, while there had been inevitable resentment and squabbling as contestants vied with each other in the emotional atmosphere which she purposefully created around herself as a woman, she had usually in the end succeeded in settling disputes before they got out of hand. Her grip was now far less confident. Essex had been for a time uncontrollable; the power the Cecils had gathered into their own hands had aroused the most dangerous envy. Quarrels at court erupted into scuffles and fights in the passages and corridors; challenges to duels were almost commonplace. "As God help me," Sir Robert Sidney's agent reported from court in 1599, "it is a very dangerous time here. . . . A man cannot tell how to govern himself."

Nor could the Queen hide from those who saw her every day that she was now an old woman, with an old woman's fears and fancies, sometimes making a spectacle of herself as she crept round the Privy Chamber plunging the ancient and rusty sword, which she kept by her bed at night, into the hangings where she suspected assassins might lurk. She rarely left her palaces now. She was, so Harington said, an old lady "shut up in a chamber from her subjects and most of her servants, and seldom seen but on holy days."

Dwelling much on the past, she had a tendency to tears when she remembered those whom she had loved and had now lost. Burghley's last illness affected her deeply. Demanding as she was and often impatiently reluctant to accept excuses of ill health as reasons for not working – once refusing to believe the Speaker, who pleaded he was too ill to come to see her late at night – she had always been sympathetic towards the old and seriously ill; and, while preferring to be served by the young and attractive, she never abandoned "any for age or other infirmity" once they had been enrolled in her service. When they could work no more, she saw to it that they received proper pensions. She had prayed for Burghley who for months now had had to be carried from room to room in an upholstered chair; she sent him repeated messages, and from time to time went to see him, sitting by his bed and feeding him his broth, holding the spoon which his own gouty hand was too crippled to grasp. His death, so Sir Robert Sidney reported, "doth often draw tears from her goodly cheeks." Another observer wrote, "She sleepeth not so much by day as she used to, neither taketh rest by night. Her delight is to sit in the dark, and sometimes with shedding tears to bewail Essex." When Essex's friend, Sir Thomas Egerton, came to receive his seals on his appointment as Lord Keeper, the Queen spoke of the first Keeper she had had, the fat and witty Nicholas Bacon – "and he was a wise man, I tell you." Then, reflecting that Egerton would be her last Lord Keeper, she burst into tears. Egerton, embarrassed and for want of anything more interesting to say, agreed that Bacon was undoubtedly a wise man. This brought forth more tears. She left the room still weeping, calling out at the door, "Swear him! Swear him. He will never be an honest man until he is sworn."

Others on occasions found the Queen less tearful than grumpy. Sir John Harington considered that "the many evil plots and designs hath overcome all her Highness's sweet temper. She walks much in her Privy Chamber, and stamps with her feet at ill news." Foreign ambassadors were warned that her propensity to loquacity was much increased and that it was advisable not to mention certain subjects in case they provoked a cantankerous dissertation. She seemed willfully to misinterpret arguments put to her and, when in peculiarly black moods, was as capable of ridiculing a diplomat as she was an incompetent servant. The French ambassador was advised to write down the gist of what he had conveyed to her and hand the précis to the Council, since the Queen might well subsequently misrepresent what he had said.

On other occasions, however, she was both attentively alert and friendly, even playful, toying with the hair of a young diplomat who knelt before her and pretending to box his ears. To de Maisse she said, "I think not to die so soon, and am not as old as they think." And, after the audience, she skipped out of the room, "half dancing," as though anxious to prove the point. She was once glimpsed in a small room at Hampton Court, attended by a single servant, energetically "dancing the Spanish Panic to whistle and tabor."

Her eyesight was growing weaker, which she denied; and she was also becoming rather forgetful, a failing likewise not to be noticed. When young men about the court were brought to speak to her, she remembered their faces but sometimes had difficulty with their names and occupations. Her memory "lapseth," one of the courtiers said, "though she will not have it." From time to time her rages became ungovernable, and once she spat at a courtier who annoyed her beyond endurance.

She could not ride as hard as she had done in the past. "When she rideth a mile or two in the park, which now she seldom doth," it was reported, "she always complaineth of the uneasy going of her horse. And when she is taken down her legs are so benumbed that she is unable to stand." A servant had to be called to massage them with "an earnest rubbing" before she could walk away.

She bridled in anger whenever comments upon her inability to ride as hard as she had done when young reached her ears, and did all she could to disprove them, galloping far longer distances than she would otherwise have felt inclined to do, and venting her wrath on anyone brave enough to hint that the time for such strenuous activity had passed. When her aged cousin, Lord Hunsdon, who was almost ten years older than herself, suggested that she should no longer ride between Hampton Court and Nonsuch, she dismissed him from her presence and refused to speak to him for two days.

At the beginning of 1602, a marked improvement was noticed in her spirits. Irish affairs were no longer a cause for deep concern, and, particularly pleasurable, was news of a brilliant victory over a Spanish fleet off the coast of Portugal won by the Earl of Nottingham's son-in-law, Sir Richard Leveson. As one encouraging report followed another, the Queen's mood lightened perceptibly. Instead of watching her ladies dance, tapping her feet and clapping her hands to the music as she had been content to do of late, she got to her feet and joined in herself. When the Venetian ambassador was given an audience soon after Christmas, he found her perfectly agreeable and gracious. She was in her Presence Chamber where musicians were playing for her, although it was a Sunday. As resplendently dressed as ever, wearing great pearls like pears and vast quantities of precious stones, she rose to greet him and spoke to him in her still fluent Italian. "I do not know if I have spoken Italian well," she said, fishing as always for a compliment, "still I think so, for I learnt it when a child, and believe I have not forgotten it."

She began to walk in the garden again almost as briskly as she had done when she was young, even in the coldest weather, leaning against the wind. Indeed, in the words of the Duke of Stettin, who saw her in the garden of Oatlands in September 1602, she strode about as though she were eighteen years old. She also rode with pleasure, covering ten to fifteen miles of a morning, the mane and tail of her horse dyed as bright an orange as the color of her wig. She hunted with all her old enthusiasm, deriding ladies who could not keep up with her, and appeared to derive as much pleasure as she had ever done from the antics of her fool, Garret. By the end of the year, however, the brief resurgence of her spirits came to an end as she lapsed into her last illness.

20

The Last Act

*"Little man, little man, the word
must is not to be used to princes."*

On 14 January 1603, in the pouring rain of a dark and windy day, the
court left Whitehall Palace for Richmond, her "warm box" to which the
Queen could "best trust her sickly old age." She had contracted a severe
cold and was excessively depressed. Harington was told that at sixty-
nine years of age she was losing the will to live. She needed help to
dismount from her horse, a stick for climbing steep stairs. Sometimes she
accepted help, at others impatiently refused it. An arm offered to assist
her step into the royal barge might be grudgingly accepted or impatiently
brushed aside. One day when she had refused help she stumbled and
hurt her leg. The robes she had to wear on state occasions had long been
proving too heavy for her; her coronation ring had become embedded in
the thickening flesh of the finger of whose slenderness she had once been
so proud. It had to be filed off, an operation which she could not but
regard as sadly symbolic.

Ill as she was at Richmond, and worse as she became, she refused to
take the medicines her doctors prescribed. They called in Robert Cecil and
Whitgift, the Archbishop of Canterbury, to support them, but neither
could persuade her: she knew her own body better than they; there was
nothing they could do to help her. When her cousin Robert Carey came to
see her she greeted him with sad affection. She had been "mightily offended" with him when he had married and he had regained her favor only
after "a stormy and terrible encounter." But he was forgiven now. She
sighed deeply and said to him, "No, Robin, I am not well."

> She discoursed with me of her indisposition [Carey recorded] and in her
> discourse she fetched not so few as forty or fifty great sighes. . . . In all my
> lifetime I never knew her fetch a sigh but when the Queen of Scottes was
> beheaded. . . . This was upon a Saturday night, and she gave command that
> the great closet should be prepared for her to go to chappell the next morn-
> ing. The next day, all things being in a readinesse, wee long expected her

coming. After eleven o'clock, one of the groomes came out and bade make ready for the private closet, she would not go to the great. There we stayed long for her coming; but, at last, she had cushions lay'd for her in the privy chamber, hard-by the closet door, and there she heard service. From that day forwards she grew worse and worse.

The Earl of Nottingham also came to see the Queen, "mourning in sad earnest" though he was after the death of his wife. "I am tied with a chain of iron about my neck," she said to him. "I am tied, I am tied, and the case is altered with me." John Harington, who had earlier found her in "a most pitiable state," tried to cheer her with some humorous verses he had written, but she smiled only once and when he had finished she said, "When thou dost feel creeping Time at thy gate, these fooleries will please thee less. I am past my relish for such matters."

She was feverish now and constantly thirsty, with what she complained of as "a great heat in her stomach," sleeping little and then with much restlessness, refusing to go to bed, sitting on a pile of cushions on the floor. "Madam, to content the people you must go to bed," Robert Cecil took it upon himself to tell her. "Little man, little man," she rebuked him with a flash of her former spirit, "the word *must* is not to be used to princes. If your father had lived ye durst not have said so much."

For four days she sat on her cushions in her Privy Chamber, speaking seldom, her eyes fixed for hours on end upon the ground, her increasingly foetid body, so the Comte de Beaumont, the French ambassador, said, "greatly emaciated by her long watching and fasting." How could she spend so much time in silence? one of her doctors asked her. "I meditate," she told him gravely. On the third day she put one of her fingers in her mouth and thereafter rarely removed it as she sat, still staring at the floor. At last she grew so weak that her doctors were able to carry her unprotesting to bed where an abscess burst in her throat. She felt slightly better after this and drank a little broth. "Soon after she began to lose her speech, and from that time ate nothing, but lay on one side, without speaking, or looking upon any person."

The Councilors gathered round her bed to ask if she agreed that her cousin, James VI of Scotland, Mary's son, should succeed her. Cecil and the Council had already made all the necessary arrangements; but the Queen, allowing the negotiations to go ahead while pretending not to know of them, had refused to commit herself till now. She found difficulty in talking, and asked for something to rinse her throat. But the Councilors said she had no need to speak: she had merely to indicate with her hand that she accepted him. The question was asked and she gave what was taken to be a sign of consent.

At six o'clock on the evening of 23 March the Archbishop of Canterbury came to say prayers at her request. He knelt by the bed and prayed for half an hour, the others in the room repeating the responses. "After he had continued in prayer, till the old man's knees were weary," Robert Carey reported,

> hee blessed her and meant to rise and leave her. The Queene made a signe with her hand. My sister Scroope [Philadelphia, Lady Scrope] knowing her meaning, told the Bishop the Queene desired hee would pray still. He did so for a long half houre after, and then thought to leave her. The second time she made signe to have him continue in prayer. He did so for halfe an hour more.
>
> She would not hear him speak of hope of her longer life, but when he prayed or spoke of heaven, and those joys, she would hug his hand. . . . It seems she might have lived if she would have used means; but she would not be persuaded, and princes must not be forced.

At length she lost consciousness. She died in the early hours of the following morning.

Robert Carey heard the sound of women weeping, then a servant came to give him the news for which he had been waiting. He stole out of the palace grounds and galloped off towards the Great North Road; and on the evening of 26 March, having ridden almost four hundred miles in less than sixty hours, he brought his last panting relay horse into the courtyard of Holyroodhouse in Edinburgh where, spattered with mud, "be-blooded with great falls and bruises," he dropped wearily from his saddle. He was the first, as he had been determined to be in the hope of reward, to bring the long-awaited news to the King of Scotland that he was King now, also, of England.

Within a week, accompanied by numerous courtiers and retainers hoping to share with him some of the profits of his new inheritance, King James was riding for the border. The farther south he reached the more his welcome excited him. The people "of all sorts rode and ran, nay rather flew" to meet him, he afterwards remembered with characteristic self-congratulation, "their eyes flaming nothing but sparkles of affection, their mouths and tongues uttering nothing but sounds of joy."

Certainly the English, disillusioned in recent years with the Queen's government, were anxious to recognize the virtues of her heir, a confirmed

Protestant, a ruler who could bring them security as well as a new dynasty, a man with an unexceptional Danish wife and two healthy sons. "The government of a woman has been a rare thing at all times," wrote Francis Bacon; "felicity in such government a rarer thing still; felicity and long continuance together the rarest thing of all." Queen Elizabeth's government had continued for almost half a century and her people were coming to feel, so the Spanish ambassador reported, that that was quite long enough. "Certain it was," the French ambassador said, "that the English would never again submit to the rule of a woman." The brightness of her popularity had been much dimmed of late. From all over the country there came reports of dissatisfaction and impatience, of the resurgence of scandalous rumors of the Queen's sexual escapades in her dotage, of plots and counterplots: Paul Hentzner had "counted on London Bridge no less than three hundred heads of persons who had been executed for high treason." A farmer rebuked by a constable for flouting the Queen's laws, burst out, "What dost thou tell me of the Queen? A turd for the Queen!" A laborer in Essex was reported to have said, "The Queen is but a woman, and ruled by noblemen, and the noblemen and gentlemen are all one, and the gentlemen and farmers will hold together so that the poor can get nothing."

Rising prices, costly wars, continuing troubles in Ireland, trade depression as well as poor harvests had overcast the glory of what had once seemed a golden and triumphant time. No longer were eulogistic tracts and ballads and approbatory speeches and sermons attended to with the complacent assent of past decades. It was recognized that the age over which she had presided had, indeed, seen many great achievements, memorable naval victories, exciting discoveries, a wonderful flowering of art and literature, architecture, drama and music. But there was now certainly much to lament, good cause to believe that the fulsome praise of Gloriana, Eliza Triumphans as the begetter rather than the patron of these achievements, was a victory of propaganda over reason. The new Poor Laws were proving inadequate in the face of rising population and increasing vagrancy and poverty; taxation was incompetently assessed and widely evaded; local government was inefficient and central government corrupt, with posts being sold to the highest bidder and granted in reversion to one rich man after another. Despite the Queen's parsimony, the financial resources of the Crown had become insufficient for the heavy demands she placed upon them; the navy was weak, its sailors ill-paid and its ships ill-equipped; the army had wasted away; the religious settlement, which Elizabeth declined to modify in the merest particular, was being attacked by militant Protestants and Catholics alike.

Yet the Queen had not long been dead when the perceived virtues of the Englishwoman who had reigned over the people for so long began to be compared with the patent shortcomings of the Scotsman who had taken her place.

"When we had experience of [King James's] government, the Queen did seem to revive," wrote Godfrey Goodman, Bishop of Gloucester. "Then was her memory much magnified: such ringing of bells, such public joy and sermons in commemoration of her, the picture of her tomb painted in many churches, and in effect more solemnity and joy in memory of her coronation than ever was for the coming-in of King James." The glories of her reign were once more attributed to her own genius; and such was the power of her extraordinary personality, the strength of her allure, that they are still seen so today.

Bibliography

PRIMARY SOURCES

Ambassades de M. de Noailles en Angleterre (Leyden, 1763)

Arber, Edward (ed.), *Sir Robert Naunton's Fragmenta Regalia* (London, 1895)

Birch, Thomas, *Memoirs of the Reign of Queen Elizabeth* (London, 1754)

Boyle, John (ed.), *Memoirs of the Life of Robert Carey* (London, 1759)

Calendar of Letters and State Papers relating to English Affairs preserved principally in the Archives of Simancas, 1558-1603 (London, 1892-9)

Calendar of Letters, Documents and State Papers relating to the Negotiations between England and Spain etc., 1485-1558 (London, 1862-95)

Calendar of State Papers relating to Scotland and Mary Queen of Scots, 1547-1603 (Edinburgh and Glasgow, 1898-1952)

Calendar of State Papers and Manuscripts relating to English Affairs in the Archives of Venice . . . etc. (London, 1864-1947)

Calendar of State Papers (Domestic Series) of the Reigns of Edward VI, Mary, Elizabeth, 1547-1603 (London, 1856-72)

Calendar of State Papers (Foreign Series) of the Reign of Elizabeth, 1558-1589 (London, 1863-1950)

Calendar of State Papers relating to English Affairs preserved principally at Rome (London, 1916-26)

Camden, William, *The Historie of the Life and Reigne of the Most Renowned and Victorious Princess Elizabeth, Late Queene of England*, new ed. (London, 1970)

Collier, J. P. (ed.), *The Egerton Papers* (London, 1840)

Collins, Arthur (ed.), *Letters and Memorials of State* (London, 1746)

Devereux, W. B., *Lives and Letters of the Devereux, 1540-1646* (London, 1853)

D'Ewes, Sir Simonds, *Journals of All the Parliaments* (London, 1693)

Digges, Dudley (ed.), *The Compleat Ambassador* (London, 1655)

Elton, G. R. (ed.), *The Tudor Constitution: Documents and Commentary* (Cambridge, 1968)

Foxe, John, *The Actes and Monuments of John Foxe*, ed. J. Pratt (London, 1877)

Giles, J. A. (ed.), *The Whole Works of Roger Ascham* (London, 1864-5)

Harington, Henry, *Nugae Antiquae* (London, 1838)

Harrison, G. B., *The Letters of Queen Elizabeth I* (new ed., Westport, Connecticut, 1968)

Harrison, G. B., and R. A. Jones (eds.), *André Hurault, Sieur de Maisse: Journal, 1597* (London, 1931)

Harrison, William, *An Historicall Description of the Iland of Britaine* (London, 1577)

Holinshed, Raphael, *Chronicles of England, Scotland and Ireland,* ed. Henry Ellis (London, 1807–8)

Le Laboureur, J. (ed.), *Les Mémoires de Messire Michel de Castelnau* (Paris, 1731)

McClure, N. E. (ed.), *Letters of John Chamberlain* (Philadelphia, 1939)

Melville, Sir James, *Memoirs of His Own Life, 1549–93,* Ed. A. F. Steuart (London, 1929)

Read, Evelyn P. and Conyers Read (eds.), *John Clapham's Elizabeth of England* (Philadelphia, 1951)

Rye, W. B., *England as Seen by Foreigners in the Days of Elizabeth and James I* (London, 1865)

State Papers Relating to the Custody of Princess Elizabeth at Woodstock in 1554 (Norfolk Archaeological Society, IV, 1855)

Stow, John, *Annales, or A Generall Chronicle of England* (London, 1631)

Teulet, Alexandre (ed.), *Correspondance diplomatique de Bertrand de Salignac de la Mothe Fénélon* (Paris, 1838–40)

Tusser, Thomas, *Four Hundred Points of Good Husbandry,* new ed. (Oxford, 1984)

Williams, Sarah, (ed.), *Letters Written by John Chamberlain during the Reign of Queen Elizabeth* (London, 1861)

Wriothesley, C., *A Chronicle of England during the Reigns of the Tudors,* ed. W. D. Hamilton (London, 1875–7)

Yorke, Philip (ed.), *Miscellaneous State Papers* (1778)

SECONDARY SOURCES

Basnett, Susan, *Elizabeth I: A Feminist Perspective* (Oxford, 1988)

Beckinsale, B. W., *Burghley: Tudor Statesman* (London 1967) *Elizabeth I* (London, 1963)

Bindoff, S. T., *Tudor England* (London, 1950)

Bindoff, S. T., Joel Hurstfield and C. A. Williams (eds.), *Elizabethan Government and Society* (London, 1961)

Black, J. B., *The Reign of Elizabeth, 1558–1603,* 2nd ed. (London, 1936)

Bowen, C. D., *Francis Bacon: The Temper of a Man* (Boston, 1963)

Bowle, John, *Henry VIII: A Biography* (London, 1964)

Bradford, C. A., *Hugh Morgan, Queen Elizabeth's Apothecary* (London, 1939)

Bradley, Henry (ed.), *Shakespeare's England* (London, 1916)

Brook, V. J. K., *A Life of Archbishop Parker* (Oxford, 1962)

Brooks, Eric St John, *Sir Christopher Hatton* (London, 1946)

Burgon, J. W., *Life and Times of Sir Thomas Gresham* (London, 1839)

Buxton, John, *Elizabethan Taste* (London, 1963)

————, *Sir Philip Sidney and the English Renaissance* (London, 1954)

Byrne, M. St Clare, *Elizabethan Life in Town and Country,* revised ed. (London, 1961)

Camden, Carrol, *The Elizabethan Woman* (London, 1952)

Cecil, Algernon, *A Life of Robert Cecil, First Earl of Salisbury* (London, 1915)

Chamberlin, Frederick, *Private Character of Queen Elizabeth* (London, 1922)

Chambers, E. K., *The Elizabethan Stage* (Oxford, 1923)

Chapman, Hester W., *The Last Tudor King: A Study of Edward VI* (London, 1958)

Cheyney, E. P., *History of England from the Defeat of the Armada to the Death of Elizabeth,* new ed., 2 vols. (New York, 1948)

Clifford, Henry, *The Life of Jane Dormer, Duchess of Feria* (London, 1887)

Collinson, Patrick, *Archbishop Grindal* (London, 1979)

————, *The Elizabethan Puritan Movement* (London, 1967)

Creighton, Mandell, *Queen Elizabeth* (London, 1896)

Cross, Claire, *The Royal Supremacy in the Elizabethan Church* (London, 1969)

Cruikshank, C. G., *Elizabeth's Army* (London, 1966)

Dewar, Mary, *Sir Thomas Smith* (London, 1964)

Dickens, A. G., *The English Reformation* (London, 1964)

Dobson, E. J., *English Pronunciation, 1500-1700* (Oxford, 1957)

Dodd, A. H., *Life in Elizabethan England* (London, 1961)

Dunlop, Ian, *Palaces and Progresses of Elizabeth I* (London, 1962)

Durant, David N., *Arabella Stuart: A Rival to the Queen* (London, 1978)

Elton, G. R., *England Under the Tudors* (Cambridge, 1969)

————, *The Parliament of England, 1559-1581* (Cambridge, 1986)

————, *Policy and Police: The Enforcement of the Reformation in the Age of Thomas Cromwell* (Cambridge, 1972)

————, *Reform and Renewal: Thomas Cromwell and the Common Weal* (Cambridge, 1973)

————, *Studies in Tudor and Stuart Politics and Government* (Cambridge, 1983)

Emmison, F. G., *Tudor Secretary* (London, 1965)

Erickson, Carolly, *Anne Boleyn* (London, 1984)

————, *The First Elizabeth* (London, 1983)

Esler, Anthony, *The Aspiring Mind of the Elizabethan Younger Generation* (Durham, 1966)

Falls, Cyril, *Mountjoy: Elizabethan General* (London, 1955)

————, *Elizabeth's Irish Wars* (London, 1950)

Fraser, Antonia, *Mary Queen of Scots* (London, 1969)

French, Peter J., *John Dee: The World of an Elizabethan Magus* (London, 1972)

Froude, J. A., *History of England from the Fall of Wolsey to the Defeat of the Spanish Armada* (1856–70)

Greenblattt, Stephen J., *Sir Walter Raleigh, The Renaissance Man and His Roles* (New Haven, 1973)

Guy, John, *Tudor England* (Oxford, 1988)

———, "The Tudor Age" in *The Oxford Illustrated History of Britain*, ed. Kenneth O. Morgan (Oxford, 1986)

Haigh, Christopher, *Elizabeth I* (London, 1988)

———, *The English Reformation Revised* (Cambridge, 1987)

———, (ed.), *The Reign of Elizabeth I* (London, 1984)

Halliday, F. E., "Queen Elizabeth I and Dr Burcot," in *History Today*, V, 8, August, 1955

Handover, P. M., *The Second Cecil: The Rise to Power of the Second Cecil, 1563–1604* (London, 1959)

Harrison, G. B., *The Life and Death of Robert Devereux, Earl of Essex* (London, 1937)

Hasler, P. W., *The House of Commons, 1558–1603* (London, 1981)

Haugaard, W. P., *Elizabeth and the English Reformation* (Cambridge, 1968)

Haynes, Alan, *Robert Cecil, First Earl of Salisbury: Servant of Two Sovereigns* (London, 1989)

———, "Supplying the Elizabethan Court," in *History Today*, XXVII, November 1978

Hayward, John, *Annals of the First Four Years of the Reign of Elizabeth* (London, 1840)

Heal, F. M., *Of Prelates and Princes. A Study of the Economic and Social Position of the Tudor Episcopate* (Cambridge, 1980)

Hill, Christopher, *Society and Puritanism in Pre-Revolutionary England* (London, 1964)

Horton-Smith, L. G. H., *Dr William Baily, Physician to Queen Elizabeth* (London, 1952)

Hughes, Philip, *The Reformation in England* (London, 1951–4)

Hume, M. A. S., *The Courtships of Queen Elizabeth* (London, 1904)

Hurstfield, Joel, *Elizabeth I and the Unity of England* (London, 1960)

———, *The Elizabethan Nation* (London, 1967)

———, *The Queen's Wards: Wardship and Marriage under Elizabeth I* (London, 1958)

Hurstfield, Joel, and A. G. R. Smith (eds.), *Elizabethan People, State and Society* (London, 1972)

Ives, E. W., *Anne Boleyn* (Oxford, 1986)

Jenkins, Elizabeth, *Elizabeth and Leicester* (London, 1962)

——, *Elizabeth the Great* (London, 1958)

Johnson, Paul, *Elizabeth I: A Study in Power and Intellect* (London, 1974)

Jones, N. L., *Faith by Statute: Parliament and the Settlement of Religion, 1559* (London, 1982)

Jordan, W. K., *Edward VI* (London, 1968, 1979)

Kendall, Alan, *Robert Dudley, Earl of Leicester* (London, 1980)

Klarwill, Victor von (ed.), *Queen Elizabeth and some Foreigners* (New York, 1928)

Lacey, Robert, *Robert, Earl of Essex: An Elizabethan Icarus* (London, 1971)

——, *Sir Walter Raleigh* (London, 1974)

Levine, Mortimer, *The Early Elizabethan Succession Question, 1558–1568* (Stanford, 1966)

Loades, D. M., *Mary Tudor: A Life* (Oxford, 1989)

——, *Two Tudor Conspiracies* (Cambridge, 1965)

Lynch, Michael (ed.), *Mary Stuart: Queen in Three Kingdoms* (Oxford, 1988)

MacCaffrey, Wallace T., *Elizabethan Government and Society* (London, 1961)

——, *Queen Elizabeth and the Making of Policy* (Princeton, 1981)

——, *The Shaping of the Elizabethan Regime* (London, 1969)

Maclean, Ian, *The Renaissance Notion of Women* (Cambridge, 1970)

MacNulty, A. S., *Elizabeth Tudor* (London, 1954)

McFarlane, K. B., *The Nobility of Late Medieval England* (Oxford, 1973)

McGrath, P., *Papists and Puritans under Elizabeth I* (London, 1967)

Martienssen, Anthony, *Queen Catherine Parr* (London, 1973)

Mattingly, Garrett, *Catherine of Aragon* (London, 1950)

——, *The Defeat of the Spanish Armada* (London, 1959)

——, *Renaissance Diplomacy* (London, 1955)

Meyer, A. O., *England and the Catholic Church under Queen Elizabeth*, trans. J. R. McKer (London, 1967)

Meyer, C. S., *Elizabeth I and the Religious Settlement of 1559* (St Louis, 1960)

Morris, Christopher, *The Tudors* (London, 1955)

Mumby, F. A., *The Girlhood of Queen Elizabeth* (London, 1909)

Neale, J. E., *Elizabeth and her Parliaments* (London, 1953 and 1957)

——, *The Elizabethan House of Commons* (London, 1949)

——, *Essays in Elizabethan History* (London, 1958)

——, *Queen Elizabeth I*, new ed. (London, 1952)

————, "The Accession of Queen Elizabeth" in *History Today,* III, 5, May 1953

Nicholas, N. H., *Life of William Davison, Secretary of State to Queen Elizabeth* (London, 1823)

————, *The Memoirs of the Life and Times of Sir Christopher Hatton* (London, 1847)

Nichols, John, *Progresses and Public Processions of Queen Elizabeth* (1823)

Osborne, June, *Entertaining Elizabeth I: The Progresses and Great Houses of her Time* (London, 1989)

Pearson, L. E., *Elizabethans at Home* (Stanford, 1957)

Pollard, A. F., *Political History of England, 1547-1603* (London, 1910)

Pollen, J. H., *The English Catholics in the Reign of Queen Elizabeth* (London, 1920)

Prescott, H. F. M., *Spanish Tudor: The Life of Bloody Mary* (London, 1940)

Pulman, M. B., *The Elizabethan Privy Council in the Fifteen-Seventies* (Berkeley, 1971)

Read, Conyers, *Lord Burghley and Queen Elizabeth* (London, 1960)

————, *Mr. Secretary Cecil and Queen Elizabeth* (London, 1955)

————, *Mr. Secretary Walsingham and the Policy of Queen Elizabeth* (Oxford, 1925)

Ridley, Jasper, *Elizabeth I* (London, 1987)

Rowse, A. L., *The Elizabethan Renaissance: The Cultural Achievement* (London, 1972)

————, *The Elizabethan Renaissance: The Life of the Society* (London, 1972)

————, *The England of Elizabeth: The Structure of Society* (London, 1950)

————, *The Expansion of Elizabethan England* (London, 1953)

————, *Ralegh and the Throckmortons* (London, 1962)

————, *Shakespeare's Southampton* (London, 1965)

————, *Simon Forman: Sex and Society in Shakespeare's Age* (London, 1974)

Ryan, Lawrence V., *Roger Ascham* (Stamford, 1963)

Scarisbrick, J. J., *Henry VIII* (London, 1968)

Simon, Joan, *Education and Society in Tudor England* (Cambridge, 1966)

Smith, A. G. R., *The Government of Elizabethan England* (London, 1967)

Smith, Lacey Baldwin, *Elizabeth I* (St Louis, 1980)

————, *Elizabeth Tudor: Portrait of a Queen* (Boston, 1975)

————, *The Elizabethan Epic* (London, 1966)

————, *Henry VIII: The Mask of Royalty* (London, 1971)

————, *Tudor Prelates and Politics* (Princeton, 1953)

Soden, Geoffrey, *Godfrey Goodman, Bishop of Gloucester, 1583–1656* (London, 1953)

Spedding, James, *An Account of the Life and Times of Francis Bacon* (London, 1878)

Starkey, David (ed.), *The English Court: From the Wars of the Roses to the Civil War* (London, 1988)

Stone, Lawrence, *The Crisis of the Aristocracy, 1558–1641* (Oxford, 1965)

———, *Family and Fortune: Studies in Aristocratic Finance in the 16th and 17th Centuries* (Oxford, 1973)

———, *The Family, Sex and Marriage in England, 1500–1800* (London, 1977)

Stone, Laurence, and Jeanne C. Fortier Stone, *An Open Elite? England 1540–1880* (London, 1984)

Stopes, C. C., *Shakespeare's Environment* (London, 1914)

Strickland, Agnes, *Lives of the Queens of England* vols. 6 and 7 (London, 1844)

Strong, Roy, *The Cult of Elizabeth: Elizabethan Portraiture and Pageantry* (London, 1977)

———, *Gloriana. The Portraits of Queen Elizabeth I* (London, 1987)

Strong, Roy, and Julia Trevelyan Oman, *Elizabeth R* (London, 1971)

Strype, John, *Annals of the Reformation* (Oxford, 1824)

Tawney, R. H., *The Agrarian Problem in the Sixteenth Century* (London, 1912)

Thomas, Keith, *Religion and the Decline of Magic* (London, 1971)

Thomson, George Malcolm, *The Crime of Mary Stuart* (London, 1967)

———, *Sir Francis Drake* (London, 1972)

Tillyard, E. M. W., *The Elizabethan World Picture* (London, 1943)

Tytler, P. R., *England under Edward VI and Mary* (London, 1856)

Waldman, Milton, *Elizabeth and Leicester* (London, 1944)

Wallace, Willard M., *Sir Walter Raleigh* (Princeton, 1959)

Ward, B. M., *The Seventeenth Earl of Oxford* (London, 1928)

Warnicke, Retha M., *The Rise and Fall of Anne Boleyn* (Cambridge, 1989)

Weinreb, Ben (ed., with Christopher Hibbert), *The London Encyclopaedia* (London, 1983)

Wernham, R. B., *After the Armada: Elizabethan England and the Struggle for Western Europe, 1588–95* (Oxford, 1984)

———, *Before the Armada: The Growth of English Foreign Policy, 1485–1588* (London, 1966)

———, *The Making of Elizabethan Foreign Policy* (Berkeley, 1980)

White, F. O., *Lives of the Elizabethan Bishops* (London, 1898)

Wickham, Glynn, *Early English Stages* (London, 1959–63)

Williams, Ethel Carlton, *Bess of Hardwick* (London, 1959)

Williams, Neville, *All the Queen's Men* (London, 1972)

——, *Elizabeth I, Queen of England* (London, 1971)

——, *Henry VIII and his Court* (London, 1971)

——, *Thomas Howard, 4th Duke of Norfolk* (London, 1964)

Williams, Penry, *Life in Tudor England* (London, 1964)

——, *The Tudor Regime* (London, 1979)

Williamson, J. A., *The Age of Drake* (London, 1938)

Wilson, C. H., *Queen Elizabeth and the Revolt of the Netherlands* (London, 1970)

Wilson, D., *Sweet Robin: A Biography of Robert Dudley, Earl of Leicester* (London, 1981)

Wilson, Thomas, *The State of England . . . 1600,* ed. F. J. Fisher (London, 1936)

Wright, Thomas (ed.), *Queen Elizabeth and her Times* (London, 1838)

Yates, Frances, *The Theatre of the World* (London, 1969)

——, *Astraea: The Imperial Theme in the Sixteenth Century* (London, 1975)

Index

The abbreviations PE and QE refer to Princess Elizabeth and Queen Elizabeth. Queen Mary Tudor is referred to as Mary Tudor, and Mary, Queen of Scots as Mary Stuart.